Making
Inclusion
Work

John Beattie ✦ LuAnn Jordan ✦ Bob Algozzine

Making
Inclusion
Work

Effective Practices for ALL Teachers

Skyhorse Publishing

Skyhorse Publishing books may be purchased in bulk at special discounts for sales promotion, corporate gifts, fund-raising, or educational purposes. Special editions can also be created to specifications. For details, contact the Special Sales Department, Skyhorse Publishing, 307 West 36th Street, 11th Floor, New York, NY 10018 or info@skyhorsepublishing.com.

Skyhorse® and Skyhorse Publishing® are registered trademarks of Skyhorse Publishing, Inc.®, a Delaware corporation.

Visit our website at www.skyhorsepublishing.com.

10 9 8 7 6 5 4 3 2 1

Library of Congress Cataloging-in-Publication Data is available on file.

Cover design by Lisa Miller

Print ISBN: 978-1-62914-667-6
Ebook ISBN: 978-1-63220-036-5

Printed in the United States of America

Contents

Preface   ix
   Making Inclusion Work   ix
   Knowledge Base   x
   Content of This Book   x

Acknowledgments   xv

About the Authors   xvii

1. What Is Special Education?   1
   What Do I Need to Know About Special Education?   2
   Where Can I Find Resources or
     More Information on Special Education?   15
   Chapter References   18

2. Why Do We Have Inclusion?   19
   What Do I Need to Know About Inclusion?   20
   What Factors Are Necessary for Inclusion to Succeed?   22
   How Does No Child Left Behind Support
     Access to the General Education Curriculum?   25
   Where Can I Find Resources or
     More Information on Inclusion?   28
   Chapter References   32

3. What Is an Individualized Education Program?   33
   How Does a Student Get an IEP?   34
   What Do I Need to Know About
     Individualized Education Programs?   37
   Where Can I Find Resources or More Information on IEPs?   55
   Chapter References   58

4. What Is Classroom Organization?   59
   Why Should My Classroom Be Organized?   60
   What Do I Need to Know About Classroom Organization?   61
   Who Needs Classroom Organization?   69

How Do I Know How Well My Classroom
   Organization Works?   70
Where Can I Find More Information
   on Classroom Organization?   71
Chapter References   72

5. What Works for Lesson Organization?   **75**
What Do I Need to Know About Lesson Organization?   75
How Do I Organize Lessons in the Inclusive Classroom?   95
What Are Some Ways to Facilitate Lesson Organization?   102
Where Can I Find Resources or
   More Information on Lesson Organization?   108
Chapter References   109

6. What Is Behavior Management and Motivation?   **111**
Why Should I Use Behavior Management
   and Motivation in My Classroom?   111
How Do I Use Behavior Management and
   Motivation in My Classroom?   112
How Do I Evaluate How Well Behavior Management
   and Motivation Activities Work in My Classroom?   124
What Are Some Commonly Used Behavior
   Management and Motivation Activities?   125
Where Can I Find Resources or More Information
   on Behavior Management and Motivation?   131
Chapter References   132

7. What Works in Teaching Reading?   **133**
   LuAnn Jordan and Jennifer A. Diliberto
What Are the Basic Components of Reading?   134
How Can I Be Sensitive to My Students'
   Reading Difficulties?   135
What Are Reading Strategies,
   and How Can I Use Them in My Classroom?   136
How Do I Use Content Enhancement in
   My Inclusive Classroom?   143
How Do I Know if Reading Strategies
   Work in My Classroom?   144
Where Can I Find Resources or More Information
   on Reading Strategies?   144
Chapter References   148

8. What Are Cognitive Strategies?   **149**
What Do I Need to Know About Cognitive Strategies?   149
Why Should I Use Cognitive Strategies in My Classroom?   150

What Is Content Enhancement, and What
  Does It Have to Do With Cognitive Strategies?   151
How Do I Know if Cognitive Strategies
  Work in My Classroom?   153
What Are Some Commonly Used Cognitive Strategies?   153
Where Can I Find Resources or More Information
  on Cognitive Strategies?   170
Chapter References   174

**9. What Are Effective Accommodations
   and Modifications?**   **177**
What Do I Need to Know About
  Accommodations and Modifications?   177
Why Should I Use Accommodations
  and Modifications in My Classroom?   178
What Are Some Commonly Used Accommodations,
  and How Do I Use Them in My Classroom?   183
What Are Some Commonly Used Modifications,
  and How Do I Use Them in My Classroom?   186
Where Can I Find Resources or More Information on
  Accommodations and Modification?   193
Chapter References   193

**10. What Works for Ongoing Assessment,
    Data Collection, and Grading?**   **195**
What Do I Need to Know About Assessment,
  Data Collection, and Grading?   196
Purposes of Assessment   197
Legal Considerations and Assessment   198
Collecting Assessment Data   202
Grading in the Inclusive Setting   208
Where Can I Find Resources or More Information
  on Assessment, Data Collection, and Grading?   209
Chapter References   210

11. What Assistance Do Parents and Families Need?   **211**
What Do I Need to Know About Parents?   211
How Do I Work With Parents to
  Maximize Their Involvement?   218
What Are Some Approaches
  That Work Effectively With Parents?   223
Where Can I Find Resources or
  More Information on Parents?   226
Chapter References   227

12. **What Works for Communicating, Consulting, and Collaborating With Other Professionals?**   **229**

What Do I Need to Know About Communicating,
  Consulting, and Collaborating?   230
Why Should I Communicate, Consult, and
  Collaborate With Other Professionals?   231
How Do I Communicate, Consult, and
  Collaborate Effectively With Other Professionals?   232
What Approaches Are Used to Communicate,
  Consult, and Collaborate?   250
Where Can I Find Resources or More Information on
  Communicating, Consulting, and Collaborating?   252
Chapter References   253

13. **The End Is Just the Beginning!**   **255**
Ensuring That No Child Is Left Behind   255

Index   **259**

Preface

MAKING INCLUSION WORK

Four special education categories account for the majority of students receiving special education services. Half of all students served are represented by the specific learning disabilities category; speech or language impairments (19%), mental retardation (11%), and emotional disturbance (8%) are the remaining high-prevalence categories. Together, these four groups of students represent almost 90% of all students with disabilities (aged 6 through 21) in public school special education programs, and large numbers of them, especially in elementary schools, are taught more often in general education than special education classrooms. While general education teacher preparation programs have adjusted to this shift in practice by providing a course or two on special education teaching strategies, a need remains for a practical, "how-to" handbook reflecting best practices for including students with disabilities in general education classrooms.

Making Inclusion Work addresses what works when teaching students with disabilities in general education classrooms. It is designed to accompany methods texts in general education, including but not limited to those in language arts, math, science, social studies, and history. Our experience is primarily in special education, with specialized methods courses in inclusion, effective teaching, behavior instruction, and attention deficit/hyperactivity disorder (ADHD). We have been consistently confronted with and impressed by the challenges that special education and general education teachers face in including students with disabilities in general education classrooms. Our approach is one of practical applications of "special education practices" (e.g., developing individualized education programs, using diagnostic testing, differentiating instruction, improving behavior and motivation, and assisting families).

KNOWLEDGE BASE

A body of literature exists on effective special education practices. This information is typically presented in special education methods courses that often are not part of the general education teacher's course of study. Our experiences over more than 30 years of preparing special education teachers and demonstrating what works in teaching students with high-incidence disabilities have illustrated continuing needs to increase understanding of special education concepts that affect general education classrooms, to apply special education concepts and skills to inclusive classroom situations, and to increase cooperation among special and general educational professionals, administrators, related-service personnel, and parents. *Making Inclusion Work* addresses these needs and is grounded in our more than 20,000 hours of professional development experience in preparing teachers as well as graduate and undergraduate students to teach students with disabilities in general education classrooms.

CONTENT OF THIS BOOK

The content of this book is a direct reflection of concerns expressed by teachers and teachers-in-training in their work with the ever-increasing numbers of students with diverse needs as well as the diverse nature of the general education classroom. Put simply, these professionals express the need to understand who these students are, how they are identified, and what to do with them in their classroom. In addition, both general and special educators express the need to understand the practice of collaboration and considerations as to how to successfully work with colleagues, families, and other professionals providing services to students with disabilities. Content addressing these needs is included in the book.

In Chapter 1 ("What Is Special Education?") we describe the current special education system (i.e., numbers of students, expectations) and critical processes related to it (e.g., factors involved in identifying students with disabilities, the prevalence of students receiving special education services, and the impact these students with disabilities have on inclusive classrooms). The goal is to start the book with everyone "on the same page" regarding contemporary special education.

In Chapter 2 ("Why Do We Have Inclusion?") we review the social, political, and legal basis for both general education and special education. We describe the history of special education with particular attention to key laws and legislation that drive contemporary practices, especially inclusion.

An individualized education program (IEP) is a defining aspect of special education services. General education teachers often have little or no knowledge of components of an IEP or their responsibilities with regard to them. In Chapter 3 ("What Is an Individualized Education Program?") we define what the IEP is and the fundamental parts of it, describe the legal implications of the IEP and the reason(s) it exists, and describe the constituents of the IEP team and the charge/goals of this group. The roles of general education personnel are highlighted.

Effective teaching involves planning for the needs of all students. General education teachers are confident in their abilities to plan for general education students, but they are much less confident in their abilities to plan for special education students. Deciding how to organize the classroom space has much to do with how successful instruction that takes place there will be for all students. Chapter 4 ("What Is Classroom Organization?") describes classroom organization in relation to instructional strategies that are effective in working with students with disabilities in general education settings (e.g., organization of the physical space to accommodate the needs of all students and considerations to enhance the climate of the classroom so as to afford opportunities for maximum academic and social growth for all students).

Effective teaching involves meeting the needs of all students with appropriate lessons, and the focus of Chapter 5 ("What Works for Lesson Organization?") is the importance of planning appropriate lessons. The chapter illustrates (a) how to use lesson plans (traditional six-step plans as well as others) in the included classroom setting, (b) how to integrate general lesson plans with the individual plans appropriate for students with disabilities, and (c) how to organize and present lessons with attention to varying learning styles and methods of instruction.

Responding positively, encouraging students, and promoting social acceptance are important to successful inclusion of students with disabilities. Chapter 6 ("What Is Behavior Management and Motivation?") discusses interventions that have proven to be successful in promoting positive behavior. The importance of consistency is emphasized, and motivational techniques that work in general education classroom settings are highlighted. Consideration is also given to creating a positive classroom climate that supports students with disabilities as productive, capable members in social groups.

Given the impact of reading on all content areas, Chapter 7 ("What Works in Teaching Reading?"), by LuAnn Jordan and Jennifer Diliberto, gives special attention to programs and techniques that foster success in early and later literacy skills. We discuss the role of direct instruction in reading in a variety of classroom settings and describe specific modifications or accommodations that increase the likelihood of success in reading.

Teaching students how to approach instructional tasks (i.e., using learning strategies) is one of the most effective approaches for students with learning disabilities. In Chapter 8 ("What Are Cognitive Strategies?")

we describe specific learning strategies that have been demonstrated to be effective by researchers at the University of Kansas (one of us has received training in the strategies approach and used her expertise to prepare this chapter). The chapter also includes descriptions of additional learning strategies and learning style considerations in relation to fostering successful academic performance of students with disabilities in general education classrooms.

A primary responsibility of classroom teachers in making inclusion work is adapting the curriculum to meet special needs of students with disabilities. This means making changes that provide learning assistance. In Chapter 9 ("What Are Effective Accommodations and Modifications?") we describe the differences between accommodations and modifications for students included in general education classrooms. We also define and discuss additional terms used with regard to adapting instruction to meet the needs of all students in the general classroom setting, and we describe commonly used modifications and accommodations, as well as where and when they are incorporated into inclusive settings. To assist general education teachers in adapting the curriculum, we provide specific examples, illustrations, and applications of modifications and accommodations.

Once students with diverse needs are placed in the classroom, it is necessary to consider monitoring progress on a daily, consistent basis and to complete and use assessment in relation to the standard course of study to the maximum degree possible. In Chapter 10 ("What Works for Ongoing Assessment, Data Collection, and Grading?") we illustrate important considerations in collecting and recording data in a simple, manageable format and provide information about presenting grades for students with disabilities, with attention to the role of all professionals involved in the process.

As parents and families are the core to a child's life, Chapter 11 ("What Assistance Do Parents and Families Need?") gives attention to issues regarding diversity and their impact on school performance. We address issues regarding poverty and its impact on school performance and provide a discussion of the importance of home-school communication, with attention to specific techniques that facilitate this process.

In Chapter 12 ("What Works for Communicating, Consulting, and Collaborating With Other Professionals?") we attend to collaboration among professionals and consider the roles of these individuals in working with students with diverse needs. We describe strategies and techniques that facilitate collaboration and communication among school personnel and others supporting students with disabilities in general education classrooms, and we provide examples of successful collaboration with attention to how and why they were successful.

No Child Left Behind is not only a law but a way of thinking. In Chapter 13 ("The End Is Just the Beginning!") we discuss the latest law to have profound impact on students with diverse needs and disabilities. We address the impact of the law on teachers and other professionals working with students with disabilities in general education classrooms. We also focus on the future as an extension of the information presented in the text.

Our intent was to provide an accessible, exciting, engaging book that would be comprehensive, compelling, and complete. We believe that our combined experiences in providing professional development in public school systems and higher education institutions across the country have created a unique partnership that makes this book an exceptional learning opportunity. We also believe that our practical experiences in the field and our continuing deep record of academic research and scholarship provide a sound basis for considering issues affecting progress in America's schools. We hope you enjoy the book!

Acknowledgments

We would like to thank our colleagues and students, whose enthusiasm about our work was a welcome driving force in prompting us to finish so they could use this book. Numerous others, especially Kathleen McLane at Corwin, were the wind beneath our wings—thank you!

We are also thankful for the unwavering support and encouragement of our families and friends. John would like to thank the following: LuAnn, for her help and support with this and other projects; Bob—while there is no way to express how much his friendship and professional guidance have meant to me, I hope he knows how I feel; my family, which has always been supportive and encouraging, even when there was no real reason for it . . . thanks Mom, Karen, Joe, Marc; Matt, the best son in the world, with love; and finally, Erika, with love, who has taught me so much about so many things. Her love and constant support, encouragement, ideas, and professional insight have been my guiding light. LuAnn would like to thank Jesus Christ; her dad Edward; her sister Amy; and her mentor and friend Cecil Mercer. Bob would like to thank Kate Algozzine, who matters greatly in all things he does.

—*John Beattie*

—*LuAnn Jordan*

—*Bob Algozzine*

About the Authors

John Beattie earned his doctorate from the University of Florida in 1981. Following a period during which he taught in the Alachua County (Florida) public schools, he joined the faculty at the University of Missouri–St. Louis in 1982. The following year a position became available at the University of North Carolina–Charlotte (UNCC), and he began his tenure at UNCC at that time. He has been at UNCC since 1983. He teaches classes, conducts research, speaks at local, state, national, and international professional conferences, provides inservice training, and consults with schools in the areas of learning disabilities, ADHD, inclusion, math, and study skills. He has served as a Field Editor for *Exceptional Children* and is currently serving a similar role for *Teacher Education and Special Education*.

LuAnn Jordan earned her doctorate from the University of Florida in 1995, working as a Research Coordinator until moving to the University of North Carolina (UNC) at Charlotte in 1997 as the Faculty Coordinator of the Distance Education Master's Program in Special Education. While at UNC Charlotte, she has served in various teaching, research, and service capacities, including Codirector of a personnel preparation program in inclusion. As Associate Professor in the UNC Charlotte Special Education Program, she teaches courses in learning disabilities, the teaching of written expression to students with learning problems, and the use of teaching strategies for teachers of students with high-incidence disabilities. She received training in the University of Kansas Strategic Instruction Model (SIM) in 1993. As a result, she is a certified trainer of the University of Kansas Learning Strategies and has trained over 100 preservice and inservice teachers in these strategies, which target middle and high school learners. She has developed a number of online courses, including courses on inclusion and attention deficit disorder. As a special education teacher, she worked with elementary students with learning disabilities, mild mental disabilities, and behavioral disabilities.

 **Bob Algozzine** earned his doctorate from Pennsylvania State University in 1975, joining the faculty there that same year and moving to the University of Florida (UF) in 1977. While at UF, he served in various teaching, research, and service capacities, including Behavior Disorders Program Coordinator. Since 1987, he has been a faculty member at the University of North Carolina at Charlotte, serving as Coordinator of the Research Program in the Department of Educational Leadership, Research Mentor for the faculty in the College of Education, and Co-Director of the Behavior and Reading Improvement Center. For 9 years, he was Coeditor of *Exceptional Children* and is widely known for his research and writing on effective teaching practices in the area of behavior disorders and critical issues in the field of special education. He has been a featured speaker at local, state, national, and international professional conferences and has conducted professional development workshops for general and special education teachers across the country.

What Is Special Education?

Outline Questions

What do I need to know about special education?

Who receives special education?

Why do students need special education?

How many students receive special education?

What does the number of students needing special education mean for inclusion?

Where is special education provided?

Where can I find resources or more information about special education?

I f education is the process of learning and changing as a result of schooling and other experiences, special education is the process of learning and changing as a result of school and other experiences designed to meet special learning needs. Some children receive special education because they have difficulty learning in general classrooms. Others do well in general classrooms; they need special education to help learn and master additional skills to reach their full potential in school.

WHAT DO I NEED TO KNOW
ABOUT SPECIAL EDUCATION?

Special education is evidence of society's willingness to recognize and respond to the individual needs of students and the limits of general school programs to accommodate those needs. To better understand special education, you need to know who receives it, why people need it, how many children receive it, and where it is provided.

Who Receives Special Education?

In the first textbook dealing with the "education of exceptional children," Horn (1924) argued that mental, temperamental, and physical differences were the basis for some students' need for special education assistance. Today, most states organize their special education departments along what has become known as categorical lines based upon exceptionality (such as "learning disability"). Since 1975, the U.S. Department of Education has collected data on the number of children served under Public Law 94-142 (and its reauthorizations). Early collections of data on the number of children with disabilities served under federal laws used nine disability categories. Through the subsequent years and multiple reauthorizations of the act, the disability categories have been increased to 13, and, although the names of the categories vary slightly from state to state, special education is generally provided for children within each of the following groups:

1. Specific Learning Disabilities (SLD)

2. Speech or Language Impairments (SI)

3. Mental Retardation (MR)

4. Emotional Disturbance (ED)

5. Multiple Disabilities (MD)

6. Hearing Impairments (HI)

7. Orthopedic Impairments (OI)

8. Other Health Impairments (OHI)

9. Visual Impairments (VI)

10. Autism (AU)

11. Deaf-Blindness (DB)

12. Traumatic Brain Injury (TMI)

13. Developmental Delay (DD)

Your state probably has a consultant or specialist responsible for the students who have these various types of disabilities. The best way to find out about them is to visit your state's department of education Web site.

Most school districts also organize their special education programs along categorical lines. For example, a district-level administrator or supervisor is probably responsible for students with disabilities in your local school district. Your local school district probably also has program options (e.g., special schools, special classes, transition programs) for students with disabilities that your state serves.

Not all states organize their services along categorical lines, but they are still required to have procedures and personnel in place to ensure a quality education for all students, including students with disabilities. One way states organize noncategorically is by serving students with "mild disabilities," "moderate disabilities," and "severe disabilities."

Our beliefs about the special education process have shaped this book. While many books about teaching students with special education needs are organized with chapters addressing each category, this book focuses on educational practices. In choosing this organization, we do not mean to downplay the importance of the categories to contemporary practice. As we have indicated, most states currently organize their special education programs along categorical lines, and we believe that most will continue that practice because it is convenient to do so.

We chose to do this book differently because we believe that categorical distinctions offer little help in deciding how to teach students with special learning needs. Teaching is a decision-making process. To teach students with disabilities is to make decisions about them, and most of those decisions have little to do with a student's special education group. When we collect information about a student, the process generally is the same whether the student has a disability or not. We have organized this book around the concepts and practices that we believe are central to making inclusion work.

Why Do Students Need Special Education?

When thinking about why students need special education, it is helpful to think about the kinds of special learning needs that exist among individuals. If the needs of students were not important, there would be no need for special education; special education exists to provide alternative educational experiences for students who require special assistance to profit in school. These needs serve as the basis for definitions used to identify seemingly distinct groups of students, and they serve as guiding principles for organizing educational programs for them.

Physical Reasons for Needing Special Education

Learning needs in areas of physical abilities (e.g., seeing, hearing, moving) are the basis for several special education categories. Most of us take normal vision and hearing for granted. The expression "20/20 vision" is used to describe normal visual functioning. Vision is measured by having people read letters or discriminate objects at a distance of 20 feet. The task is not very difficult for most people. There are people, however, who must stand closer than others do to see what others see easily from 20 feet away. These differences in visual functioning are the basis for deciding if a student is blind or visually impaired. There are also people who cannot hear at a louder volume what others hear easily. Between normal hearing and total deafness are various degrees of hearing loss, and differences in these degrees of hearing are the basis for another category (i.e., those who are deaf or hard of hearing).

How different does vision or hearing have to be before a person is classified with a disability? Even with correction (e.g., glasses), a person who must be 20 feet from a target that a person with normal vision can see at 200 feet or more is considered *blind.* People with corrected vision better than 20/200 but not better than 20/70 are considered *visually impaired.* Ability to hear is measured along two scales: intensity and frequency. Intensity or loudness is measured in decibels (dB), and frequency or pitch is measured in hertz (cycles per second). Moores (2001) defined *deaf* and *hard of hearing* in terms of the effects on hearing loss; his perspective is evident in current federal definitions for disabilities related to hearing [20 U.S.C. 1401(3)(A) and (B); 1401(26)]:

> **Deafness** means a hearing impairment that is so severe that the child is impaired in processing linguistic information through hearing, with or without amplification, that adversely affects a child's educational performance.

> **Hearing impairment** means an impairment in hearing, whether permanent or fluctuating, that adversely affects a child's educational performance but that is not included under the definition of deafness in this section.

For practical purposes, *deafness* means the absence of hearing in both ears; people who are deaf have great difficulty hearing conversational speech without the assistance of a hearing aid. People who are *hard of hearing* experience hearing loss to a lesser extent but still have significant difficulties in hearing.

Sometimes people experience a physical injury to the brain that results in a total or partial disability that may adversely affect school or life performance. *Traumatic brain injury* is the term used to create a category for providing special education for these individuals. *Autism* is another physical disability that adversely affects verbal and nonverbal communication and social interaction.

There are also health problems that provide the basis for special education grounded in special learning needs that are physical. For example, arthritis is a measurable inflammation of a joint that limits movement and makes it painful. Cerebral palsy is paralysis due to brain damage; it produces differences in motor control that are observable in movement of large and small muscle groups. Epilepsy is also a brain disorder that results in measurable convulsive episodes and periods of unconsciousness. Other health impairments include severe orthopedic problems that adversely affect educational performance and limit strength, vitality, or alertness. Special education is also provided to people with physical differences caused by congenital anomalies (e.g., clubfoot, spina bifida, absence of a body member) or other causes (e.g., amputation, infections) as well as other general health problems (e.g., heart disease, asthma, diabetes).

Cognitive Reasons for Needing Special Education

Differences in intellectual performance or mental abilities are the basis for other groups of students needing special education. To be classified with mental retardation, a person must perform very poorly on an intelligence test and also demonstrate deficits in adaptive behavior. There is no formal definition of adaptive behavior, but it can be generally taken to refer to the way an individual functions in his or her social environment. The requirement that people demonstrate deficits in adaptive behavior is a part of the definition of mental retardation so that people who perform poorly on intelligence tests but manage to adapt or adjust to their environment and function adequately outside school will not be classified with mental retardation.

How different do intellectual scores have to be before a person is classified with *mental retardation?* Differences in scores on intelligence tests and measures of adaptive behavior are evaluated in the same way as differences in scores on hearing, vision, or physical performance tests. Standards for normal intelligence and adaptive behavior are set by testing large groups of individuals. Professionals then set criteria for retardation that are based on differences from normal intelligence or adaptive behavior. For example, the common standard for normal performance is a score of 90 to 110 on an intelligence test; scores below 70 are considered reflective of mental retardation.

Academic Reasons for Needing Special Education

For students with mental retardation, it is assumed that their performance on achievement tests will be consistent with their performance on intelligence tests. This means that if students perform poorly on intelligence tests, then their achievement test scores will also be low. In contrast, there are students whose performance on achievement tests is not consistent with their performance on intelligence tests. When these differences between ability (i.e., intelligence test performance) and achievement (i.e., achievement test performance) are substantial, the student is classified with *learning disabilities.*

How different do scores on ability tests and scores on achievement tests have to be before learning disabilities are identified? Determining which students have learning disabilities is different from determining which students are blind or deaf or have mental retardation. While officials of the federal government have provided guidelines for use in identifying students with learning disabilities, no specific criteria have been provided for deciding when discrepancies between ability and achievement are great enough to classify students as having learning disabilities. This decision is left to individual states. State education agency personnel have undertaken the task of refining the specific learning disabilities definition; specific criteria exist in each state for deciding when differences between ability and achievement warrant an identification of a learning disability. However, different states may (and do) have different criteria. Thus a student may have a learning disability in one state and not have a learning disability in another state, without any loss or gain in his or her learning.

In light of current legislation, the discrepancy model is now not the only choice in identifying a learning disability. According to the Individuals with Disabilities Education Act (IDEA) Amendments of 2004, students may also be identified with learning disabilities as a result of "failure to respond to scientific research-based intervention." This method of identification was proposed in answer to years of dissatisfaction with the discrepancy model, which relies on standardized intelligence and achievement tests. These standardized tests can be unfair to students, especially culturally diverse students. "Failure to respond" is a concept still under development, but the core principle is that if general education teachers are using research-based interventions under appropriate conditions, then students who continue to have learning problems may have learning disabilities.

Just as there are differences in reading, writing, and mathematics skills of students, there are differences in the ways students speak and express themselves. Some people speak clearly, pronouncing each part of their speech exactly as it should be said. Others speak quickly, making it difficult for others to understand them. Some children use speech as a means of making their desires, feelings, and opinions known. Others rely very little on speech as a means of communicating. There are accepted points at which children are expected to demonstrate use of various forms of communication. For example, most children understand about 1,000 words, combine their words into simple sentences, and understand concepts related to language (e.g., "on," "off," "later") by the time they are 2 years old. By the age of 7, children are expected to use proper grammar when constructing sentences; language at this age is very much like that used by adults. Differences in language and communication skills are measured by performance on tests. Differences in language development and communication skills are commonly observed in children of all ages. When these differences adversely affect educational performance, the individual is entitled to special services provided for *speech or language impairments.*

How different does speech and language have to be before a student is classified with a disability? Many students in this category receive special services for problems such as lisping, stuttering, and word pronunciation problems (e.g., they say "wabit" instead of "rabbit," "pasketti" instead of "spaghetti," or "bud" for "bird"); some of these students have voice tones that are too low, too high, too nasal, too harsh, or too hoarse. There are no standards for determining when an individual's speech is "too" nasal or "too" harsh or when it will adversely affect educational performance. Some teachers are better than others at understanding differences in the language produced by their students. Similarly, the context in which speech occurs influences the judgments made about it. Recent government figures indicate that there were more students in the speech or language impairments category than in any other, except learning disabilities and "other health impairments" (which includes attention deficit/hyperactivity disorder [ADHD]). These numbers are probably not surprising for a category based on differences in speech clarity and/or tone.

Behavioral Reasons for Needing Special Education

Just as standards for normal intellectual performance have evolved within the educational system, standards for how students should act in school and society also have evolved. And while standards for normal behavior are based more on judgments of what is acceptable than on judgments about performance on a test, the effect of deviating from the standards is much the same. Demonstrating intellectual performance that is sufficiently above or below normal is the basis for being identified as gifted or mentally retarded. Demonstrating inappropriate behavior in or out of school is the basis for being identified with *serious emotional disturbance.*

How different does behavior have to be before a student is identified with a disability? On the basis of what you have learned about the other conditions of special education, you probably expect the answer to be "significantly different from the behavior of other people." You would be right, but how would you objectively define the differences? Defining emotional disabilities is not like defining blindness or retardation because there are no numerical standards for "normal" behavior. There are no tests to measure the normality or acceptability of behavior. Defining emotional disabilities is like defining beauty; the activity is highly subjective. More often than not, "normal or acceptable" is in the eye of the beholder. For example, what is acceptable behavior at home may not be acceptable in school. What is acceptable behavior for one teacher may be unacceptable for another. What is acceptable in one class (e.g., physical education) may not be acceptable in another (e.g., music).

What About ADHD?

You may have noticed that ADHD is not listed in the disability categories presented earlier. There are many students with ADHD in today's schools, an estimated 3% to 7% of the school population (American Psychiatric Association, 2000). Students with ADHD often experience challenges in both learning and behavior. They usually have problems maintaining attention and effort in completing tasks, knowing when to "slow down" motor activity, and organizing themselves to finish tasks (American Psychiatric Association, 2000). Other negative characteristics such as anxiety, depression, and behavior problems may also be present (Whalen & Henker, 1991).

ADHD is not included in the category list because it is a medical diagnosis versus a category that is used for educational programming. Children are "identified" or diagnosed with ADHD by doctors, usually pediatricians. Most students who have ADHD receive all of their instruction in the general education classroom. Students who have ADHD and receive special education services are usually classified under "other health impairments" (OHI).

How Many Students Receive Special Education?

Currently the federal government recognizes 12 categories of students eligible for special education. *Mental retardation* is used to refer to students with cognitive disabilities. *Specific learning disabilities, speech or language impairments,* and *serious emotional disturbance* are used to refer to students with academic disabilities. *Deafness-blindness, hearing impairments, visual impairments, orthopedic impairments, other health impairments, multiple disabilities, autism,* and *traumatic brain injury* are used to refer to students with physical disabilities.

The number of children with disabilities receiving special education and related services has steadily grown since passage of Public Law 94-142, and the *Twenty-Second Annual Report to Congress* (U.S. Department of Education, 2000) marked the 25th anniversary of reporting progress in "meeting the mandates" of the act. The number of students ages 6 through 21 receiving special education reached 5,541,166 in 1998–99, a 2.7% increase over the previous year. In the previous decade, the number of students served grew 30.3%, from 4,253,018 in 1989–90 to 5,541,166 in 1998–99. The numbers of children served in 1991–92 and 2000–2001 and the percentage change by disability category are illustrated in Table 1.1.

On the silver anniversary of Public Law 94-142, specific learning disabilities continued to be the most prevalent disability among students ages 6 through 21 (U.S. Department of Education, 2000). Over half of the students with disabilities served under IDEA were categorized as having specific learning disabilities (2,817,148, or 50.8%). Speech and language impairments (1,074,548, or 19.4%), mental retardation (611,076, or 11.0%), and emotional disturbance (463,262, or 8.4%) were the next most common disabilities. This pattern of prevalence has been observed for some time; in fact, there have been only slight variations in disability prevalence since 1989–90 (see Table 1.2). The largest increase, a jump of 318.8%, occurred in the "other health impairments" category, which accounted for only 1.2% (or 52,733) of the children served in 1989–90 and in 1998–99 accounted for 4.0% (or 220,808). States have reported that the increase in the number of children with other health impairments is largely a function of increased identification and service provision to children with attention deficit/hyperactivity disorder (ADHD).

What Do All These Numbers Mean for Inclusion?

If you haven't figured it out by now, consider this: Special education is the subsystem of general education that has evolved to provide services to students who fail to profit from the menu of experiences provided in

Table 1.1 Numbers of Students Receiving Special Education

Disability	1991–92	2000–01	% Change in Number
Specific learning disabilities	2,247,004	2,887,217	28.5
Speech or language impairments	998,904	1,093,808	9.5
Mental retardation	553,262	612,978	10.8
Emotional disturbance	400,211	473,663	18.4
Multiple disabilities	98,408	122,559	24.5
Hearing impairments	60,727	70,767	16.5
Orthopedic impairments	51,389	73,057	42.2
Other health impairments	58,749	291,850	396.8
Visual impairments	24,083	25,975	7.9
Autism	5,415	78,749	1,354.3
Deaf-blindness	1,427	1,320	−7.5
Traumatic brain injury	245	14,844	5,958.8
Developmental delay	—	28,935	—
All disabilities	4,499,824	5,775,722	28.4

SOURCE: U.S. Department of Education (2002, Table II-4, p. II-20).

NOTE: Reporting in the autism and traumatic brain injury categories was optional in 1991–92 and required beginning in 1992–93. Data from 1991–92 include children with disabilities served under the Chapter 1 Handicapped Program.

Table 1.2 Percentage of Students Ages 6 Through 21 Receiving Special Education

	1989–90	1998–99
Specific learning disabilities	48.5	50.8
Speech and language impairments	22.9	19.4
Mental retardation	13.3	11.0
Emotional disturbance	9.0	8.4
Multiple disabilities	2.1	1.9
Hearing impairments	1.4	1.3
Orthopedic impairments	1.1	1.3
Other health impairments	1.2	4.0
Visual impairments	0.5	0.5
Autism	NA	1.0
Deaf-blindness	>0.1	>0.1
Traumatic brain injury	NA	0.2
Developmental delay	NA	0.2

SOURCE: U.S. Department of Education (2000, p. II-21).

general education classrooms. Each category for students needing special education has a definition that indicates the area of special need that separates students with disabilities from their peers. In most states, the names assigned to the categories are also the names assigned to the places where the students receive their special education or to the programs of individualized education that they receive. For example, there are special education programs in most states for students with learning disabilities. Recall that some states do not organize their special education programs along categorical lines. This is largely due to the concern among professionals that the categories are not satisfactory reflections of the special learning needs of the students. This is also due to concern for the negative impact that classifying the students may have on the students and their families (e.g., most of us don't want to be identified as "special," especially if being special has negative connotations). Noncategorical special education arose as an alternative means of providing services to exceptional students without having to group and label them with specific names.

The general guidelines that drive special education practices are provided in federal legislation (originally Public Law 94-142, reauthorized in 2004 as amendments to the Individuals with Disabilities Education Act). The law states that students with disabilities are entitled to a free, appropriate public education. To the maximum extent appropriate, children with disabilities should be educated with children without disabilities. Special classes, separate schooling, or other removal of children with disabilities from the general educational environment should occur only when the nature or severity of the child's disability is such that education in general classes with the use of supplementary aids and services cannot be achieved satisfactorily.

Where Is Special Education Provided?

The federal government reports information about students with disabilities in its annual reports to Congress (see U.S. Department of Education, 1999, 2000, 2001, 2002). The reports represent the "latest" figures but may be several years out of date as a result of publication lags and approvals required for release of information. Also, the categories of numbers available in these resources vary from year to year as a result of efforts to meet different reporting requirements. Below, we provide a sampling of information represented in these resources.

In recent years, the percentage of students with disabilities served in schools and classes with their peers without disabilities has gradually increased, and at least 50% of children with disabilities ages 6 through 21 are being served in general education classrooms 80% of the day or more (U.S. Department of Education, 2002). Of course, as the percentage of students served in settings with students without disabilities rises, the number of special education and general education teachers prepared to provide inclusive services must also increase. A continuing objective of the U.S. Department of Education is to increase the percentage of children with disabilities served in settings with their peers without disabilities to the maximum extent appropriate by providing needed supports and accommodations in general education (U.S. Department of Education, 1999, 2000, 2001, 2002). Toward this goal, we examine the environments in which students with disabilities received services and explore factors, such as age and type of disability, that may affect the service delivery environment. State-reported data are presented to describe the extent to which students with disabilities received special education and related services in settings with their peers without disabilities.

During the 1997–98 school year (U.S. Department of Education, 2000), 46.4% of students ages 6 through 21 with disabilities were served outside the regular classroom for less than 21% of the school day (i.e., the most inclusive category). Moving from more inclusive to less inclusive settings, another 29.0% were served outside the regular classroom for 21% to 60% of the school day and approximately 20% spent more than 60% of the school day outside the regular classroom. The remaining students were served in less inclusive setting such as either a separate or residential facility or a home or hospital environment. The trend favoring less restrictive placements is illustrated in Figure 1.1.

From the 1988–89 school year to the 1997–98 school year, the percentage of students ages 6 through 21 with disabilities who were served outside the regular classroom for more than 60% of the day decreased 3.9% (from 24.3% to 20.4%), and the percentage served outside regular school buildings declined by 2.1% (from 6.2% to 4.1%). Again, these data show a gradual movement of students with disabilities from separate schools and classes to general education schools and classes.

The environments in which students receive special education and related services vary by student age and disability. In 1997–98, 97.8% of students ages 6 through 11 with disabilities were served in schools with their peers without disabilities, versus 94.7% of students ages 12 through 17 with disabilities and 87.2% of students ages 18 through 21 with disabilities. The pattern of serving more elementary-aged students in schools with their natural neighbors and peers holds for all disability categories and is most pronounced among students with other health impairments, visual impairments, and deaf-blindness (cf. U.S. Department of Education, 2000, 2001, 2002, 2003).

Students ages 6 through 21 with speech or language impairments (85.6%) were more likely than students with other disabilities to receive

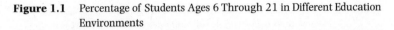

Figure 1.1   Percentage of Students Ages 6 Through 21 in Different Education Environments

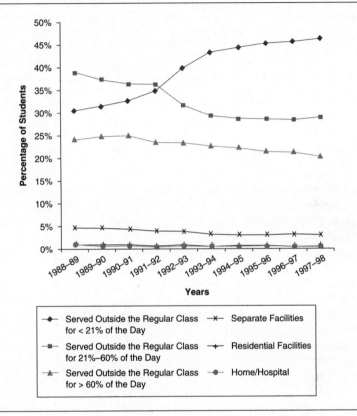

services outside the regular class for less than 21% of the school day, while students with multiple disabilities (12.1%) and students with mental retardation (13.2%) were the least likely to receive services in these inclusive settings. Students with multiple disabilities (26.4%) and students with deaf-blindness (37.8%) were more likely than students with other disabilities to receive services in separate schools or residential facilities, while students with speech or language impairments (0.9%) and students with specific learning disabilities (1.0%) were the least likely to be served in these separate settings (see Table 1.3).

Progress in serving students in less restrictive settings has varied by disability over the past decade. From 1988–89 to 1997–98, in several disability categories, the percentage of students ages 6 through 21 with disabilities

Table 1.3   Percentage of Students Ages 6 Through 21 With Disabilities
Served in Different Educational Environments During the
1997–98 School Year

	Served Outside the Regular Classroom					
	0%–21% of the Day	21%–60% of the Day	>60% of the Day	Separate Facilities	Residential Facilities	Home/ Hospital
All disabilities	46.4	29.0	20.4	2.9	0.7	0.6
Specific learning disabilities	43.8	39.3	16.0	0.6	0.2	0.2
Speech or language impairments	87.8	7.3	4.4	0.3	0.04	0.1
Mental retardation	12.6	29.6	51.7	5.2	0.6	0.4
Emotional disturbance	25.0	23.3	33.5	13.1	1.6	1.6
Multiple disabilities	10.0	17.3	45.1	22.3	2.9	2.5
Hearing impairments	38.8	19.1	25.4	7.4	9.2	0.2
Orthopedic impairments	46.6	21.3	26.2	3.7	0.3	2.0
Other health impairments	41.4	33.8	18.3	1.7	0.3	4.7
Visual impairments	48.1	20.1	17.3	6.7	7.1	0.7
Autism	18.3	12.7	52.1	14.6	1.8	0.5
Deaf-blindness	13.6	11.3	39.0	19.9	14.8	1.5
Traumatic brain injury	29.8	26.2	30.1	9.8	1.6	2.5

SOURCE: U.S. Department of Education (2000, Table III-1, p. III-4).

who received special education and related services outside the regular classroom for less than 60% of the school day has increased considerably. In other disability categories, percentages have remained relatively constant. The percentage of students with orthopedic impairments served in classrooms with their natural neighbors and peers for most of the school day rose 20% (from 47.8% to 67.8%), as did the percentage of students with mental retardation (13.7%; from 28.4% to 42.1%) and other health impairments

(24.8%; from 50.3% to 75.1%). From 1988–89 to 1997–98, the majority of students with speech or language impairments received services outside the regular class for less than 60% of the school day; this figure was relatively unchanged (U.S. Department of Education, 2000).

Progress continues to be made toward providing services to students with disabilities in more inclusive settings. In recent years, the number of students served outside regular school buildings has steadily decreased, and "inclusion" has become the intervention of choice in many school districts across the country; however, the percentage of students in different educational environments within regular school environments remains variable across disability and age groups, with some age and disability groups served primarily in classes with their peers without disabilities and others served largely outside those classrooms (cf. U.S. Department of Education, 2000, 2001, 2002). Concerns of parents and school professionals regarding the quality of educational experiences received by individuals with disabilities have been a driving force in looking to inclusive settings as the place to provide access to the general education curriculum that is essential for everyone.

WHERE CAN I FIND RESOURCES OR MORE INFORMATION ON SPECIAL EDUCATION?

The following general resources about special education were accessed from the "Inclusion" Web site maintained by the Special Education Program at the University of Northern Iowa (www.uni.edu/coe/inclusion/resources/resources.html). For more information, contact:

Dr. Sandra Alper, Department Head
Department of Special Education
University of Northern Iowa
Cedar Falls, IA 50614
Phone: (319) 273-6061
E-mail: sandra.alper@uni.edu

Books

Algozzine, B., & Ysseldyke, J. E. (2005). *Introduction to special education.* Longmont, CO: Sopris West.

Resource Books for General Education Teachers

Cohen, J. J., & Fish, M. C. (1993). *Handbook of school-based interventions.* San Francisco: Jossey-Bass.

McIntyre, Thomas. (1989). *A resource book for remediating common behavior and learning problems.* Allyn & Bacon.
Metcalf, L. (1999). *Teaching towards solutions.* West Nyack, NY: Center for Applied Research in Education.
Shore, Kenneth. (1998). *Special kids: Problem solver.* Paramus, NJ: Prentice Hall.
Watson, G. (1998). *Classroom discipline problem solver.* West Nyack, NY: Center for Applied Research in Education.

Web Sites

Centre for Studies on Inclusive Education (United Kingdom; http://inclusion.uwe.ac.uk/csie/csiehome.htm). CSIE is an independent organization working in the United Kingdom and overseas to promote inclusion and end segregation. The Web site provides abundant information about inclusive education and related issues.

Family Village: A Global Community of Disability-Related Resources (www.familyvillage.wisc.edu/). A site for individuals with disabilities and their families and friends that brings information together in a organized, easy-to-use resource.

IDEA 2004 Resources (www.ed.gov/offices/OSERS/IDEA/updates.html). Sponsored by the Office of Special Education and Rehabilitative Services (OSERS). Provides up-to-date news and information on IDEA 2004.

Inclusion . . . Yours, Mine Ours (www.rushservices.com/Inclusion). The Florida Inclusion Network sponsors this Web site of ideas, inspiration, and resources for including children with special needs in the regular classroom. It contains specific ideas about how teachers have made inclusion work and examples of schools where inclusion works.

Our Kids (www.our-kids.org/). At this site, a "family" of parents, caregivers, and others who are working with children with physical and/or mental disabilities and delays can discuss children's accomplishments and defeats; get some ideas of how others address specific problems/concerns with feeding, learning, schools, medical resources, techniques and equipment; and share problems and questions.

Project CHOICES (www.projectchoices.org/). Provides information on Project CHOICES, a "least restrictive environment" initiative funded by the Illinois State Board of Education that supports preschool-age and school-age children by increasing the capacities of school districts and educational personnel to educate and provide supports and services in environments in which they would participate if not identified as having a disability. Site includes information and resources on inclusion.

World Association of Persons with Disabilities Newsletter (www .wapd.org/news/index.html). An association that advances the interests of persons with disabilities at national, state, local, and home levels. The Web site is a rich resource for materials and information.

Wrightslaw Special Education Law and Advocacy (www.wrightslaw .com/). Provides parents, advocates, educators, and attorneys with accurate, up-to-date information about special education law and advocacy so that they can be effective catalysts. The site is a repository for articles, cases, newsletters, and resources about dozens of topics.

Organizations

Association for Supervision and Curriculum Development (ASCD)
1250 N. Pitt St.
Alexandria, VA 22314
(703) 549-9110
Web: www.ascd.org/

Council for Exceptional Children (CEC)
1110 N. Glebe Rd., Suite 300
Arlington, VA 22201
(800) 224-6830
Web: www.cec.sped.org/index.html

National Association of State Boards of Education (NASBE)
1012 Cameron St.
Alexandria, VA 22314
(800) 220-5183
Web: www.nasbe.org/

National Information Center for Children and Youth with Disabilities
    (NICHCY)
P.O. Box 1492
Washington, DC 20013-1492
(800) 695-0285
Web: www.nichcy.org/index.html

The Association for Persons with Severe Handicaps (TASH)
29 W. Susquehanna Avenue
Suite 210

Baltimore, MD 21204
Phone: (410) 828-8274
Fax: (410) 828-6706
Web: www.tash.org/

CHAPTER REFERENCES

American Psychiatric Association. (2000). *Diagnostic and statistical manual of mental disorders DSM-IV-TR (Text Revision)* (4th ed.). Washington, DC: Author.

Horn, J. L. (1924). *The education of exceptional children: A consideration of public school problems and policies in the field.* New York: Century.

Moores, D. (2001). *Educating the deaf: Psychology, principles, and practices* (5th ed.). Boston: Houghton Mifflin.

U.S. Department of Education. (1999). *U.S. Department of Education FY 2000 annual plan.* Vol. 2. Washington, DC: Author. Retrieved November 16, 2005, from www.ed.gov/pubs/AnnualPlan2002/index.html#vol2.

U.S. Department of Education. (2000). *Twenty-second annual report to Congress on the implementation of the Individuals with Disabilities Education Act.* Washington, DC: Author. Retrieved September 29, 2005, from www.ed.gov/about/reports/annual/osep/2000/index.html.

U.S. Department of Education. (2001). *Twenty-third annual report to Congress on the implementation of the Individuals with Disabilities Education Act.* Washington, DC: Author. Retrieved September 29, 2005, from www.ed.gov/about/reports/annual/osep/2001/index.html.

U.S. Department of Education. (2002). *Twenty-fourth annual report to Congress on the implementation of the Individuals with Disabilities Education Act.* Washington, DC: Author. Retrieved September 29, 2005, from www.ed.gov/about/reports/annual/osep/2002/index.html.

U.S. Department of Education. (2003). *Twenty-fifth annual report to Congress on the implementation of the Individuals with Disabilities Education Act.* Washington, DC: Author. Retrieved September 29, 2005, from www.ed.gov/about/reports/annual/osep/2003/index.html.

Whalen, C. K., & Henker, B. (1991). Social impact of stimulant treatment for hyperactive children. *Journal of Learning Disabilities, 24,* 231–241.

Why Do We Have Inclusion?

Outline Questions

Why do we have inclusion?

What do I need to know about inclusion?

What factors are necessary for inclusion to succeed?

What is the importance of positive attitudes toward inclusion?

What is the importance of parents?

What is the importance of professional development?

What is the importance of collaboration among teachers and other staff?

How does No Child Left Behind support access to the general education curriculum?

Where can I find resources or more information on inclusion?

Most classrooms contain three types of students: students who typically demonstrate superior performance on measures of intelligence and achievement (*academically gifted*, or *gifted and talented*), students with disabilities, and students who neither are gifted nor have disabilities. This last group is referred to as *normal*, *average*, or *normally* *achieving.* Some school districts and organizations group students who are gifted and students with disabilities in a group labeled *exceptional students.* The term *exceptional* applies to students who do not fall into the "normal" category.

While the term *exceptional children* is occasionally used in material quoted from other authors to refer to children with disabilities, our focus is on students who need special education to make adequate yearly progress in school, and we consistently refer to them as *students (or children) with disabilities.* We will usually favor the term *student* rather than *child* in this book because this book is so focused on school concerns. Sometimes, however, we will use *child* or *children*, especially when speaking to family concerns.

Students with disabilities require special education to meet individual learning needs and be successful in school. In this book, we are concerned with how to meet the individual learning needs of students with disabilities in the same classrooms as their peers without disabilities and those who are gifted.

There was a time when children with disabilities were not treated very well. They were not allowed to go to school with their neighbors and friends, and many spent most of their lives in institutions. In 1975, the federal government passed a law, the Individuals with Disabilities Act (IDEA), that mandated a *free, appropriate education* for all children with disabilities. Because this landmark legislation was designed to correct the problems of the past for individuals with disabilities, one of the foundations of Public Law 94-142 was its *least restrictive environment* provisions. The intention of lawmakers was that the free, appropriate education for children with disabilities be provided in classrooms as much like those of children without disabilities *as possible.* The law did not require that children with disabilities be educated in general education classrooms but directed that they be included in those classrooms as much as possible. Subsequent revisions of Public Law 94-142 (e.g., the IDEA Amendments of 1997 and 2004) have maintained the "least restrictive environment" provision, language, and intention. Today, this practice of teaching students with disabilities in the same classrooms as their peers is known as *inclusion.*

WHAT DO I NEED TO KNOW ABOUT INCLUSION?

Including students with disabilities in classes with their natural neighbors and peers is a relatively new educational practice. Prior to 1975, it did not occur on a systematic, recommended, or expected basis in most schools in the United States. When law directed that students with disabilities spend as much of their school day as possible in the same instructional and social activities as their peers without disabilities, inclusion became more popular (or at least more frequent).

Early efforts to include students with disabilities in general education classes were known as *mainstreaming.* In the 1970s and 1980s, mainstreaming was the placement of choice for many children with disabilities, and there was no shortage of definitions driving then-current practices:

- "[T]he temporal, instructional, and social integration of eligible exceptional children with normal peers based on an ongoing, individually determined, educational planning programming process . . . requires clarification of responsibilities among [general] and special education administrative, instructional, and supportive personnel" (Kauffman, Gottlieb, Agard, & Kukic, 1975, p. 5).
- "[A] belief which involves an educational placement procedure and process for exceptional children, based on the conviction that each such child should be educated in the least restrictive environment in which his educational and relational needs can be satisfactorily provided for" (Council for Exceptional Children, 1976, p. 43).
- "[T]he social and instructional integration of [students with disabilities] in a [general] education class for at least a portion of the school day" (Schulz & Turnbull, 1983, p. 49).
- "[M]aximum integration in the [general education] class combined with concrete assistance for the [general] class teacher" (Gearheart, Weishahn, & Gearheart, 1988, p. 5).
- "[T]he integration of children with learning, behavioral, and/or physical problems in [general] education settings and programs unless their problems are so severe that they cannot be accommodated in [general] programs" (Cartwright, Cartwright, & Ward, 1989, p. 10).

Mainstreaming became inclusion when teachers, parents, and other professionals observed that students with severe disabilities were still being excluded and segregated in America's schools (Stainback & Stainback, 1985, 1990, 1992).

Today, inclusion is the special education practice of choice in most school districts:

The percentage of students ages 6 through 21 with disabilities served in both [general] schools and in [general] education classes within those schools has continually increased. During the 1984–85 school year, only one-quarter of students with disabilities were served outside the [general] class [for] less than 21 percent of the school day. By 1998–99, that percentage [of students] had increased to almost half (47.4 percent) [and] *virtually all students (96 percent) are now served in [general] school buildings.* (U.S. Department of Education, 2001, p. III-2, emphasis added)

To participate fully in inclusion practices, you need to know about the broad system of special education that provides services for children who will be included in your classroom. This means being familiar with concepts that are driving contemporary special education practices such as access to the general education curriculum and what works in inclusive classrooms.

WHAT FACTORS ARE NECESSARY FOR INCLUSION TO SUCCEED?

Achievement in any curriculum comes about through the use of effective programs and procedures. For students with disabilities, it requires that special and general education teachers, parents, other school representatives, and representatives of other agencies take part in the student's educational planning, with improved learning in the general education curriculum as a goal. In addition, teachers must be trained in and then use well-founded, research-based instructional practices in their classrooms. The attitudes toward inclusion that are held by teachers, administrators, and other professionals; parents' involvement; professional development; and collaboration among all parties concerned are also important (Beckman, 2001).

Importance of Positive Attitudes Toward Inclusion

Effective inclusion practices often require that teachers, administrators, and other professionals give up traditional attitudes and expectations. Successful inclusion in the general education curriculum is most likely to happen when the following beliefs are fostered:

- Responsibility for positive outcomes for special education students is equally shared by all school personnel.
- General and special education classroom teachers both feel and are held responsible for identifying appropriate educational goals and providing instruction to help the student reach them.
- Teachers know the strengths and weaknesses of all of their students.

- Administrators recognize that teachers need time and support to adequately teach diverse groups of students.
- Administrators recognize that teachers need to have time set aside to work with other teachers and parents to identify best practices and approaches for all students.
- Teachers recognize that a special education label does not direct how much or how well a student will learn or perform, so assignments and activities are not based primarily on a student's educational category.
- All parties concerned recognize that good teaching involves sometimes alternative methods, activities, expectations, and approaches to meet the diverse learning strengths and weaknesses prevalent in today's classrooms.

Importance of Parents

Education has become more complex as directives and expectations for accountability have increased. In light of increased accountability, the importance of including families and broad support systems has grown; as in all areas of education, parents are an integral part of effective inclusive practices. Parent participation has been part of special education mandates since the first law requiring a free, appropriate education for all children with disabilities. These mandates have consistently reflected the belief that an inclusive school involves parents and their communities as meaningful contributors to the education of its students. The following activities lead to productive collaboration between parents and schools:

- Sharing information at the beginning of the school year
- Contacting parents frequently and informing them of successes more than failures
- Contacting parents before problems reach "critical" levels and asking for support in efforts to solve them
- Including parents in any meeting involving making decisions about their child
- Valuing parents, families, and communities as equal partners in efforts to provide effective inclusive education

Importance of Professional Development

Professional development that empowers both special education and general education teachers and encourages them to work together is critical to successful inclusion. One of the most important ways to provide all children with a great education is to provide them with great teachers. Studies have shown that the single greatest effect on student achievement is teacher quality (Darling-Hammond, 2003). For this reason, ensuring that every classroom has a highly qualified teacher has become a national priority (see the U.S. Department of Education's Web page for No Child Left Behind at www.ed.gov/nclb/landing.jhtml). Ensuring that all students gain access to the general education curriculum in inclusive settings requires support for efforts to improve teacher skills. Each teacher has his or her own set of unique strengths and weaknesses. When teachers identify and address their own teaching needs, they are better equipped to make inclusion work.

The fact that you are reading this text indicates that you are involved in professional development to increase your understanding and skills in inclusion. Teachers must have high-quality training and support to be successful inclusive teachers. The following are skills that help teachers support inclusion and access to the general curriculum for all of their students:

- Organizing classrooms and physical space to support diverse learning styles
- Planning, organizing, and presenting lessons that encourage diverse learning styles
- Managing behavior and motivation to keep students actively engaged
- Teaching reading relentlessly to support learning in other content areas
- Teaching cognitive strategies to support diverse learning styles and typical learning problems
- Providing accommodations and modifications to encourage all students to learn
- Monitoring progress frequently with appropriate assessments and grading practices
- Providing family-friendly educational experiences
- Collaborating, consulting, and communicating with other professionals

Importance of Collaboration Among Teachers and Other Staff

Schools with successful inclusion programs have teachers and other staff members who work together. Everyone contributes to planning and making decisions about students. General education teachers are usually specialists in curriculum; special education teachers (and related service personnel such as speech clinicians and therapists) are usually specialists in the unique learning and behavior needs of all students, especially those with special learning needs. Other professionals bring skills that support inclusive practices. All these important professionals contribute to inclusive efforts that make students the ultimate winners.

Effectively bringing all of this expertise to the classroom requires adhering to organizational principles designed to help all students learn while supporting individual differences. Classroom instruction should be tied to accepted curriculum standards and objectives that are appropriate for all students.

HOW DOES NO CHILD LEFT BEHIND SUPPORT ACCESS TO THE GENERAL EDUCATION CURRICULUM?

An important goal facing all teachers is helping all students, with or without disabilities, including English-language learners and students who are "falling between the cracks," to achieve in the general education curriculum (Beckman, 2001). For students with disabilities, access to the general education curriculum is mandated by the Individuals with Disabilities Education Act Amendments of 2004 (IDEA). Another strong mandate is included in federal legislation known as No Child Left Behind (see the U.S. Department of Education Web site on this legislation at www.ed.gov/nclb), a landmark in education reform designed to improve student achievement and change the culture of America's schools.

The U.S. Department of Education is committed to ensuring that all children— including children with disabilities—receive a high-quality education. Before the passage of No Child Left Behind, students with disabilities were expected to be included in state and districtwide assessment programs. No Child Left Behind further develops this expectation by ensuring that these assessments measure how well students with disabilities have learned required material in reading and mathematics. For students with the most significant cognitive disabilities (e.g., severe mental retardation), results from specially designed alternate assessments may be used in accountability decisions instead.

With the passage of No Child Left Behind, Congress authorized a sweeping overhaul of federal efforts to support elementary and secondary education in the United States. It is built on four commonsense pillars: accountability for results; an emphasis on doing what works based on scientific research; expanded parental options; and expanded local control and flexibility. These foundations are supported by continuing and important practices.

Supporting Learning in the Early School Years

Children who enter school with language skills and prereading skills (e.g., understanding that print reads from left to right and top to bottom) are more likely to learn to read well in the early grades and succeed in later years. In fact, research shows that most reading problems faced by adolescents and adults could have been prevented with good instruction in their early childhood (Snow, Burns, & Griffin, 1998). It is never too early to start building language skills by talking with and reading to children. No Child Left Behind targets resources for early childhood education so that all youngsters get the right start.

Providing Frequent, Positive Information for Parents About Their Child's Progress

Under No Child Left Behind, each state must measure every public school student's progress in reading and math in each of Grades 3 through 8 and at least once during Grades 10 through 12. By school year 2007–08, assessments (or testing) in science will be underway. These assessments must be aligned with state academic content and achievement standards and are intended to provide parents with objective data on where their child stands academically.

Using Information on the Performance of the Child's School to Prompt Change

No Child Left Behind requires states and school districts to give parents easy-to-read, detailed report cards on schools and districts, telling them which ones are succeeding (and which ones are not) and why. Included in the report cards are student achievement data broken out by race, ethnicity, gender, English-language proficiency, migrant status, disability status, and socioeconomic status, as well as important information about the professional qualifications of teachers. With these provisions, No Child Left Behind ensures that parents have important, timely information about the schools their children attend—whether they are performing well or not for *all* children, regardless of their background.

Giving Children and Parents a Lifeline

When inclusive practices are effective, children will no longer be trapped in the dead end of ineffective schooling. Under No Child Left Behind, poorly producing schools must use their federal funds to make needed improvements. In the event of a school's continued poor performance, parents have options to ensure that their children receive the high-quality education to which they are entitled. That might mean that children can transfer to higher-performing schools in the area or receive supplemental educational services in the community, such as tutoring, after-school programs, or remedial classes.

Providing Better Information to Teachers and Principals

Annual tests to measure students' progress provide teachers with independent information about each student's strengths and weaknesses. With this knowledge, teachers can craft lessons to make sure each student meets or exceeds the standards. In addition, principals can use the data to (a) assess exactly how much progress each teacher's students have made and (b) inform decisions about how to run their schools.

Building Programs With High-Quality Teachers

No Child Left Behind defines the qualifications needed by teachers and paraprofessionals who work on any facet of classroom instruction. It requires that states develop plans to achieve the goal that all teachers of core academic subjects be highly qualified by the end of the 2005–06 school year. States must include in their plans annual, measurable objectives that each local school district and school must meet in moving toward the goal; they must report on their progress in the annual report cards.

Giving More Resources to Schools

Today, more than $7,000 on average is spent per pupil by local, state, and federal taxpayers. States and local school districts are now receiving more federal funding than ever before for all programs under No Child Left Behind: $23.7 billion, most of which was used during the 2003–04 school year. This represents an increase of 59.8 percent from 2000 to 2003. A large portion of these funds is for grants under Title I of the Elementary and Secondary Education Act (ESEA): Improving the Academic Achievement of the Disadvantaged. Title I grants are awarded to states and local education agencies to help states and school districts improve the education of disadvantaged students, turn around low-performing schools, improve teacher quality, and increase choices for parents. For fiscal year (FY) 2003, funding for Title I alone was $11.7 billion—an increase of 33% since the passage of No Child Left Behind. President Bush's FY 2004 budget request would increase spending on Title I by 48% since he took office.

Allowing More Flexibility

In exchange for the strong accountability, No Child Left Behind gives states and local education agencies more flexibility in the use of their federal education funding. As a result, principals and administrators spend less time filling out forms and dealing with federal red tape. They have more time to devote to students' needs. They have more freedom to implement innovations and allocate resources as policy makers at the state and local levels see fit, thereby giving local people a greater opportunity to affect decisions regarding their schools' programs.

Focusing on What Works

No Child Left Behind puts a special emphasis on implementing educational programs and practices that have been clearly demonstrated to be effective through rigorous scientific research. Federal funding will be targeted to support such programs. For example, the Reading First program makes federal funds available to help reading teachers in the early grades strengthen old skills and gain new ones in instructional techniques that scientifically based research has shown to be effective.

Since ESEA first passed Congress in 1965, the federal government has spent billions of dollars supporting the education of children with learning problems and those at risk for failure in school. Yet the achievement gap between rich and poor and white and minority students remains wide. For example, according to the most recent National Assessment of Educational Progress (NAEP) on reading in 2000, only 32% of fourth graders can read at a proficient level and thereby demonstrate solid academic achievement; and while scores for the highest-performing students have improved over time, those of America's lowest-performing students have declined (NAEP, 2001). The good news is that some schools in cities and towns across the nation are supporting high achievement for children with a history of low performance. If some schools can do it, then all schools should be able to do it, and effective inclusive practices are an important part of the "mix."

WHERE CAN I FIND RESOURCES OR MORE INFORMATION ON INCLUSION?

The following resources were accessed from the "Inclusion" Web site maintained by the Special Education Program at the University of Northern Iowa: www.uni.edu/coe/inclusion/resources/resources.html.

For more information, contact:
Dr. Sandra Alper, Department Head
Department of Special Education
University of Northern Iowa
Cedar Falls, IA 50614
Phone: (319) 273-6061
E-mail: sandra.alper@uni.edu

Books

DeBettencourt, L. U. (1999). General educators' attitudes toward students with mild disabilities and their use of instructional strategies: Implications for training. *Remedial and Special Education, 20,* 27–35.

Giangreco, M. F. (1997). *Quick-guides to inclusion.* Baltimore: Paul H. Brookes.

Hamill, L. B., & Dever, R. B. (1998). Preparing for inclusion: Secondary teachers describe their professional experiences. *American Secondary Education, 27,* 18–26.

McDonnell, L. M., McLaughlin, M. J., & Morison, P. (Eds.). (1997). *Educating one and all: Students with disabilities and standards-based reform.* Washington, DC: National Academy Press.

Putnam, J. W. (1998). *Cooperative learning and strategies for inclusion: Celebrating diversity in the classroom* (2nd ed.). Baltimore: Paul H. Brookes.

Salend, S. J., & Garrick Duhaney, L. M. (1999). The impact of inclusion on students with and without disabilities and their educators. *Remedial and Special Education, 20,* 114–126.

Vitello, S. J., & Mithaug, D. E. (1998). *Inclusive schooling: National and international perspective.* Mahwah, NJ: Lawrence Erlbaum.

Other Books and Articles

Alder, L. (2000). How can special education students access the Utah Core Curriculum? *Utah Special Educator, 21*(2), 10–11.

Beckman, P. (2000). Utah's school-to-school project: Aiming for student success. *Utah Special Educator, 21*(2), 19–20.

Costa, A. L., & Kallick, B. (2000). *Habits of mind.* Alexandria, VA: Association for Supervision and Curriculum and Development.

Orkwis, R., & McLane, K. (1998). *A curriculum every student can use: Design principles for student access.* ERIC/OSEP Topical Brief. Reston, VA: ERIC/OSEP Special Project. Retrieved September 30, 2005, from www.cec.sped.org/osep/ude sign.html

Pressley, P., & Woloshyn, V. (1995). *Cognitive strategy instruction.* Cambridge, MA: Brookline.

Tomlinson, C. A. (1999). *The differentiated classroom: Responding to the needs of all learners.* Alexandria, VA: Association for Supervision and Curriculum Development.

Ysseldyke, J. (2001). Reflections on a research career: Generalizations from 25 years of research on assessment and instructional decision making. *Exceptional Children, 67*(3), 295–308.

Books for General Education Teachers

Alper, S., & Ryndak, D. L. (1996). *Curriculum content for students with moderate and severe disabilities in inclusive settings.* Needham, MA: Allyn & Bacon.
Berres, M. S. (1996). *Creating tomorrow's schools today: Stories of inclusion, change, and renewal.* New York: Teachers College Press.
Cohen, J. J., & Fish, M. C. (1993). *Handbook of school-based interventions.* San Francisco: Jossey-Bass.
McIntyre, T. (1989). *A resource book for remediating common behavior and learning problems.* Needham, MA: Allyn & Bacon.
Metcalf, L. (1999). *Teaching towards solutions.* West Nyack, NY: Center for Applied Research in Education.
Shore, K. (1998). *Special kids: Problem solver.* Paramus, NJ: Prentice Hall.
Watson, G. (1998). *Classroom discipline problem solver.* West Nyack, NY: Center for Applied Research in Education.

Web Sites

IDEA 2004 Resources (www.ed.gov/offices/OSERS/IDEA/updates.html). Sponsored by the Office of Special Education and Rehabilitative Services (OSERS). Provides up-to-date news and information on IDEA 2004.

Inclusion Press (www.inclusion.com/). Creates person-centered materials for professional development events, schools, community colleges, universities, human service agencies, health organizations, government agencies, and families. A great resource for media on all disabilities.

Inclusion . . . Yours, Mine Ours (www.rushservices.com/Inclusion). The Florida Inclusion Network sponsors this Web site of ideas, inspiration, and resources for including children with special needs in the regular classroom. It contains specific ideas about how teachers have made inclusion work and examples of schools where inclusion works.

Our Kids (www.our-kids.org/). A general Web site with information about children with disabilities. Its e-mail list consists of over 800 people representing children of varying diagnoses—everything from indefinite developmental delays and sensory integration problems, to cerebral palsy, to rare genetic disorders.

World Association of Persons with Disabilities Newsletter (www.wapd.org/news/index.html). An association that represents individuals with disabilities regardless of the term used to categorize them and advances their interests at national, state, local, and home levels. The Web site is a rich resource for materials and information.

Wrightslaw Special Education Law and Advocacy (www.wrightslaw .com/). Provides up-to-date information about special education law and advocacy for children with disabilities, including articles, cases, newsletters, and resources about dozens of topics in its Advocacy Libraries and Law Libraries.

Organizations

Association for Supervision and Curriculum Development (ASCD)
1250 N. Pitt St.
Alexandria, VA 22314
(703) 549-9110
Web: www.ascd.org/

Council for Exceptional Children
1110 N. Glebe Rd., Suite 300
Arlington, VA 22201
(800) 224-6830
Web: www.cec.sped.org/index.html

Inclusion Press/Centre for Integrated
    Education and Community
24 Thome Crescent
Toronto, Ontario M6H 2S5
Canada
(416) 658-5363
Web: www.inclusion.com/

National Association of State Boards of Education (NASBE)
1012 Cameron St.
Alexandria, VA 22314
(800) 220-5183
Web: www.nasbe.org/

National Dissemination Center for Children with
    Disabilities (NICHCY)
P.O. Box 1492
Washington, DC 20013-1492
(800) 695-0285
Web: www.nichcy.org/index.html

The Association for Persons with Severe Handicaps (TASH)
29 W. Susquehanna Ave.
Suite 210
Baltimore, MD 21204
Phone: (410) 828-8274
Fax: (410) 828-6706
Web: www.tash.org/

University of Kansas Center for Research on Learning
3061 Dole
Lawrence, KS 66045
(785) 864-4780
Web: www.ku-crl.org/

CHAPTER REFERENCES

Beckman, P. (2001). *Access to the general education curriculum for students with disabilities.* Arlington, VA: Council for Exceptional Children, ERIC Clearinghouse on Disabilities and Gifted Education.

Cartwright, G. P., Cartwright, C. A., & Ward, M. E. (1989). *Educating special learners* (3rd ed.). Belmont, CA: Wadsworth.

Council for Exceptional Children. (1976). *Policy statement of the delegate assembly.* Reston, VA: Author.

Darling-Hammond, L. (2003). Keeping good teachers. *Educational Leadership, 60,* 6–8.

Gearheart, B. R., Weishahn, M. W., & Gearheart, C. J. (1988). *The exceptional student in the regular classroom* (4th ed.). New York: Merrill/Macmillan.

Kauffman, J. M., Gottlieb, J., Agard, J. A., & Kukic, M. D. (1975). Mainstreaming: Toward an explication of the concept. In E. L. Meyen, G. A. Vergason, & R. J. Whelan (Eds.), *Alternatives for teaching exceptional children* (pp. 35–54). Denver, CO: Love.

Schulz, J. B., & Turnbull, A. P. (1983). *Mainstreaming handicapped students* (2nd ed.). Boston: Allyn & Bacon.

Stainback, S., & Stainback, W. (Eds.). (1985). *Integrating students with severe handicaps into regular schools.* Reston, VA: Council for Exceptional Children.

Stainback, S., & Stainback, W. (Eds.). (1990). *Support networks for inclusive classrooms.* Baltimore, MD: Paul H. Brookes.

Stainback, S., & Stainback, W. (1992). *Curriculum considerations in inclusive classrooms.* Baltimore, MD: Paul H. Brookes.

U.S. Department of Education. (2001). *Twenty-third annual report to Congress.* Washington, DC: Author. Retrieved September 27, 2005, from www.ed.gov/about/reports/annual/osep/2001/index.html.

What Is an Individualized Education Program?

Outline Questions

What is an Individualized Education Program (IEP)?

How does a student get an IEP?

What elements must be included in an IEP?

How can the IEP be connected to inclusive classroom instruction?

Who participates in developing IEPs?

What are some strategies for dealing with IEPs effectively?

How can IEP paperwork be reduced?

Where can I find resources or more information about IEPs?

E very child in public school who receives special education and related services must have an Individualized Education Program (IEP). Each IEP must be designed for one student and must be a truly *individualized* document. The IEP creates an opportunity for teachers, parents, school administrators, related services personnel, and students (when appropriate) to work together to improve educational results for children with disabilities. The IEP is the cornerstone of a quality education for each child with a disability, and it is an important part of efforts to make inclusion work.

To create an effective IEP, parents, teachers, education professionals, and often the student him- or herself work together to evaluate the individual needs of the student. Then they pool their knowledge, experience, and commitment to design an educational program that will support inclusion and progress in the general curriculum. The IEP guides the delivery of special education supports and services for the student with a disability. Without a doubt, writing—and implementing—an effective IEP is a critical part of making inclusion work.

HOW DOES A STUDENT GET AN IEP?

The writing of each student's IEP takes place within the larger picture of the special education process according to current federal guidelines (i.e., IDEA 2004). The 10 steps of the basic special education process have been expertly represented in *A Guide to the Individualized Education Program* (U.S. Department of Education, 2000a). A summary of that document follows.

Step 1: The Child Is Identified as Possibly Needing Special Education and Related Services

The state must identify, locate, and evaluate all children with disabilities in the state who need special education and related services. To do so, states conduct "Child Find" activities. For example, a child is identified by "Child Find," and then parents are asked if the "Child Find" system can evaluate their child. Parents can also call the "Child Find" system and ask that their child be evaluated. Or a school professional may ask that a child (student) be evaluated to see if he or she has a disability. Parents may also contact the child's teacher or other school professional to ask that their child be evaluated. This request may be verbal or in writing. Parental consent is needed before the child may be evaluated. Evaluation needs to be completed within a reasonable time after the parent gives consent. An overview of the remaining nine steps of the basic special education process is presented in Table 3.1.

Step 2: The Child Is Evaluated

The evaluation must assess the child in all areas related to the child's suspected disability. The evaluation results will be used to decide the

Table 3.1   Overview of Steps Taken by the Teacher Assistance Team (TAT) to
Review a Referral for Evaluation

- Once a referral has been received from the teacher or other professional, the TAT chair schedules a meeting as soon as possible to review information on folder and discuss strategies being used or new strategies to try.

- At this meeting, if the teacher has been using appropriate strategies for 4 to 6 weeks with no change in student performance, the team will recommend permission to screen. If the team feels that the teacher needs to do more strategies or allow more time for strategies to work, the team will meet in approximately 2 to 3 weeks.

- If screening is to take place, a request for permission is sent home to the parents. Once the team receives permission to screen, the student is screened within the week or as soon as possible.

- The TAT chair schedules the second TAT meeting. At this follow-up meeting, the team will review the screening results and discuss results of the strategies used. At this point, the team will make a decision based on all information received as to whether to refer to the IEP team for further evaluation. Many school districts recommend that the TAT complete this process within 65 days of receiving the referral.

- If the team decides not to refer to the IEP team, the student is closely monitored. The team may recommend other services for the student.

- The TAT chair meets the following week or as soon as possible with the school psychologist for students being referred for further evaluation.

The IEP team may accept or reject the referral. If the referral is accepted, the IEP team has 90 days to complete the evaluation. If the referral is rejected, the TAT chair consults with the school psychologist for recommendations.

child's eligibility for special education and related services and to make decisions about an appropriate educational program for the child. If the parents disagree with the evaluation, they have the right to take their child for an Independent Educational Evaluation (IEE). They can request that the school system pay for this IEE.

Step 3: Eligibility Is Decided

A group of qualified professionals and the parents look at the child's evaluation results. Together, they decide if the child is a "child with a disability," as defined by IDEA. Parents may ask for a hearing to challenge the eligibility decision. If the child is found to be a "child with a disability," as defined by IDEA, he or she is eligible for special education and related services.

Step 4: An IEP Meeting Is Scheduled

The IEP team is required to meet to write an IEP for the student within 30 calendar days after a student is determined eligible. The school system schedules and conducts the IEP meeting. School staff must do the following:

- Contact the participants, including the parents.
- Notify parents early enough to make sure they have an opportunity to attend.
- Schedule the meeting at a time and place agreeable to parents and the school.
- Tell the parents the purpose, time, and location of the meeting.
- Tell the parents who will be attending.
- Tell the parents that they may invite people to the meeting who have knowledge or special expertise about the child.

Step 5: The IEP Meeting Is Held, and the IEP Is Written

The IEP team gathers to talk about the student's needs and write his or her IEP. Parents and the student (when appropriate) are part of the team. If the student's placement is decided by a different group, the parents must be part of that group as well.

Before the school system may provide special education and related services to the student for the first time, the parents must give consent. The student begins to receive services as soon as possible after the meeting.

If the parents do not agree with the IEP and placement, they may discuss their concerns with other members of the IEP team and try to work out an agreement. If they still disagree, parents can ask for mediation, or the school may offer mediation. Parents may file a complaint with the state education agency and may request a due process hearing, at which time mediation must be available to them.

Step 6: Services Are Provided

The school makes sure that the student's IEP is being carried out as it was written. Parents are given a copy of the IEP. Each of the student's teachers and service providers has access to the IEP and knows his or her specific responsibilities for carrying out the IEP. This includes the accommodations, modifications, and supports that must be provided to the student, in keeping with the IEP.

Step 7: Progress Is Measured and Reported to the Parents

The student's progress toward the annual goals is measured, as stated in the IEP. The parents are regularly informed of their child's progress and whether that progress is enough for the child to achieve the goals by the end of the year. These progress reports must be given to parents at least as often as parents are informed of their other children's progress.

Step 8: The IEP Is Reviewed

Traditionally, the student's IEP is reviewed by the IEP team at least once a year, or more often if the parents or school ask for a review. If necessary, the IEP is revised. Parents, as team members, must be invited to attend these meetings. Parents can make suggestions for changes, agree or disagree with the IEP goals, and agree or disagree with the placement.

If parents do not agree with the IEP and placement, they may discuss their concerns with other members of the IEP team and try to work out an agreement. There are several options, including additional testing, an independent evaluation, mediation (if available), or a due process hearing. They may also file a complaint with the state education agency at this point.

IDEA 2004 allows local education agencies (LEAs), with the written consent of the parent, to develop comprehensive multiyear IEPs, not to exceed a 3-year span. There are certain provisions for these multiyear IEPs, including consideration for access to the general curriculum, measurable annual goals, and a process for doing more frequent reviews as necessary. The government will issue a report on multiyear IEP success in 2007 (Council for Exceptional Children, 2005).

Step 9: The Child (Student) Is Reevaluated

At least every 3 years the child must be reevaluated. This evaluation is often called a "triennial," or a 3-year reevaluation. Its purpose is to find out if the child continues to be a "child with a disability," as defined by IDEA, and what the child's educational needs are. Individuals with disabilities must be reevaluated more often if conditions warrant or if the child's parent or teacher asks for a new evaluation.

WHAT DO I NEED TO KNOW ABOUT INDIVIDUALIZED EDUCATION PROGRAMS?

By law, the IEP must include certain information about the child and the educational program designed to meet his or her unique needs

(U.S. Department of Education, 2000b). This information includes the following:

- Current levels of educational performance
- Measurable goals and measurable objectives or benchmarks
- Special education and related services
- The extent of participation with children without disabilities
- A statement of how the child's progress will be measured and how parents will be informed of that progress
- The extent of modification of participation in state and districtwide tests
- The dates and location of services to be provided
- Beginning at age 16 (or younger), a statement of transition services the student will need to reach postschool goals
- Beginning at age 16 (or younger), a statement of transition services to help the child prepare for leaving school
- Beginning at least 1 year before the child reaches the age of maturity, a statement that the student has been told of any rights that will transfer to him or her

In defining the IEP and making these requirements, the intent of education professionals was to bring together teachers, parents, and students to develop a program that would be tailored to the student's needs and provides documentation of inclusive educational experiences based on those individual needs. Over the years, however, complying with the explicit tenets of the law (i.e., procedures related to developing and documenting an IEP) has taken precedence over developing a high-quality program that educators can implement for each student who has special needs. Planning and implementing a procedurally sound IEP will always be a challenge: The developers of IEPs must deliver a high-quality framework to help teachers perform at their best in providing specially designed instruction for each of their students with disabilities.

Connecting the IEP With Inclusive Classroom Instruction

The law clearly states that a relationship should exist between the IEP and classroom activities. Each student's present level of performance should serve as the basis for IEP annual goals and objectives. This basic link between the student's needs and his or her program represents the essentials of special education and specially designed instruction.

Every effort should be made to ensure that each annual goal and short-term objective is directly related to the statement of the student's present level of performance. In this way, annual goals and objectives are based on assessment data and not on unfounded beliefs about programs thought to be beneficial to the student.

The IEP should contain goals and objectives for all areas in which the student cannot substantially benefit from inclusive education programs, including related services. In some areas, state and local officials recommend three to four short-term objectives for each annual goal in the document.

In planning interventions, the IEP team needs to take into account the student's current skill level, the teacher's skill, the resources, and the likelihood that the intervention will be implemented. This last factor often depends upon (a) the effectiveness of the intervention, (b) the length of time and skill required for the intervention, and (c) the significance of the student's needs.

The IEP must be reviewed at least annually, and goals and objectives are modified as the student continues to demonstrate mastery. The attainment of the stated objectives is measured by daily performance as determined by the teacher and frequent objective measures of the student's ability to perform the skills needed to attain the goal. The criteria for mastery should be of a type and level appropriate to the behavior being learned. If the objectives subordinate to a goal are sequenced by a task analysis (i.e., breaking down a task into its components), the standard for mastery should be the level of the skill needed to address the next objective.

Participants in Developing IEPs

By law, certain individuals must be involved in writing a child's Individualized Education Program (U. S. Department of Education, 2001). These are the following:

- The child's parents
- At least one of the child's special education teachers or providers
- At least one of the child's regular education teachers (if the student is, or may be, participating in the regular education environment)
- A representative of the school system
- An individual who can interpret the evaluation results
- Representatives of any other agencies that may be responsible for paying for or providing transition services (if the student is 16 years or, if appropriate, younger)
- The student, as appropriate
- Other individuals who have knowledge or special expertise about the child

An IEP team member may fill more than one of the team positions if properly qualified and designated. For example, the school system representative may also be the person who can interpret the child's evaluation results. These people must work together as a team to write the child's IEP. As stated previously, a meeting to write the IEP must be held within 30 calendar days of deciding that the child is eligible for special education and related services. Each team member brings important information to the IEP meeting. Members share their information and work together to write the child's IEP. Each person's information adds to the team's understanding of the child and what services the child needs.

Parents are key members of the IEP team. They know their child very well and can talk about their child's strengths and needs as well as their ideas for enhancing their child's education. They can offer insight into how their child learns, what his or her interests are, and other aspects of the child that only a parent can know. They can listen to what the other team members think their child needs to work on at school and share their suggestions. They can also report on whether the skills the child is learning at school are being used at home.

Teachers are vital participants in the IEP meeting as well. At least one of the child's *general education teachers* must be on the IEP team if the child is (or may be) participating in inclusive education experiences. The "inclusion" teacher has a great deal to share with the team. For example, he or she might talk about the following:

- The general curriculum
- The aids, services, or changes to the educational program that would help the child learn and achieve
- Strategies to help the child with behavior, if behavior is an issue

The general education teacher may also discuss with the IEP team the supports for school staff that are needed so that the child can accomplish the following:

- Advance toward his or her annual goals
- Be involved and progress in the general curriculum
- Participate in extracurricular and other activities
- Be educated with other children, both with and without disabilities

Professional development and training are important for teachers, administrators, bus drivers, cafeteria workers, and others who provide services for students with disabilities.

Strategies for Dealing With IEPs Effectively

While a general education teacher must be a member of the IEP team if the child is, or may be, participating in inclusive education experiences, he or she does not (depending upon the child's needs and the purpose of the specific IEP team meeting) have to participate in all decisions made as part of the meeting, or be present throughout the entire meeting, or attend every meeting. For example, the general education teacher who is a member of the IEP team must participate in discussions and decisions about how to modify the general curriculum in the inclusion classroom to ensure the child's involvement and progress in the general curriculum and participation in the general education environment. Depending upon the specific circumstances, of course, it may not be necessary for the general education teacher to participate in discussions and decisions regarding, for example, the physical therapy needs of the child if the teacher is not responsible for implementing that portion of the child's IEP.

Reducing Paperwork in Developing IEPs

Professionals responsible for teaching special education students are required to record large amounts of information. For example, teachers surveyed about their administrative duties reported that each month they spend an average of 2 hours on each IEP, 1.5 hours attending each IEP meeting, 4 hours per month printing or copying special education forms, 2 hours per month scheduling IEP meetings, 1 hour per month mailing notices to parents, and 4 hours per month tracking paperwork from other teachers that is required for the IEP process or other aspects of special education (Carlson, Chen, Schroll, & Klein, 2003). The ranges on these figures were quite large. For example, work on the IEP ranged from 0 to 30 hours; 99.7% of respondents reported that they worked on IEPs between 0 and 20 hours per month.

As the U.S. Congress was revising the Individuals with Disabilities Education Act, many special educators and school advocacy groups were asking for relief from burdens of the large amount of legal paperwork that they had to do. Easing the paperwork burden has been a driving force in current legislation (i.e., IDEA 2004). But in the special education world, where distrust and fear of litigation often create adversarial relationships between parents and educators, some parents see paperwork as their only evidence that their children's needs are recognized and their educational rights respected.

While the need for paperwork in special education is often viewed as burdensome, it has value and cannot be eliminated. There are strategies that teachers can use to handle paperwork more effectively and efficiently without reducing its value.

Here are a few suggestions from Carlson, Chen, Schroll, and Klein (2003) for ways for teachers and other educational leaders to reduce stress associated with IEPs and other special education paperwork:

- Assign other school personnel (e.g., school psychologists) the responsibility for initial and triennial evaluations, or to the extent that teachers must retain these duties, adjust their teaching responsibilities to allow sufficient time.
- Credit special education teachers for the time needed for case management when defining job responsibilities.
- Consider the potential value of allowing teachers to select from lists of annual goals when writing IEPs.
- Re-examine the process for IEP review. Encourage teachers to update only those portions of the IEP that require changes at annual review rather than rewriting the entire document.
- Limit administrative duties and paperwork to 3 or 4 hours a week unless teaching responsibilities are reduced proportionally.
- Invest in hardware, software, and technological support so teachers have access to reliable computers to manage paperwork responsibilities. (p. 19)

Here are some other ways to "deal with paperwork" that is often seen as a primary deterrent for making inclusion work.

Strategy 1: Focus on the Student

When teachers focus on the needs of the students, they can make the most sense out of paperwork requirements. Commitment to students requires that teachers take the time to step back, reflect on their students' needs, and provide leadership in developing and implementing the instructional plan. The time we spend reflecting and planning at the front end of the process will ensure that greater benefits are derived from subsequent time spent doing paperwork.

When considering special education paperwork, you should consider the nature of the information that must be collected and systematically maintained for instructional as well as compliance reasons (i.e., planning for, monitoring, and reporting student progress). For example, what are the common data elements needed to fulfill IEP data requirements, make quarterly progress reports, or communicate with other professionals? Might the data collected for local progress monitoring or assessment results be used for these purposes?

It is helpful to remember that all instructional goals and objectives need to be developed and planned against a reference point—the curriculum. Most typically, this will be the general education curriculum unless an approved alternative curriculum has been agreed upon. When outcome measures and monitoring forms are available through the district, they can be used to save time and help maintain alignment with general education frameworks and practices.

Strategy 2: Use One Source of Information to Communicate With Different Audiences

A simple way to reduce paperwork is to use a single source of information for communicating with parents, teachers, other professionals, and students. One example would be to use assessment information gathered for planning instructional programs as part of IEP evaluations and reevaluations. The language of IDEA (2004) directs professionals to "use a variety of assessment tools and strategies to gather relevant functional and developmental information (20 U.S.C. sec. 1414 (b)(2)(A)) . . . and assessment tools and strategies that provide relevant information that directly assist persons in determining the educational needs of the child" (20 U.S.C. sec. 1414 (b)(3)(D)). Formal and informal assessment measures used for designing and redesigning instruction are in line with this directive and also provide valuable information and monitoring of student progress. In addition, data from specific areas of student need as described in IEP goals would be appropriate for quarterly progress reports to parents and for communication with other professionals.

Strategy 3: Save Time in Keeping Informal Records

Because grading, promotion, graduation, and program changes are based on individual goals and related progress, individualized and often informal records must be kept for students. These typically include informal monitoring of student progress, student schedules, work samples, and anecdotal records.

Evaluating, recording, and maintaining student records may create additional paperwork. A number of time-saving suggestions are offered by Kronowitz (1992), including the following:

- Plan to assess every other response (e.g., odd-numbered or even-numbered items) on activities with multiple examples of similar tasks or problems.
- Use a scoring key, and have students score their own work.
- Create portfolios and progress charts that allow students to complete selected recording tasks themselves.

Also consider commercial, technologically based proficiency measures. Many textbooks are accompanied by assessment measures, some of which may be completed by the student electronically. When this is appropriate and available, the computer maintains the scores and can generate many different types of data reports, including item analysis and progress reports.

Strategy 4: Understand Formal Paperwork Requirements

Considerable documentation is needed to comply with federal, state, and local policies for educating students with disabilities. The IEP and the individualized family service plan (IFSP—for children who are not yet in the school system) are two critically important documents that have been expanded significantly in recent years. Other formally required documents include reports from locally adopted progress monitoring systems, testing and assessment results, reports for related service providers, and other required student performance reports such as behavior reports or medical observations.

Often, to protect themselves from litigation, state and local educational agencies require additional documentation beyond that required by federal regulations, resulting in even more paperwork. In discussing the review by the U.S. Department of Education's Office of Special Education Programs of paperwork required by states, the National Education Association (NEA) reported that "[o]ne IEP package that was sent in was 43 pages long. . . . [T]he educators were told that most of what they were documenting was unnecessary under the new federal law" (Green, 2000). In fact, the U.S. Department of Education's sample IEP form is only five pages long (see Exhibit 3.1).

Strategy 5: Encourage Student Participation in IEPs

When the IEP is incorporated into lesson planning so that students take an active role in developing and monitoring their own educational programs, student skills in such areas as self-determination, awareness, and advocacy are developed (National Information Center for Children and Youth with Disabilities [NICHCY], 2002). This also provides a means of remaining focused on the student while maintaining legally compliant documents.

There are a variety of ways students can participate in the IEP process. The format and procedures for participation must be tailored to the student's age and degree of disability. NICHCY (2002) has published activities, audiotapes, and workbooks to encourage collaboration between teachers and older students with disabilities. *A Student's Guide to the IEP* (NICHCY, 2002) provides step-by-step guidelines for walking students through the process of participating in the writing of their own IEPs. In general, the idea is to begin the process of IEP planning at the beginning of the year. After discussing what an IEP is and some of the language that is used, older students may participate in reviewing their own IEP. It is a good idea to discuss key ideas with them, such as what the general education curriculum is or terms such as *present level of performance* and *accommodations*. Students who are able can go a step further by having revisiting their IEPs periodically to provide feedback based on guided discussions. Sample questions for these discussions include the following:

- Are there annual goals and/or objectives or benchmarks that the student has met that need to be updated? (Objectives and benchmarks contribute to the annual goals and address the student's progress in the general curriculum and progress toward any other educational goals.)
- Are there other goals or objectives that the student would like to address?
- Is the student able to recognize the connections between goals and objectives or benchmarks and his or her schoolwork?

This process may take the form of class discussions, individual seatwork, one-on-one conferences with the teacher and/or paraprofessional, and even homework with parental support. Then, when it comes time for an annual review, the teacher can draft various sections of the IEP using data gathered throughout the year, rather than in a last-minute dash to the deadline. In all of this, privacy issues and age appropriateness play a major role, and, as always, it is a good idea to inform parents of the plan and include them in the process as much as they are able to participate.

Perspectives on Individualized Education Programs

Current federal regulations regarding the IEP process specify that

1. The IEP team for each child with a disability must include at least one regular education teacher of the child (if the child is, or may be, participating in the regular education environment; see §300.344(a)(2)); and

2. The teacher must, to the extent appropriate, participate in the development, review, and revision of the child's IEP, including

3. The determination of appropriate positive behavioral interventions and strategies for the child and

4. The determination of supplementary aids and services, program modifications, and supports for school personnel that will be provided for the child consistent with the IEP content requirements in §300.347(a)(3). (See §300.346(e))

While at least one general education teacher of a child with a disability must be a member of the IEP team (if the child is, or may be, participating in inclusive education experiences), the teacher is not required to participate in all decisions made as part of the meeting or be present at all meetings or throughout an entire meeting. The following guidelines will help you decide what is appropriate for supporting IEP development in efforts to make inclusion work (U.S. Department of Education, 2000c):

- The teacher would participate in discussions about the child's involvement and progress in the general curriculum and participation in the regular education environment (as well as discussions about the supplementary aids and supports for teachers and other school staff that are necessary to ensure the child's progress in that environment).
- The teacher need *not* participate in discussions about certain other matters in the IEP meeting (e.g., the physical therapy needs of the child if the teacher is not responsible for implementing that portion of the child's IEP).
- Whether the teacher must be physically present at each meeting and the extent to which the teacher must participate in all phases of the IEP process are matters that must (a) be determined on a case-by-case basis by the public agency, the parents, and the other members of the IEP team, and (b) be based on a variety of factors.
- Only one teacher is required on the IEP team, but others may attend. If a child with a disability has more than one regular education teacher, only one of the teachers is required to be on the IEP team. However, if the participation of more than one of the teachers would be beneficial to the child's success in school (e.g., in terms of enhancing the child's participation in the general curriculum), it may be appropriate under the act and regulations for them to be members of the team and participate.
- Local education agencies (LEAs) may designate which teacher will be on the IEP team. If a child has more than one regular education teacher, the LEA may designate which teacher or teachers will be on the IEP team.
- In a situation in which all of the child's regular education teachers are not members of the IEP team, the LEA is strongly encouraged to seek input from the teachers who will not be attending.

Exhibit 3.1   Sample IEP Form Provided by the U.S. Department of Education

Use of this IEP form, or any other form, will not, in and of itself, ensure compliance with IDEA's Part B requirements. Whether or not a state or local education agency chooses to require or recommend that teams use this form for IEPs, all IEP team participants including parents need to receive clear guidance and training regarding Part B requirements and to understand the importance of the IEP in focusing instruction to meet the unique needs of each child with a disability.

Individualized Education Program (IEP)

Student Name:

Date of Meeting to Develop or Review IEP:

Note: For each student with a disability beginning at age 14 (or younger, if appropriate), a statement of the student's **transition service needs** must be included under the applicable parts of the IEP. The statement must focus on the courses the student needs to take to reach his or her post-school goals.

❖

From the Regulations:

Statement of Transition Service Needs—34 CFR §300.347(b)(1)

"The IEP must include . . . [f]or each student with a disability beginning at age 14 (or younger, if determined appropriate by the IEP team), and updated annually, a statement of the transition service needs of the student under the applicable components of the student's IEP that focuses on the student's courses of study (such as participation in advanced-placement courses or a vocational education program)."

❖

Present Levels of Educational Performance

❖

(Continued)

(Continued)

From the Regulations:

Statement of Present Levels of
Educational Performance—34 CFR §300.347(a)(1)

"The IEP for each child with a disability must include . . . a statement of the child's present levels of educational performance, including

"(i) How the child's disability affects the child's involvement and progress in the general curriculum (i.e., the same curriculum as for nondisabled children); or

"(ii) For preschool children, as appropriate, how the disability affects the child's participation in appropriate activities."

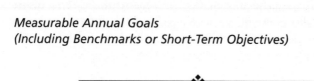

Measurable Annual Goals
(Including Benchmarks or Short-Term Objectives)

———————————— ❖ ————————————

From the Regulations:

Statement of Measurable Annual
Goals, Including Benchmarks or
Short-Term Objectives—34 CFR §300.347(a)(2)

"The IEP for each child with a disability must include . . . a statement of measurable annual goals, including benchmarks or short-term objectives, related to

"(i) Meeting the child's needs that result from the child's disability to enable the child to be involved in and progress in the general curriculum (i.e., the same curriculum as for children without disabilities), or for preschool children, as appropriate, to participate in appropriate activities; and

"(ii) Meeting each of the child's other educational needs that result from the child's disability."

———————————— ————————————

Special Education and Related Services

- Start Date:
- Location:
- Frequency:
- Duration:

Supplementary Aids and Services

- Start Date:
- Location:
- Frequency:
- Duration:

Program Modifications or Supports for School Personnel

- Start Date:
- Location:
- Frequency:
- Duration:

───────────── ❖ ─────────────

From the Regulations:

*Statement of the Special Education and
Related Services, Supplementary Aids and
Services, Program Modifications, and
Supports for School Personnel—34 CFR §300.347(a)(3)*

"The IEP for each child with a disability must include . . . a statement of the special education and related services and supplementary aids and services to be provided to the child, or on behalf

(Continued)

(Continued)

of the child, and a statement of the program modifications or supports for school personnel that will be provided for the child

"(i) To advance appropriately toward attaining the annual goals;

"(ii) To be involved and progress in the general curriculum in accordance with 34 CFR §300.347(a)(1) and to participate in extracurricular and other nonacademic activities; and

"(iii) To be educated and participate with other children with disabilities and nondisabled children in the activities described in this section."

—ALSO—

Beginning Date, Frequency,
Location, and Duration of Services
and Modifications—34 CFR §300.347(a)(6)

"The IEP for each child with a disability must include . . . the projected date for the beginning of the services and modifications described in 34 CFR §300.347(a)(3), and the anticipated frequency, location, and duration of those services and modifications."

Explanation of Extent, if Any, to Which Child
Will Not Participate With Nondisabled Children

From the Regulations:

Explanation of Extent, if Any, to
Which Child Will Not Participate
With Nondisabled Children 34 CFR §300.347(a)(4)

"The IEP for each child with a disability must include . . . an explanation of the extent, if any, to which the child will not participate with nondisabled children in the regular class and in the activities described in 34 CFR §300.347(a)(3)."

Administration of State and District-wide Assessments of Student Achievement

Any Individual Modifications in Administration Needed for Child to Participate in State or District-wide Assessment(s)

From the Regulations:

Statement of Any Individual Modifications in Administration of State or District-wide Assessments 34—CFR §300.347(a)(5)(i)

> "The IEP for each child with a disability must include . . . a statement of any individual modifications in the administration of State or district-wide assessments of student achievement that are needed in order for the child to participate in the assessment."

If IEP Team Determines That Child Will Not Participate in a Particular State or District-Wide Assessment

- Why isn't the assessment appropriate for the child?

- How will the child be assessed?

From the Regulations:

If Child Will Not Participate in State or District-wide Assessment—34 CFR §300.347(a)(5)(ii)

> "If the IEP team determines that a child with a disability will not participate in a particular State or district-wide assessment

(Continued)

(Continued)

of student achievement (or part of an assessment), the IEP must include a statement of

"(A) Why that assessment is not appropriate for the child; and

"(B) How the child will be assessed."

❖

*How Child's Progress Toward Annual
Goals Will Be Measured*

❖

From the Regulations:

*How Child's Progress Will
Be Measured—34 CFR §300.347(a)(7)(i)*

"The IEP for each child with a disability must include . . . a statement of how the child's progress toward the annual goals described in 34 CFR §300.347(a)(2) will be measured."

❖

*How Child's Parents Will Be Regularly
Informed of Child's Progress Toward
Annual Goals and Extent to Which Child's
Progress Is Sufficient to Meet Goals by End of Year*

❖

From the Regulations:

*How Parents Will Be Informed of
Their Child's Progress—34 CFR §300.347(a)(7)(ii)*

"The IEP for each child with a disability must include . . . a statement of how the child's parents will be regularly informed (through such means as periodic report cards), at least as often as parents are informed of their nondisabled children's progress, of

"(A) Their child's progress toward the annual goals; and

"(B) The extent to which that progress is sufficient to enable the child to achieve the goals by the end of the year."

(Beginning at age 16, or younger if determined appropriate by IEP team)

Statement of Needed Transition Services, Including, if Appropriate, Statement of Interagency Responsibilities or Any Needed Linkages

From the Regulations:

Statement of Needed Transition Services—34 CFR §300.347(b)(2)

"The IEP must include . . . for each student with a disability beginning at age 16 (or younger, if determined appropriate by the IEP team), a statement of needed transition services for the student, including, if appropriate, a statement of the interagency responsibilities or any needed linkages."

Definition of "Transition Services"—34 CFR §300.29

"(a) As used in [Part B], "transition services" means a coordinated set of activities for a student with a disability that:

"(1) Is designed within an outcome-oriented process, that promotes movement from school to post-school activities, including post-secondary education, vocational training, integrated employment (including supported employment), continuing and adult education, adult services, independent living, or community participation;

"(2) Is based on the individual student's needs, taking into account the student's preferences and interests; and

"(3) Includes: (i) Instruction; (ii) Related services; (iii) Community experiences; (iv) The development of employment and other post-school adult living objectives; and (v) If

(Continued)

(Continued)

appropriate, acquisition of daily living skills and functional vocational evaluation.

"(b) Transition services for students with disabilities may be special education, if provided as specially designed instruction or related services, if required to assist a student with a disability to benefit from special education."

(In a state that transfers rights to the student at the age of majority, the following information must be included beginning at least one year before the student reaches the age of majority.)

The student has been informed of
the rights under Part B of IDEA, if any,
that will transfer to the student on
reaching the age of majority. Yes [box to check]

From the Regulations:

Age of Majority—34 CFR §300.347(c)

"In a State that transfers rights at the age of majority, beginning at least one year before a student reaches the age of majority under State law, the student's IEP must include a statement that the student has been informed of his or her rights under Part B of the Act, if any, that will transfer to the student on reaching the age of majority, consistent with 34 CFR §300.517."

SOURCE: U.S. Department of Education (2000d).

- The IEP of each child with a disability is accessible to each regular education teacher (as well as each special education teacher, related service provider, and other service provider) who is responsible for implementing the IEP.
- Each teacher and provider is informed of (a) his or her specific responsibilities related to implementing the IEP and (b) the specific

accommodations, modifications, and supports that must be provided to the child in accordance with the IEP.

With proper implementation of the child's IEP, the provision of effective instructional practices is increased and the likelihood of making inclusion work is greatly enhanced.

WHERE CAN I FIND RESOURCES OR MORE INFORMATION ON IEPs?

If you would like more information about special education, children with disabilities, the IEP process, or the IDEA, contact your state education agency or your local education agency. Additional sources of information include the following:

Agencies

Office of Special Education Programs
ERIC Clearinghouse on Disabilities and Gifted Education (ERIC EC)
1920 Association Drive
Reston, VA 20191-1589
(800) 328-0272
E-mail: ericec@cec.sped.org
Web: http://ericec.org

Families and Advocates Partnership for Education (FAPE)
PACER Center
4826 Chicago Avenue South
Minneapolis, MN 55417-1098
(888) 248-0822; (612) 827-2966; (612) 827-7770 (TTY)
E-mail: fape@pacer.org
Web: www.fape.org

National Dissemination Center for Children with Disabilities
   (NICHCY)
P.O. Box 1492
Washington, DC 20013
(800) 695-0285 (Voice/TTY); (202) 884-8200 (V/TTY)
E-mail: nichcy@aed.org
Web: www.nichcy.org

Office of Special Education and Rehabilitative Services
Policy Maker Partnership (PMP) for Implementing IDEA 97
National Association of State Directors of Special Education
1800 Diagonal Road, Suite 320
Alexandria, VA 22314
(703) 519-3800; (703) 519-7008 (TTY)
E-mail: nasdse@nasdse.org
Web: www.nasdse.org

Regional Resource Centers:

Mid-South Regional Resource Center (MSRRC)
Human Development Institute
University of Kentucky
126 Mineral Industries Building
Lexington, KY 40506-0051
(859) 257-4921; (859) 257-2903 (TTY)
E-mail: msrrc@ihdi.uky.edu
Web: www.ihdi.uky.edu/msrrc
Serving: Delaware, Kentucky, Maryland, North Carolina, South
    Carolina, Tennessee, Virginia, Washington DC, and West Virginia.

Southeast Regional Resource Center (SERRC)
School of Education
Auburn University, Montgomery
P.O. Box 244023
Montgomery, AL 36124
(334) 244-3100; (334) 244-3800 (TTY)
E-mail: bbeale@edla.aum.edu
Web: http://edla.aum.edu/serrc/serrc.html
Serving: Alabama, Arkansas, Florida, Georgia, Louisiana, Mississippi,
    Oklahoma, Puerto Rico, Texas, and the U.S. Virgin Islands.

Mountain Plains Regional Resource Center (MPRRC)
Utah State University
1780 North Research Parkway, Suite 112
Logan, UT 84341
(435) 752-0238; (435) 753-9750 (TTY)
E-mail: cope@cc.usu.edu
Web: www.usu.edu/mprrc
Serving: Arizona, Bureau of Indian Affairs, Colorado, Kansas,
    Montana, Nebraska, New Mexico, North Dakota, South Dakota,
    Utah, and Wyoming.

Western Regional Resource Center (WRRC)
1268 University of Oregon
Eugene, OR 97403-1268
(541) 346-5641; (541) 346-0367 (TTY)
E-mail: wrrc@oregon.uoregon.edu
Web: http://interact.uoregon.edu/wrrc/wrrc.html
Serving: Alaska, American Samoa, California, Commonwealth of the
  Northern Mariana Islands, Federated States of Micronesia, Guam,
  Hawaii, Idaho, Nevada, Oregon, Republic of the Marshall Islands,
  Republic of Palau, and Washington.

Technical Assistance Alliance for Parent Centers
PACER Center
4826 Chicago Avenue South
Minneapolis, MN 55417-1098
(888) 248-0822; (612) 827-2966
(612) 827-7770 (TTY)
E-mail: alliance@taalliance.org
Web: www.taalliance.org

U.S. Department of Education
Mary E. Switzer Building
330 C Street SW
Washington, DC 20202
(202) 205-5507 (Voice/TTY)
Web: www.ed.gov/offices/OSERS/OSEP

Books and Articles

Bateman, B. D., & Linden, M. A. (1998). *Better IEPs: How to develop legally correct and educationally useful programs.* Longmont, CO: Sopris West. (800) 547-6747.

Council for Exceptional Children. (1998). *IDEA 97: Let's make it work.* Reston, VA: Author. (888) 232-7733.

Smith, S. W. (1990). Individualized education programs: From intent to acquiescence. *Exceptional Children, 57*(1), 6-14.

Smith, S. W., & Brownell, M. T. (1995). Individualized education programs: Considering the broad context for reform. *Focus on Exceptional Children, 28*(1), 1-12.

U.S. Department of Education. (2000). *A guide to the individualized education program.* ED444279. Washington, DC: Author. ERIC Document Reproduction Service, (800) 443-3742. Retrieved from www.ed.gov/parents/needs/speced/iepguide/index.html.

CHAPTER REFERENCES

Carlson, E., Chen, L., Schroll, K., & Klein, S. (2003). *SPeNSE: Study of Personnel Needs in Special Education.* Washington, DC: Office of Special Education Programs. Retrieved September 30, 2005, from http://ferdig.coe.ufl.edu/spense/index.htm.

Council for Exceptional Children. (2005). *Initial summary of selected provisions from Part B Proposed Regulations for the Individuals with Disabilities Education Act.* Retrieved July 17, 2005, from www.cec.sped.org/pdfs/Initial_ Summary.pdf.

Green, M. Y. (2000, November). Taming the paper tiger. *NEA Today Online,* cover story. Retrieved October 11, 2002, from www.nea.org/neatoday/0011/cover.html.

Kronowitz, E. L. (1992). *Your first year of teaching* (2nd ed.). White Plains, NY: Longman.

National Information Center for Children and Youth with Disabilities. (2002). *A student's guide to the IEP.* Retrieved October 11, 2002, from www.nichcy.org/pubs/stuguide/st1book.htm.

U.S. Department of Education. (2000a). "The Basic Special Education Process Under IDEA." In *A guide to the individualized education program.* Washington, DC: Author. Retrieved September 30, 2005, from www.ed.gov/parents/needs/speced/iepguide/index.html.

U.S. Department of Education. (2000b). "Contents of the IEP." In *A guide to the individualized education program.* Washington, DC: Author. Retrieved September 30, 2005, from www.ed.gov/parents/needs/speced/iepguide/ index.html.

U.S. Department of Education. (2000c). "The IEP Team Members." In *A guide to the individualized education program.* Washington, DC: Author. Retrieved September 30, 2005, from www.ed.gov/parents/needs/speced/iepguide/ index.html.

U.S. Department of Education. (2000d). "Sample Form." In *A guide to the individualized education program.* Washington, DC: Author. Retrieved September 30, 2005, from www.ed.gov/parents/needs/speced/iepguide/index.html.

What Is Classroom
Organization?

Outline Questions

What is classroom organization?

Why should my classroom be organized?

What do I need to know about classroom organization?

What do I need to know about the physical layout of the classroom?

What are some examples of inclusive arrangements for grouping students for team teaching?

How can I guide classroom interactions and activities with rules and procedures?

What do I need to know about organizing myself?

Who needs classroom organization?

How do I evaluate how well my classroom organization works?

Where can I find resources or more information on classroom organization?

Classroom organization is the coordination of people, objects, and space within a classroom to support teacher-student, student-student, and teacher-assistant interactions, including how your room is designed, where you keep the things you need, and how you plan for traffic flow within the room. Organizing your classroom is one of the most important aspects of your job as a teacher. The more diverse your class is, the more important your organization will be. Principals look for qualities of a good classroom organizer as early as the initial interview. Efficient classroom organization reflects a mature, "together" teacher, and these qualities are highly attractive, no matter how long (or how little) you have been teaching.

WHY SHOULD MY CLASSROOM BE ORGANIZED?

Consider your class as a body. Just as the body has parts and systems to keep it working efficiently, the class body is a group of individuals working together to make the class work. The class body works together to learn important information and skills, to learn how to get along with other students and its teacher, and to experience various aspects of school life together, such as events, field trips, programs, and experiments.

There are three principles about the classroom body to keep in mind. First, no part of the body is any more important that any other part of the body. Each student in your classroom, whether gifted or having a learning disability, or a speech impairment, or a behavior disorder, or no special identification at all, is just as important as everyone else. This assumption requires you to treat everyone in your classroom *fairly*. This does not mean that you have to treat everyone *the same*. You are not expected to treat every student the same, because each student will have different needs.

Rick Lavoie provides a wonderful example of this principle in his *F.A.T. City* video (available from PBS). He describes a class where a student has a seizure and is in need of CPR. The fictional teacher who wants to treat everyone the same refuses to help, saying, "Sorry, kid, if I give you CPR, I'll have to give *everyone* CPR!" Fair treatment is not treating everyone the same; fair treatment is giving every student what he or she needs to the best of your ability.

Second, while no one is more important than another, each person is vitally important and has a special contribution to make. Each person in your classroom will possess some gift. Your charge as his or her teacher is to help each student identify and use that gift. In a classroom the obvious gifts are academic: good reading, good spelling, good writing, or math talent. Other gifts include athleticism or talent in art or music. Less obvious gifts will be the ability to get others to listen, or cooperate, or smile. Finding and appreciating your students' gifts will be a joy of your teaching experience.

The last principle is about you. Keep in mind that your role in the classroom is pivotal. Not only your students but you yourself bring special gifts to your classroom, and your classroom would not be the same without you.

With the recognition of your gifts comes a reminder of your responsibility: Your *decisions* will affect the entire classroom body, and your *attitude* will affect its mental and emotional health. You are at the head of the body, and the rest of the body will take its cue from you.

WHAT DO I NEED TO KNOW ABOUT CLASSROOM ORGANIZATION?

The term *classroom organization* is broad and has different definitions. Many people focus on the *behavior management* aspect of classroom organization, which includes rules, procedures, and their enforcement. Behavior management is addressed later in this book. Others focus on the *physical layout* of the classroom, including traffic patterns and furniture arrangement. In general, if you hear that a teacher has "poor classroom organization," it usually means he or she is having trouble with behavior management rather than selecting the wrong bookcases. However, how well the teacher has planned and arranged the classroom can have great impact on the behavior that is exhibited.

In this chapter, the focus is first on physical layout of the classroom and then on classroom interactions as guided by rules and procedures, with a final word on how you "organize" yourself. Your classroom may include students who have cognitive disabilities, physical disabilities, and/or behavioral disabilities, as well as students with no disabilities and those who are gifted. Their needs will affect your classroom organization in visible and invisible ways. Good classroom organization is critical to the successful inclusion of students with (or without) disabilities. Examples of how you can respond to individual needs in your classroom organization are provided in this chapter.

Physical Layout of the Classroom

When you see your classroom for the first time, you will have many questions. Where will you put your students? Where will your materials go? Where will assistants and/or volunteers sit? What will you put on your walls and bulletin boards? How will traffic flow within the room? The physical organization of your classroom can promote peace or invite disaster.

One great beginning step in planning your classroom is to take time to see how other teachers have organized their classrooms and borrow ideas from them. You can learn from their mistakes and successes. You will also need to consider the type of content and age level you teach (science vs. social studies, elementary vs. secondary) in your classroom arrangement. Finally, IEP considerations will influence how you arrange your classroom.

Table 4.1   Accommodations and Modifications in IEPs

Modified grading	Abacus
Modified assignments	Dictation to a scribe
Alternative materials	Magnification devices
Graphic organizers	Interpreting/transliterating
Technical assistance/inservice	Demonstration teaching
Reading aloud	Assistive devices
Extended time	Computer/typewriter/
Portfolio	word processor
Large print	Permission to mark in books
Audiotapes	Study guides
Braille/Braillewriter	Multiple test sessions
Preferential seating	Separate room for testing
Videocassettes	One test item per page

SOURCE: North Carolina State Board of Education (2004).

The beginning of your work to organize your classroom is the best time to consider the needs of your students with disabilities so that you can plan for their needs rather than having to react to them later. As you learned in Chapter 3, students with disabilities are provided with an IEP that ensures that their education is appropriate. The IEP often includes accommodations and modifications, which are meant to assist the learner with special needs in various aspects of the school day. These accommodations and modifications often affect physical space. Your classroom organization will reflect your ability to implement accommodations and modifications successfully. See Table 4.1 for an example of accommodations and modifications that are incorporated into IEPs. More on accommodations and modifications is presented in Chapter 9.

Physical Space and Furniture Arrangement

Availability of physical space varies from school to school. Some teachers receive an entire classroom in a building; others share classroom space or have a classroom in a mobile unit. Beginning teachers sometimes fall to the bottom of the "pecking order" in assignment of classroom space. The type of classroom you are assigned will affect your options for arranging your physical space. However, talking to other teachers with similar spaces and visiting other classrooms will help you make good design decisions.

A teacher's personal preferences will influence classroom design. Some teachers like lots of color and movement; others like a very orderly appearance with minimal distractions. If you are a beginning teacher, administrators' opinions and mentors' influences may also affect your decisions about how your classroom looks.

Although the design of your classroom is ultimately your responsibility as the teacher, you need to consider that you are going to have a variety of learners, both with and without disabilities, who will be sharing the space. You may also have a teacher assistant, a classroom volunteer, or some other adult using your classroom space. You will want to design a space that all the people who use it will find comfortable and useful. The world of interior design can teach us a lot about how to organize our classroom space. The interior design principles of variety, balance, proportion, and scale are described here.

Variety is defined as the use of opposing, contrasting, changing, elaborating, or diversifying elements in a composition to add individualism and interest. You can use variety to promote interest in target areas of your classroom, such as centers, student work areas, and student display areas.

In the world of interior design, *balance* is defined as a feeling of equilibrium in weight. A balanced classroom will have traffic patterns where you and your students will be able to move about freely in the classroom without their crowding each other (which can easily lead to misbehavior such as pushing or hitting). Students and teaching activity will not be clustered in one place. Small group and/or individual work areas will have plenty of room for students to get into and leave.

If any of your students use a special apparatus to ambulate throughout your classroom, such as a wheelchair or walker, then storage space and traffic routes will require planning. A good rule in planning for students with physical disabilities is that these students need to be able to go *everywhere* in your classroom that other students go. If you have centers in your classroom, special study areas, or special interest areas, all your students should be able to access them.

Proportion is defined as the relationship of object sizes in a space, and *scale* is defined as the relationship of object sizes to the size of the human body. Remember that in your classroom your goal is to design a space that is comfortable for everyone in there. If you teach young students, you will be considering child-size bodies as well as adult-size bodies; therefore, you will need furniture and storage spaces for both. When proportion and/or scale are not present, spaces will feel awkward. You will use proportion and scale throughout your classroom to design work spaces that promote efficiency. Furniture pieces that have enough space between them, bulletin boards that complement student work spaces nearby, and arrangement of your work area for your private work and meeting with students are examples of appropriate use of proportion and scale.

The disabilities and special needs of your students will require your careful consideration when you arrange your classroom. The most obvious instance needing your attention will be your students who have physical and/or sensory disabilities. Your guiding principle should be that if an area is to be used or accessible to *any* of your students, those areas should be used and accessible to *all* of your students. Students who have physical and/or sensory disabilities and/or use specialized equipment should be able to ambulate freely within the classroom. You may need to store some of the special equipment (such as wheelchairs or braces, or mats used in therapy) in your classroom. Some of these accommodations may be spelled out in the IEP; some needs may emerge after the school year starts. Talking to teachers who have had the student with a physical disability and the student's parents can yield helpful information in dealing with physical space issues.

Other students with disabilities such as learning disabilities, ADHD, or behavior disorders will usually benefit from ample space and space that is orderly. While their physical space needs are not as complicated as those of students with physical and/or sensory disabilities, your careful consideration of space can prevent problems later. For example, you will not want to put student desks so close together that physical contact is easy (or tempting).

Student Arrangement

Your students' space in the classroom is of prime importance. Student space becomes their center for organization and communication within the classroom. Mercer and Mercer (2005) present five considerations for arranging student space:

1. Students should be able to both see and hear teacher presentations with ease.

2. The teacher should have easy access to every student.

3. The teacher should be able to scan the room and see each and every student. Frequent scanning (e.g., every 10–15 seconds) communicates to students that you are aware of them.

4. Arrange desks so that students face where you want them to pay attention (i.e., toward instructional areas and away from

distractions, including each other). For example, although clustering desks together in groups can be a positive arrangement for socialization, it tends to keep students' attention on each other rather than the teacher.

5. Students who have trouble paying attention should sit where they can be easily monitored, or front and center of the room. Teachers can use their presence (i.e., proximity control) to discourage misbehavior.

Materials Arrangement

The types of materials that you will use and store in your classroom will vary according to your teaching assignment. You may have some materials that need to be under lock and key, such as student files or chemicals. Some of your materials you will want to be available to your students at all or certain times of the day. Supplies such as paper and writing instruments are usually stored where students can have access. In addition, seatwork materials, self-correcting materials, and instructional games should be placed in areas where students can get to them. Art supplies, paper for copying, colored paper, and materials that are not used on a daily basis are usually stored where the teacher has primary access. Visits to other classrooms can give you ideas about how and where to store materials.

Your students with disabilities will benefit from consistency and simplicity in materials arrangement. Having a place for everything will help students know where to get materials and, after the activity, where to put them back. Use of color coding, labels, files, and containers may be helpful. Mercer and Mercer (2005) provide two considerations in materials arrangement: (a) Materials that are used frequently need to be easily accessible, and (b) high-traffic areas should be kept free of congestion.

Special Areas

Parts of your classroom may be devoted to special activities such as small group instruction, individual study, and learning or enrichment activities. Good organization of these areas can positively influence the efficiency and attractiveness of your classroom. The special areas in your classroom will need to provide a place for students and a place for materials storage. In addition, the placement of these special areas of your classroom is important; any special area should be a place where the teacher can readily see the students and their activities. Emmer, Evertson, and Worsham (2000) recommend providing displays at the beginning of the school year for essential information such as daily assignments, school information, and content-related information on an upcoming unit or topic. Student study areas are designed for students to be able to complete work away from their classroom desk. Mercer and Mercer (2005) caution that students may view these study areas as punishment because they are out of the mainstream of activity. You as the teacher can communicate that the study area is a positive place to learn, not punishment.

Examples of Inclusive Arrangements

Different types of inclusive arrangements can support various team teaching activities. Descriptions of these arrangements follow. In the first three models, teachers group students according to their learning needs. In the next two models, students remain together in heterogeneous groups.

In *station teaching*, each teacher delivers instruction to one small group at a time while the students are arranged at "stations" around the classroom. In this model, students switch from one station to another. Often one station is set up for independent work (Cook & Friend, 1995). This model provides for small group instruction. Remediation and individualized instruction are possible because of the small numbers in the groups. Student movement between the stations needs to be planned for, as transitions are often challenging to classroom management.

In *parallel teaching*, the special education teacher instructs a small group of students in a designated area of the general education classroom while the general education teacher instructs the larger group. Each teacher has a group and provides instruction in the same room at the same time. The same topic is addressed by each teacher, but in different formats and/or levels. Parallel teaching should be used only when there is a good reason to separate the students. In this arrangement, the special education teacher may teach a mix of students with and without disabilities. The general education teacher may also have students with disabilities in his or her group. Students are placed in the larger or smaller group according to their learning needs in the target subject or topic. General operating procedures of the classroom need to be agreed upon by both teachers (Cook & Friend, 1995).

Alternative teaching is much like parallel teaching, except that the roles of the special educator and general educator may switch, with the special educator teaching the large group while the general educator pulls out the smaller group. One teacher will manage the majority of the class while the other teacher pulls a small heterogeneous group aside to preview, review, assess, or provide enrichment. The purpose and membership of the small group are subject to constant change (Friend & Cook, 2000). In this arrangement, the teacher provides general instruction in concepts. Meanwhile, students who struggle are pulled out in small groups for additional instruction and/or review. In the next two models, teachers teach and manage the entire group rather than separating students.

When *teaching together,* the two teachers manage and instruct the class at the same time. Flexibility is a must as the two teachers employ various instructional formats such as small group instruction, partner work, or individual instruction (Friend & Cook, 2000). This model allows the general and special education teachers to manage and instruct together.

The *coteaching* model allows the two teachers to take advantage of each others' strengths as they prepare, teach, and evaluate student learning. In coteaching, the general education teacher and special education teacher cooperatively teach the lesson, going back and forth in presentation, questioning, leading activities, and so forth. This service delivery model exemplifies the height of collaboration, as teachers partner in instruction from beginning to end. Coteaching, while sharing some elements with *teaching together,* differs in that it reflects the most collaborative of presentation styles, as coteachers work with the same students simultaneously.

Classroom Interactions and Activities

In addition to the physical arrangement of your classroom, your classroom organization will include guidelines for how you and your students will behave and accomplish routine class activities. These guidelines can be constructed in the forms of "rules" and "procedures." Mercer and Mercer (2005) explain that rules and procedures help students deal with social and emotional factors in the classroom, which can be quite complex.

Clearly stated *rules* teach expectations for behavior in the classroom. Students know what they are expected to do, and teachers are provided with a standard for measuring, reinforcing, and correcting behavior. Many schools have their own set of school rules and require teachers to develop classroom rules. Experts (e.g., Randy Sprick, 1985) recommend developing a few rules (four to six). Providing fewer rules to remember allows for greater simplicity in reinforcing and redirecting behavior. Few rules are also more easily remembered than many rules. Rules can be general, such as "Cooperate with others" and "Respect others' property."

In contrast, *procedures* can be specific and numerous. Stated procedures are appropriate for any activity you find in a school. Any of the following can have procedures attached to them:

- Putting your name and date on your paper
- Entering the classroom to begin class

- Exchanging papers for grading
- Moving into peer tutoring teams
- Leaving the room to go to lunch
- Sharpening pencils
- Lining up for recess
- Getting permission to go to the bathroom
- Preparing for assemblies
- Lunchroom behavior
- Completing seatwork

Procedures should be used to minimize confusion in a classroom. You can incorporate procedures anywhere, any time that you want your students to have clear ideas of what you expect of them. An example of a procedure for collecting homework papers is provided below:

When the teacher requests last night's homework . . .
- Each student will check to make sure that his or her name and homework integrity statement are at the top of his or her homework paper.
- Each student will fold his or her homework paper lengthwise.
- Each student will pass his or her homework paper to the student in front of him or her.
- The student at the front of the row will hold the group of homework papers until the homework monitor or teacher comes by to get them.
- Homework papers will go into teacher's homework file to await grading and return to students.

This may seem like a lot of detail for a relatively simple act, but it is amazing how much chaos can ensue when groups of people do not know what they are expected to do.

You may want to prioritize your development of classroom procedures by first developing procedures for the activities you engage in most frequently or for the activities where your students will most likely misbehave or get off task. For example, the cafeteria is notorious for instances of misbehavior. In addition, transitions between activities can be problematic. When students have "down time," they are more likely to break classroom rules, get in arguments or fights, or lose track of what they should be doing. This can be especially true for students who have ADHD or behavior problems.

In most cases IEPs will have very little effect on rules in your classroom because they are so general. But your development of procedures may be affected by IEP goals and accommodations, and procedures can be very effective in including all students in your classroom. For example, if you have a student with epilepsy, you may develop a procedure for your class in the event of a seizure. Students would need to know to give the student space, call for help, remain calm and quiet, and so on.

Unfortunately, there are no perfect sets of rules and procedures, and misbehavior results when rules are broken. Measuring and addressing problem behavior is addressed in Chapter 6 of this book. You are encouraged to spend a significant amount of time teaching your rules, procedures, and expectations at the beginning of the year and then to review them at various times during the school year. If students do not learn what you expect of them early in the year, they are prone to forget easily, and time will be spent reteaching.

Organizing Yourself

Finally, it is very important that as part of your classroom organization you include strategies to balance your time and energy. Teaching can be a draining activity, and every year many teachers decide to leave the classroom, often citing stress as the cause. Developing interests outside your job, developing and maintaining relationships as part of a support system, and focusing on your mental, physical, and spiritual well-being are important aspects of bringing your best into the classroom.

WHO NEEDS CLASSROOM ORGANIZATION?

Everyone in your class needs classroom organization. First, you need some level of order in your workplace so that you can do your job well. Next, you owe your students (and administrator) a safe, pleasant, and orderly environment that is conducive to learning. Finally, if you have assistants, volunteers, or visitors in your classroom, they will also benefit from your classroom organization.

In a typical inclusive classroom, there will be variation in ability, behavior, and personality. Students will excel in some subjects and struggle in others. You will have some students that take charge and some that shy away. Some students will comply easily, and others will stubbornly resist. Some students will have homes where they want for nothing, and others will have homes where each purchase threatens the household economy. The environment of an inclusive classroom multiplies these variations.

Your efforts in organizing your classroom begin long before your students arrive as you consider classroom space and traffic and organization of materials for yourself and for your students. You will also learn, as you gain experience, when it is time to make changes and rearrange. It is wise to consider your classroom rules and procedures before the school year starts and to work on these diligently in the beginning days of school. Finally, your efforts in maintaining positive interactions and developing a positive classroom climate will pay off in better student outcomes and increased satisfaction in your work.

HOW DO I KNOW HOW WELL MY CLASSROOM ORGANIZATION WORKS?

Evaluation of classroom organization comes from many sources. Kame'enui and Darch (1995) advocate evaluating classroom organization both before and after instruction. They recommend a rating system that allows the teacher to decide that a part of his or her classroom organization (a) is acceptable, (b) needs to be monitored, or (c) needs to be changed.

First, ask yourself if your class activities are running smoothly and if you think your students feel safe and comfortable in your classroom. Ask yourself if you feel safe and comfortable in your classroom. You can ask your students how they feel about being in your class and whether they feel they know what is expected of them. Finally, your administrators will be assessing your skills in classroom organization and may note certain areas where you excel or where you can improve. Other more specific questions include the following:

- Do transitions between lessons go smoothly?
- Are students getting to and beginning class on time?
- Are students prepared for class?
- Can everyone find necessary materials efficiently?
- Are all students able to access all areas of the classroom?
- Are there congested areas in the classroom?

Evaluation will be ongoing, and there will always be room for improvement and change. As you continue to teach, you will continue to grow in classroom organization skills. As your classroom organization improves, you can focus increasing attention on other aspects of your teaching such as your lesson planning. Lesson organization is addressed in the next chapter.

WHERE CAN I FIND MORE INFORMATION ON CLASSROOM ORGANIZATION?

Research Articles

Anderson-Inman, L. (1986). Bridging the gap: Student centered strategies for promoting the transfer of learning. *Exceptional Children, 52,* 562–572.

Bender, W. N., Vail, C. O., & Scott, K. (1995). Teachers' attitudes toward increased mainstreaming: Implementing effective instruction for students with learning disabilities. *Journal of Learning Disabilities, 28,* 89–94, 120.

Brigham, F. J., Scruggs, T. E., & Mastropieri, M. A. (1992). Teaching enthusiasm in learning disabilities classrooms: Effects on learning and behavior. *Learning Disabilities Research and Practice, 7,* 68–73.

Giangreco, M. F., Dennis, R. E., Edelman, S. W., & Cloninger, C. J. (1994). Dressing your IEPs for the general education climate: Analysis of IEP goals and objectives for students with multiple disabilities. *Remedial and Special Education, 15,* 288–296.

Kline, F. M., Schumaker, J. B., & Deshler, D. D. (1991). Development and validation of feedback routines for instructing students with learning disabilities. *Learning Disability Quarterly, 14*(3), 191–207.

Descriptive Articles

Alderman, M. K. (1990). Motivation for at-risk students. *Educational Leadership, 48*(1), 27–30.

Baker, E. T., Wang, M. C., & Walberg, H. J. (1994/1995). The effects of inclusion on learning. *Educational Leadership, 52*(4), 33–35.

Reynolds, M. C., Wang, M. C., & Walberg, H. J. (1992). The knowledge bases for special and general education. *Remedial and Special Education, 13*(5), 6–10, 33.

Showers, B. (1990). Aiming for superior classroom instruction for all children: A comprehensive staff development model. *Remedial and Special Education, 11*(3), 35–39.

Books

Emmer, E. T., Evertson, C. M., & Worsham, M. E. (2000). *Classroom management for secondary teachers* (5th ed.). Boston: Allyn & Bacon.

Goodlad, J. I. (1984). *A place called school.* New York: McGraw-Hill.

Kame'enui, E. J., & Darch, C. B. (2004). *Instructional classroom management: A proactive approach to behavior management* (2nd ed.). Upper Saddle River, NJ: Merrill.

Lovitt, T. C. (1995). *Tactics for teaching* (2nd ed.). Upper Saddle River, NJ: Merrill/Prentice Hall.

Mercer, C. D., & Mercer, A. R. (2005). *Teaching students with learning problems* (7th ed.). Upper Saddle River, NJ: Merrill.

Sprick, R. S. (1981). *The solution book: A guide to classroom discipline.* Blacklick, OH: Science Research Associates.

Wolfe, P. (2001). *Brain matters: Translating research into classroom practice.* Alexandria, VA: Association for Supervision and Curriculum Development.

Web Sites

Children and Adults with Attention Deficit/Hyperactivity Disorder (www.chadd.org). Contains information and support for families and teachers of people with ADHD.

Internet4Classrooms, "Classroom Organization and Workstations" (www.internet4classrooms.com/classroom_organization.htm). Includes various topics in classroom organization.

LD Online (www.ldonline.org). Contains information and support for families and teachers of people with learning disabilities. Articles and newsletters are included.

Montana Public Schools, MEA-MFT, "Classroom Organization" (www.mea-mft.org/assist/classroom_org.html). Assists new teachers.

Parent Magic (www.parentmagic.com/newsletter-view.cfm). Contains tips directed toward parents in managing behavior.

Project PARA, University of Nebraska–Lincoln, "Organization and Management of the Classroom" (www.para.unl.edu/para/Organization/Intro.html). Presents a unit on classroom organization for paraprofessionals.

ProTeacher (www.proteacher.com). ProTeacher is a professional community for elementary school teachers, specialists, and student teachers in prekindergarten through Grade 8. The open membership includes visitors from across the United States and guests from around the world. The site features over two dozen active discussion boards and an extensive archive and directory of teacher-selected lesson plans, teaching ideas, and resources.

Saskatchewan Learning, "Classroom Organization" (www.sasked.gov.sk.ca/docs/elemsci/corgesc.html). Includes classroom organization (including procedures) in an elementary science classroom.

CHAPTER REFERENCES

Cook, L., & Friend, M. (1995). Co-teaching: Guidelines for creating effective practices. *Focus on Exceptional Children, 28,* 1–16.

Emmer, E. T., Evertson, C. M., & Worsham, M. E. (2000). *Classroom management for secondary teachers* (5th ed.). Boston: Allyn & Bacon.

Friend, M., & Cook, L. (2000). *Interactions: Collaboration skills for school professionals* (3rd ed.). New York: Longman.

Kame'enui, E. J., & Darch, C. B. (2004). *Instructional classroom management: A proactive approach to behavior management* (2nd ed.). Upper Saddle River, NJ: Merrill.

Mercer, C. D., & Mercer, A. R. (2005). *Teaching students with learning problems* (7th ed.). Upper Saddle River, NJ: Merrill.

North Carolina State Board of Education, Department of Public Instruction. (2004). Individualized Education Plan Form. Retrieved September 30, 2005, from www.ncpublicschools.org/ec/policy/forms/statewide/.

Sprick, R. S. (1985). *Discipline in the secondary classroom: A problem-by-problem survival guide.* West Nyack, NY: Center for Applied Research in Education.

What Works for Lesson Organization?

Outline questions

What do I need to know about lesson organization?

How do I organize lessons in the inclusive classroom?

What are some approaches that are used to facilitate lesson organization and successful implementation of the plan?

Where can I find resources or more information on lesson organization?

WHAT DO I NEED TO KNOW ABOUT LESSON ORGANIZATION?

Lesson organization in an inclusive setting is the process by which general educators and special educators meet to develop a plan that will guide their classroom. The lesson plan is initially developed with regard to the standard course of study (SCOS), most likely by the state's department of education. These professionals develop plans that reflect the needs of the students with and without special needs. It is important to remember that the students with special needs are placed in the inclusive setting because it is deemed to be the least restrictive placement for them. The Individualized

Education Program (IEP), which will be completed before any placement decision is to be made for a student with special needs, must indicate that the inclusive setting is the least restrictive placement for him or her. Once the inclusive setting is determined to be the most appropriate placement option for a student with special needs, the lesson plan becomes the document that directs and guides the instruction to be completed cooperatively by the general educator and special educator.

Lesson plans are viewed differently by the professionals using them. The content area, experience of the teacher(s) involved in lesson planning, skill or developmental levels of the students in the inclusive classroom, and individual teaching styles are factors that determine the simplicity or complexity of the lesson plan (Maroney & Searcy, 1996). Many teachers have reported to us that the only time they ever completed a formal lesson plan was when it was required for specific coursework during their academic training. In fact, practicing teachers report that they have learned to streamline their lesson plans and that they seldom write plans as detailed as those of the student or beginning teacher (Maroney & Searcy, 1996). If this is the "state of the art," it is legitimate to question the rationale for continuing to use a lesson plan format. While the intent of this chapter is not to discuss or debate the pros and cons of lesson plans, it is crucial to consider the intent of lesson plans. These plans are the blueprint for teaching that guides the professional educator through the maze of curriculum standards and high-stakes testing criteria in our schools. This is particularly true when instruction is to take place in an inclusive classroom. The lesson plan provides the coteachers with the content of the instruction, the techniques to be used during instruction, and the roles of each teacher during the presentation of the lesson.

Although lesson planning is a crucial step in the instructional process in an inclusive classroom, no single approach or form will be appropriate in each classroom. The decision as to which format to use should be made on the basis of specific districtwide or school-based requirements. If there are no such requirements, the individual coteaching groups should select the lesson plan format that most appropriately fits their particular inclusion approach. The traditional six-point plan, however, continues to serve as the foundation for most of the lesson plan formats used in schools. The six-point plan (See Table 5.1 for an example of a plan for teaching one potentially effective technique, the first-letter mnemonic clue *PLEASE*, used by many teachers in a variety of settings) identifies six (cleverly enough!) specific steps that should be followed when presenting information to students. The six-point plan suggests that a lesson should begin with a *focus and review* in which the teacher reminds the students of the work that was completed in the previous class. This step provides students with information that not only helps them remember what was previously covered but also enables them to use the previous information as a foundation for the current day's topic. The focus is followed by a statement of the *objectives* for the current class. The second step in the plan is intended to provide students with a statement about what they will learn or be able to do upon completion of the lesson. This essentially "sets the table" for the class as they begin to extend their previous learning. Instruction at this point usually involves the teacher(s) providing some model or demonstration of the new material being introduced. The *teacher input* can be accomplished through a traditional lecture format, a role-play situation, or any other means by which the teacher(s) conveys the information to the class. Once exposed to the content, the students begin to master the material through a series of *guided practice* activities. These activities are designed to give students the opportunity to practice the new skills learned under the supervision of the teacher(s). Once the teacher(s) is satisfied that the students have assimilated the material at an appropriate level, they are provided with tasks that require them to demonstrate their content understanding independent of direct teacher supervision. These *independent practice* activities may be completed as homework assignments or may be measured through a class quiz during the next class period. Finally, *closure* is presented to the students in the form of a synopsis or overview of the lesson, with attention given to the skill or content that was to be learned during the lesson.

Good lesson plans take time to develop, but they are essential to success in teaching. The six-point lesson plan may be viewed as guiding the teacher(s) as he or she connects previous learning to new learning opportunities. There is a common misconception that all six steps in the lesson plan must be included in each daily lesson, but this is simply not the case. In planning, think of the best way to involve students in the lesson and in the sequence of learning something new, then use the above steps as they aid the outlining of a learning plan.

While it is not necessary to use the six-point plan, most attempts at developing lesson plan formats consider the six steps described above. Many examples of lesson plan formats simply provide a blank space in which the teacher(s) writes the activities that are to be completed during the school day. This is true with many "Lesson Planners" that are purchased at office or teacher supply stores. The class week is divided into squares, with each square essentially representing an individual lesson. While this example is simple, plans are often far more complex and require a considerable amount of preparation to complete. One is the new format that has been instituted at the University of North Carolina at Charlotte. This lesson plan format is required of all undergraduate teachers-in-training as well as

Table 5.1   Sample Six-Point Lesson Plan

1. Focus and Review
   - The teacher restates the learning mind-set from the previous instruction, linking it to the new lesson.

   Example:

   "You'll remember that yesterday we began to discuss ideas that we can use to help with our writing. What did we begin talking about when we stopped yesterday? Yes, that's right, Mike. We talked about something called first-letter mnemonic cues. What is a first-letter mnemonic cue? Great, Katherine! It is a way to help us remember some things we need to do when we write a story. Today we are going to learn about one first-letter mnemonic cue."

2. Objectives
   - Provides a statement of what the students will be able to do following the lesson that they could not do before it
   - May or may not be stated to students

   Example:

   "After we are done today, we will be able to use a six-letter mnemonic cue to help us every time we write a story. We will learn to write the six letters on our papers and then use the ideas to write our story."

3. Teacher Input
   - The direct instruction by the teacher; the new data that are presented to the student
   - Typically involves modeling or demonstrating by the teacher

   Example:

   "The first-letter mnemonic cue we are going to learn about today uses the word PLEASE. Each letter in the word PLEASE helps us remember something we need to do when writing. What is the first letter in PLEASE? Right! It's a **P** (teacher writes a P on the overhead). When we write a story, the **P** helps us remember to **P**ick a topic, audience, and appropriate format (e.g., cause/effect)." After this first step, the teacher continues to describe the remaining letters in the mnemonic. These are presented below:

   L —List information relative to the topic.

   E —Evaluate whether the list is complete.

   A—Activate the paragraph with a short and simple topic sentence.

   S —Supply supporting sentences based on items from the list.

   E —End with a concluding sentence and evaluate the passage for punctuation, capitalization, and appearance.

4. Guided Practice
   - The students try to complete items involving skills learned during class.
   - During this step the teacher monitors student progress.
   - Teacher checks for student understanding and answers individual questions.

Example:

After completing the input stage, the teacher instructs students to list PLEASE vertically and to write the procedure for each of the steps/letters. Students begin writing, focusing on the specific elements of the mnemonic. The teacher(s) provide feedback relative to the needs of the individual students.

5. Independent Practice
   - Students demonstrate independent mastery of the skill
   - This step is frequently done as homework

   Example:

   Students are given a homework assignment in which they write a story using the PLEASE mnemonic. If appropriate, ask the students to explain the mnemonic to their parents/guardians. Feedback from the parents/guardians would be helpful with future homework tasks as well as serving as a measure of the students' understanding of the mnemonic.

6. Closure
   - Restating or practicing what was learned in the lesson
   - Often tied to the objectives as a final check for understanding

   Example:

   "We have learned to use a mnemonic cue to help us when we write. What mnemonic cue did we learn? Tell me what the **P** reminds us to do [continue through each letter]. Every time we write, remember to use the reminders to help us write a better story. We may learn some more mnemonic cues, but we can always remember our PLEASE cue."

SOURCE: Adapted from Welch (1992).

individuals working toward advanced licensure or degrees. The eighteen-step plan (See Tables 5.2(A) and (B)) is clearly designed to give students with limited experience the opportunity to understand the lesson-planning process as well as identify a specific progression that should be in place during effective instruction. Close inspection of the plan and its rubric reveals that each of the six steps of the six-point plan is considered in the UNC Charlotte plan (i.e., Steps 5, 6, 7–10, 12, 13, and 14). The additional steps in the more complex UNC Charlotte plan are designed to help less experienced teachers focus on critical instructional elements as they prepare the lesson itself. This model is by no means included here in an attempt to suggest that schools adopt it; it is merely presented as an example of the degree of complexity possible when planning lessons. Regardless of the format used, the lesson plan continues to serve as a guideline or road map for teachers as they develop strategies and techniques to provide instruction that will take full advantage of the skills and abilities of all students.

Table 5.2(A) UNC Charlotte 18-Step Lesson Plan Format: Instructional Lesson Plan Rubric

COED Common Work Sample—Instructional Lesson Plan Rubric

Student Name: _____ Course: _____ Date: _____

Title of Lesson: _____ Intended Grade Level: _____

	Developing (Level 1)	Acceptable (Level 2)	Exemplary (Level 3)	Level	Points	Weight	Program Standards
	Point Value = ____	Point Value = ____	Point Value = ____				
I. Initial Planning							
Brief description of classroom context and student(s) characteristics, including ESL, IEP, and 504 accommodations.	No description given for one or more of the following: classroom and available resources, characteristics of class, and accommodations necessary for special needs.	Basic information about the classroom, resources, characteristics of the class, and accommodations provided.	Candidate provides complete description of classroom including resources available for use during instruction, characteristics of the class, and description of accommodations necessary for any special needs student(s).				INTASC 2,7,8 COED CF 1,4
Identification of specific learning objective(s)	More than one of the elements is missing, unclear, or	Objective(s) clearly stated and provides purpose. Standards	Candidate develops objectives based upon student data (Present				INTASC 1,2,7 COED CF 1,2,4

	Developing (Level 1)	Acceptable (Level 2)	Exemplary (Level 3)	Level	Points	Weight	Program Standards
	Point Value = ___	Point Value = ___	Point Value = ___				
(outcomes) and standards addressed.	inappropriate. Stated as activities rather than learning outcomes.	alignment is correct. One of the elements may be missing, unclear, or inappropriate.	Level of Performance). Objectives are measurable with precise outcomes at a mastery level that matches the developmental stage of student(s). Aligned with required standards (NC-SCOS), scope and sequence of curriculum, and accommodations.				
Identification of what the students must know prior to this lesson (prerequisites) that you will build upon.	Prerequisite skills and concepts not clearly identified and/or incorrect for lesson objective.	Most prerequisite skills and concepts are clearly articulated but some important skills may have been missed.	Prerequisite skills and concepts are clearly articulated, complete, and are correct for the stated lesson objective(s).				INTASC 1,2,3,7,8 COED CF 1,2

(Continued)

Table 5.2(A) (Continued)

	Developing (Level 1) Point Value = ___	Acceptable (Level 2) Point Value = ___	Exemplary (Level 3) Point Value = ___	Level	Points	Weight	Program Standards
Identification of resources needed to teach this objective including appropriate technology to use.	Listing of resources incomplete and not clearly thought out. Technology either missing or inappropriate for objective.	Listing of necessary resources given. Technology used within the lesson.	Resources used are integrated into the lesson and make a significant contribution to student learning. Technology well integrated into lesson or a strong rationale given for not using technology.				INTASC 4, 6, 7 COED CF 1
II. Lesson Introduction							
Focus or review	States pre-skills rather than using questions to gauge readiness. Misses opportunity to motivate students and help them make connections.	Individual students checked for pre-skills. Limited questions used to gauge readiness for lesson. Focusing activity somewhat sets stage for	Background knowledge and skills key to student success in this lesson checked to gauge readiness for the lesson. Clear connections made to prior learning or knowledge. If				INTASC 1,2,7 COED CF 1

	Developing (Level 1) Point Value = ___	Acceptable (Level 2) Point Value = ___	Exemplary (Level 3) Point Value = ___	Level	Points	Weight	Program Standards
		attending to the lesson, but important connections missed.	completely new instruction, focus has the potential to stimulate interest and motivate student to pay attention.				
Statement of objective in student terms	Objective is unclear with no specific performance set for what students will know how to do. Students not given an idea of what candidate will look for in his or her performance.	Objective is briefly stated and provides clear purpose. Limited performance expectations given. What candidate expect students to do as a part of the lesson may or may not be given.	Connections made between earlier learning and present lesson. New skill, concept, or purpose is clearly stated for the student in behavioral terms and is specific to performance. Relevance is established for the student and informally tells what you expect to observe students doing as a result of your lesson.				INTASC 1,2,7 COED CF 1,2

(Continued)

Table 5.2(A) (Continued)

	Developing (Level 1)	Acceptable (Level 2)	Exemplary (Level 3)	Level	Points	Weight	Program Standards
	Point Value = ___	Point Value = ___	Point Value = ___				
III. Lesson Development (Input, Modeling, Checking for Understanding)—What the teacher does to teach the lesson.							
Content development	Content and skills lack sequential presentation. No planned examples. Lesson focuses more on an activity than on development of content or skills.	Content and skills sequential but lack basis on assessment data. Some attention to examples and vocabulary planned for use during the lesson.	Content and skills are selected, based on assessment data ("present level of performance"), and are presented in a sequential manner that facilitates student learning. A broad range of examples and non-example are planned as necessary. Vocabulary is appropriate to the learner(s).				INTASC 1,2,6,7,8 COED CF 1,2,3
Methods, strategies, and resources used	Methods and strategies to be used in this lesson are unclear or	Most methods and strategies are appropriate and marginally match	Methods and strategies are appropriate for the instructional objective, are research-based, and				INTASC 2,4,6,7 COED CF 1,2,4

	Developing (Level 1)	Acceptable (Level 2)	Exemplary (Level 3)	Level	Points	Weight	Program Standards
	Point Value = ___	Point Value = ___	Point Value = ___				
	inappropriate for the content or stated student needs. Resources and technology are either ineffective or inappropriate for the objective and lesson fails to include modeling.	student needs. Resources and technology are appropriate. Limited use of modeling.	there is a good instructional match to the students and the skills being taught. Resources and technology included in the plan are essential and make a significant contribution to student understanding. Modeling of new learning and application of the learning are a key part of the instructional presentation.				
Structure and sequence of the lesson	Lesson focuses on how to complete an activity rather than	Lesson sequence is clear and time is allowed for student	Sequence and organization of lesson are effective, logical, and				INTASC 3,4,5 COED CF 1,2,3,4

(Continued)

Table 5.2(A) (Continued)

	Developing (Level 1) Point Value = ___	Acceptable (Level 2) Point Value = ___	Exemplary (Level 3) Point Value = ___	Level	Points	Weight	Program Standards
	developing student understanding of content and skills.	questions and practice, but segments may be missing from the lesson.	structured to increase student understanding. Lesson sequence allows for student questions, practice, and success during each important segment.				
Instructional decision-making	Plans do not indicate when and how student understanding will be checked.	Lesson segmented to allow for student understanding to be checked. No options included for lesson modification if needed.	Frequent checks of student understanding are planned to guide instruction. Teaching options indicated in plans as to how the lesson might be modified based upon student performance.				INTASC 3,4,5 COED CF 1,2,3,4
Differentiation	Strategy for student support is unrealistic to classroom context	One to two strategies that allow for additional	Candidate plans for at least 3 levels of diverse student needs and indicates				INTASC 3,4,5,7 COED CF 1,4

Developing (Level 1)	Acceptable (Level 2)	Exemplary (Level 3)	Level	Points	Weight	Program Standards
Point Value = ___	Point Value = ___	Point Value = ___				
or no differentiation present in the lesson.	support or early acquisition of the skills are planned to address student needs. Lesson may or may not present a plan for building upon student successes or accommodations.	how student needs will be accommodated (varying levels of instructional intensity, scaffolding, rate of completion, peer support, output, grouping patterns, time allocation, and/ or skill level). Accommodations are indicated in the plans for all students who have IEPs, 504 plans, or speak English as a second language. Lesson builds in success for students who have more difficult time learning.				

(Continued)

Table 5.2(A) (Continued)

	Developing (Level 1)	Acceptable (Level 2)	Exemplary (Level 3)	Level	Points	Weight	Program Standards
	Point Value = ___	Point Value = ___	Point Value = ___				
IV. Lesson Implementation – What the students do to practice the new learning.							
Guided Practice	Candidate does not present a plan for leading students through the steps necessary to perform the skill. No practice is provided.	Candidate presents a plan for leading students through the steps necessary to perform the skill, but some steps may be missing or insufficient number of tasks prepared. Scaffolding may be limited or not indicated. Plan for student response missing.	Candidate plans how to lead the students through the steps necessary to perform the skill using the tri-modal approach—hear/see/do—and to allow all students to respond and receive feedback on success with learning objective throughout the lesson. Practice is scaffolded with the gradual removal of support. Sufficient number of tasks necessary for extended practice is present. Plans to model application and how to allow all students the opportunity to respond.				INTASC 3,4,5 COED CF 1,2,3

	Developing (Level 1)	Acceptable (Level 2)	Exemplary (Level 3)	Level	Points	Weight	Program Standards
	Point Value = _____	*Point Value = _____*	*Point Value = _____*				
Independent Practice	Plan does not indicate instructions students will be given. Product or activity does not relate to stated objective(s).	Instructions present but may lack clarity. Product or activity may not be at the level of the objective but do relate to the stated objective(s).	Instructions are clear. Tasks ensure that individual students are knowledgeable or have the skills needed for independent success at objective level for this lesson. Candidate anticipates student questions.				INTASC 4,5 COED CF 1,2,3
Closure	Does not relate to key points of the lesson.	Some key points indicated for summary/review but not all critical attributes key to understanding are included.	Provisions are made for key points/critical attributes of the lesson to be summarized and reviewed using student responses, if appropriate.				INTASC 4,5 COED CF 1,2

(Continued)

Table 5.2(A) (Continued)

	Developing (Level 1)	Acceptable (Level 2)	Exemplary (Level 3)	Level	Points	Weight	Program Standards
	Point Value = ___	Point Value = ___	Point Value = ___				
V. Lesson Evaluation							
Evaluation	Evaluation strategy does not relate to the objective.	Strategy gauges group learning of the objective(s) but may not give individual levels of mastery or directly match conditions or behaviors of the objective(s).	Candidate effectively proposes strategy for determining individual levels of mastery of lesson objective(s). Task matches the conditions set in the objective. Results can be compared to the criterion(a) set for lesson objective(s).				INTASC 7,8 COED CF 1.2
VI. Lesson Reflection							
Reflection—To be completed only when lesson is actually implemented	Fails to identify important factors related to success or failure of lesson and/or student	Partially identifies key factors related to success or failure of the lesson and/or student	Success of lesson judged on student outcomes. Explores multiple hypotheses for why some children				INTASC 9 COED CF 1,2,3,4,5

	Developing (Level 1)	Acceptable (Level 2)	Exemplary (Level 3)	Level	Points	Weight	Program Standards
	Point Value = ___	Point Value = ___	Point Value = ___				
with a group of students	outcomes. Recommendations for future lessons missing or vague.	outcomes. Recommendations for future lessons not clearly related to outcomes.	did not meet the objective(s). Key factors that lead to the success or lack of success are identified. Ideas are provided for redesigning objectives, instruction, and evaluation as well as how changes would improve student learning.				

(Continued)

Table 5.2(A) (Continued)

		Developing (Level 1)	Acceptable (Level 2)	Exemplary (Level 3)	Level	Points	Weight	Program Standards
		Point Value = ___	Point Value = ___	Point Value = ___				
VII. Student Writing and Conventions								
Mechanics		5 or more mechanics errors found in the lesson plan. Word processor not used.	No more than 4 mechanics errors found. Word processor used.	No mechanics errors found in the lesson plan. Word processor used.				INTASC 6 COED CF 1,6
Grammer/ Usage		3 or more grammar or usage errors found in lesson plan.	No more than 2 grammar or usage errors found in lesson plan. Phrases used as needed.	No grammar or usage errors found in the lesson plan. Complete sentences used as appropriate but phrases acceptable and used as needed.				INTASC 6 COED CF 1,6

Table 5.2(B) UNC Charlotte 18-Step Lesson Plan Format: Scoring Sheet

COED Common Work Sample—Scoring Sheet

Student Name: _____

Course: _____   Date: _____

Title of Lesson: _____

Intended Grade Level: _____

Section Scores				Comments
Rubric Level	Total Score	Rubric Level	Total Score	
1._____	_____	11._____	_____	
2._____	_____	12._____	_____	
3._____	_____	13._____	_____	
4._____	_____	14._____	_____	
5._____	_____	15._____	_____	
6._____	_____	16._____	_____	
7._____	_____	17._____	_____	
8._____	_____	18._____	_____	
9._____	_____			
10._____	_____			
		Total Score: _____		
				Instructor/Supervisor Signature: _____ Date: _____
Scoring Guide: _____ = Exemplary _____ = Acceptable			Less Than _____ = Developing	

Several factors may affect the overall ease with which the planning process for developing lessons is completed. These tend to fall into specific categories related to teachers, the school environment, and the students involved:

- Teacher-Related Factors
  - Attitudes and beliefs of teachers that are directly related to planning for students with special needs. Teachers who do not see the value of the inclusion model should not be teaching in an inclusive setting. But if they are, their beliefs should be strongly considered in the planning process. Teachers may consciously or

unconsciously treat the planning session as an opportunity to sabotage the instruction in an effort to remove the students with special needs from the inclusive setting.

- General educators' knowledge and skills in planning and making modifications or accommodations for students with special needs. While many of the adaptations are identified in the IEP, the coteachers must plan for and appropriately implement these adaptations. Specific teaching arrangements should consider the individual ability of each teacher to successfully incorporate the modifications/accommodations.
- Knowledge and interest level of the special educator regarding the specific material. Hopefully, changes in coteaching responsibilities can be changed if knowledge or interest is lacking. If not, these factors should be carefully considered in the planning process.

• School Environment Factors
- Any state-level, school-level, grade-level, or subject area guidelines that may exist regarding planning. If specific requirements or policies exist, these must be taken into consideration.
- State-adopted textbooks or other curriculum materials. If requirements exist that force teachers to use specific instructional materials, these must be addressed in the lesson plan.
- Access to specialists. If students with or without special needs require the support of counselors, reading specialists, or other related service personnel, the time and place in which these services are provided must be included in the plan.
- Scheduling of special classes (e.g., music, art, and physical education) as well as special events

• Student-Related Factors
- Class size, which may dictate certain instructional practices while eliminating others
- Individual student learning styles. Material should be presented in a manner that incorporates as many different modalities as possible.
- Specific patterns of behavior exhibited by any students in the inclusive classroom. If a male student becomes overly aggressive when placed in a group with female students, it is important to reflect the need to avoid this type of grouping in the development of the lesson plan.
- Language and/or cultural differences that may exist in the classroom

HOW DO I ORGANIZE LESSONS IN THE INCLUSIVE CLASSROOM?

In the beginning stages of planning lessons for the inclusive classroom, several factors must be considered. These include the support of the school's administration, the roles of each professional working in the inclusive classroom, the specific material to be taught, student knowledge and responses, and how the coteaching will take place.

Administrative Support

As stated throughout this book, inclusion is less likely to succeed without the support of the building administration. Administrative support is crucial to the successful completion of lesson plans because of the need for scheduling. Planning can be truly effective only if the coteachers have the opportunity to plan together, and this will occur only if the building administration provides the coteachers with common planning periods. The common planning time provides the coteachers with the opportunity to meet together and jointly plan the activities for the classes to be taught. If common planning time is impossible, Murawski and Dieker (2004) suggest alternative options, such as having a substitute teacher occasionally cover classes or meeting during student activity periods, during student field-trips or assemblies, during lunch, or before or after school. While viable, these alternatives may not be optimal for teachers, as they are likely not to occur due to financial limitations (e.g., hiring substitute teachers), limitations on the teachers (e.g., missing assemblies that might be of interest to an individual teacher), or the requirement that the teachers give up their free time (e.g., lunch or before/after school). The support of the school administration from the outset will help eliminate or at least reduce the scheduling problems that might negatively affect joint planning.

Roles of the Professionals Involved in Planning

The training provided to general education specialists typically includes significant attention to specific content information. General education teachers know the content to be taught in their assigned classroom setting. As an obvious example, general education teachers assigned to teach algebra to middle school students have a strong mathematics background and significant exposure to the content of math in general and algebra in particular. Thus general educators are aware of the curricular materials that are appropriate and have been trained in methodologies designed to enable them to present the curriculum to their classes. These classes are much larger than those with which the special educator is familiar. Hence the general education teacher is the curriculum or content specialist with specific skills and strategies that enable the presentation of the content to classes with larger numbers of students. The special education teacher, on the other hand, has received greater training emphasis in areas involving behavior management, modification of instruction, consideration of learning styles and learning strategies, and instructional techniques designed for smaller groups of students. During planning, careful consideration of and attention to the areas of expertise of each professional will lead to far greater success in the inclusive classroom setting. The general educator can provide a general overview of the content to be presented, while the special educator can suggest modifications to the material/presentation that adhere to the IEP provisions and meet the individual demands of the students with special needs. By planning together, the general and special educators can use each team member's expertise to enhance the classroom presentation for all students in the inclusive setting.

What Material Will Be Taught?

It is important to remember that, although the goals and objectives of the IEP continue to guide the instruction, students with special needs are placed in the inclusive classroom because this setting is deemed to be the most appropriate or least restrictive for them. Given the placement in the general education/inclusion classroom, however, the expectation is that students with special needs will receive instruction based on specific SCOS criteria.

Consequently, the specific content to be covered during each individual lesson will be determined by adherence to the SCOS in each school. The SCOS is usually developed by each state department of education and identifies a specific scope and sequence of skills to be considered when instruction is delivered. An example of the curricular expectations in a standard course of study is presented in Table 5.3. This SCOS lists mathematics skills and concepts that are presented to students in kindergarten through eighth grade in North Carolina.

Pacing guides, also provided by the state or local education department, suggest the rate at which material should be presented. For example, a pacing guide may indicate that Skills X through Y should be taught during a 2-week instructional period (see Table 5.4 for an example of a Pacing Guide).

Table 5.3   Standard Course of Study: Mathematics, Grade 4

Major Concepts

Addition, subtraction, and multiplication with multidigit numbers

Division with single-digit divisors

Points, lines, angles, and transformations in geometry

Non-numeric symbols to represent quantities

Range, median, and mode

Bar, picture, and circle graphs; stem-and-leaf plots and line plots

Probability

Students will create and solve relevant and authentic problems using appropriate technology and applying these concepts as well as those developed in previous years.

Computational Skills to Maintain

Use counting strategies

Add and subtract multidigit numbers

Read and write word names for numbers

Addition, subtraction, multiplication facts/tables

Identify, explain, and apply the commutative and identity properties for multiplication and addition

Number Sense, Numeration, and Numerical Operations

Goal 1: The learner will read, write, model, and compute with rational numbers.

1.01 Read and write numbers less than 1 million using standard and expanded notation.

1.02 Use estimation techniques in determining solutions to problems.

1.03 Model and identify the place value of each digit in a multidigit numeral to the hundredths place.

1.04 Model, identify, and compare rational numbers (fractions and mixed numbers).

1.05 Identify and compare rational numbers in decimal form (tenths and hundredths) using models and pictures.

1.06 Relate decimals and fractions (tenths and hundredths) to each other using models and pictures.

1.07 Use models and pictures to add and subtract decimals, explaining the processes and recording results.

(Continued)

Table 5.3 (Continued)

1.08 Use models and pictures to add and subtract rational numbers with like denominators.

1.09 Find the fractional part of a whole number using models and pictures.

1.10 Model and explain associative and distributive properties.

1.11 Memorize the division facts related to the multiplication facts/tables through 10.

1.12 Identify missing factors in multiplication facts.

1.13 Round rational numbers to the nearest whole number and justify.

1.14 Estimate solutions to problems.

1.15 Multiply two- or three-digit numbers by one-digit numbers or a two-digit multiple of 10.

1.16 Divide using single-digit divisors, with and without remainders.

1.17 Use order of operations with addition, subtraction, multiplication, and division.

1.18 Solve multistep problems; determine if there is sufficient data given, then select additional strategies, including making a chart or graph; looking for patterns; making a simpler problem; using logic; working backwards; and breaking into parts. Verify and interpret results with respect to the original problem; use calculators as appropriate. Discuss alternate methods for solution.

Spatial Sense, Measurement, and Geometry

Goal 2: The learner will demonstrate an understanding and use of the properties and relationships in geometry and of standard units of metric and customary measurement.

2.01 Identify points, lines, and angles (acute, right, and obtuse).

2.02 Use manipulatives, pictorial representations, and appropriate vocabulary (e.g., sides, angles, and vertices) to identify properties of plane figures; identify in the environment.

2.03 Use manipulatives, pictorial representations, and appropriate vocabulary (e.g., faces, edges, and vertices) to identify properties of polyhedra (solid figures); identify in the environment.

2.04 Identify intersecting, parallel, and perpendicular lines and line segments and their midpoints; identify in the environment.

2.05 Recognize congruent plane figures after geometric transformations such as rotations (turns), reflections (flips), and translations (slides).

2.06 Use designs, models, and computer graphics to illustrate reflections, rotations, and translations of plane figures and record observations.

2.07 Estimate and measure length, capacity, and mass using these additional units: inches, miles, centimeters, and kilometers; milliliters, cups, and pints; kilograms and tons.

2.08 Write and solve meaningful, multistep problems involving money, elapsed time, and temperature; verify reasonableness of answers.

2.09 Use models to develop the relationship between the total number of square units contained in a rectangle and the length and width of the figure.

2.10 Measure the perimeter of rectangles and triangles. Determine the area of rectangles and squares using grids; find areas of other regular and irregular figures using grids.

Patterns, Relationships, and Functions

Goal 3: The learner will demonstrate an understanding of patterns and relationships.

3.01 Identify numerical and geometric patterns by stating their rules; extend the pattern, generalize, and make predictions.

3.02 Identify the pattern by stating the rule, extend the pattern, generalize the rule for the pattern, and make predictions when given a table of number pairs or a set of data.

3.03 Construct and order a table of values to solve problems associated with a given relationship.

3.04 Use non-numeric symbols to represent quantities in expressions, open sentences, and descriptions of relationships. Determine solutions to open sentences.

Data, Probability, and Statistics

Goal 4: The learner will demonstrate an understanding and use of graphing, probability, and data analysis.

4.01 Interpret and construct stem-and-leaf plots.

4.02 Display data in a variety of ways, including circle graphs. Discuss the advantages and disadvantages of each form, including ease of creation and purpose of the graph.

4.03 Collect, organize, and display data from surveys, research, and classroom experiments, including data collected over time. Include data from other disciplines such as science, physical education, social studies, and the media.

4.04 Interpret information orally and in writing from charts, tables, tallies, and graphs.

(Continued)

Table 5.3 (Continued)

4.05 Use range, median, and mode to describe a set of data.

4.06 Plot points that represent ordered pairs of data from many different sources such as economics, science experiments, and recreational activities.

4.07 Investigate and discuss probabilities by experimenting with devices that generate random outcomes such as coins, number cubes, and spinners.

4.08 Use a fraction to describe the probability of an event and report the outcome of an experiment.

Table 5.4   Sample Pacing Guide

September 2005

Monday	Tuesday	Wednesday	Thursday	Friday
			1 Variables and Expressions Text: 1-1 Goal 1.01	2 Variables and Expressions Text: 1-1 Text: 1-02
5 Order of Operations and Open Sentences Text: 1-2 & 1-3 Goal: 1.01	6 Order of Operations and Open Sentences Text: 1-2 & 1-3 Goal: 1.02	7 Properties Text: 1-4 Goal: 1.01	8 Properties Text: 1-5 Goal: 1.02	9 Properties Text: 1-6 Goal: 4.01

The material to be taught in the inclusive classroom may be modified, or the students with special needs may receive specific and appropriate accommodations. However, the coursework itself emanates from and is a reflection of the SCOS or any other scope and sequence of skills used by a school district. While all students are to be exposed to curriculum that is designed to meet the mandates of No Child Left Behind (i.e., providing all students with the opportunity to succeed), there remains a need to consider the unique requirements of students with special needs. In planning for lessons in an inclusive classroom, it is crucial to consider the additional requirements that might exist due to the presence of students with special needs. For example, fourth graders are expected to learn to divide using single-digit divisors, with and without remainders (see Table 5.3, Skill 1.16). But before skills involving division with and without remainders can be introduced, students with special needs may require certain modifications or accommodations to their instruction and/or materials. These should be considered in the lesson plan, and the coteachers must determine how the adaptations will be infused into the classroom instruction.

Student Knowledge and Responses

Successful planning also considers information designed to give the students opportunities to demonstrate their understanding of the material presented. Lesson plans should describe the importance of the knowledge to the overall concept being taught. This knowledge includes learning the basic facts or principles involved in the curricular material being presented (Jitendra, Edwards, Choutka, & Treadway, 2002). For example, a lesson plan in mathematics may focus on the multiplicative properties of 0 and 1. Once the "basics" are in place, subsequent lesson plans should consider how students are to respond to the target material. Jitendra et al. (2002) suggest that lesson plans should identify if students are to reiterate, summarize, illustrate, predict, evaluate, and/or apply the new information learned. Using the multiplicative properties of 0 and 1, for example, students may learn to apply these principles to problem solving.

Once the decision has been made as to what to teach, the coteachers must decide how the information will be presented to the class. There are several coteaching models from which to choose when planning for instruction (see Chapter 12 for a more detailed description). However, the approaches generally are established such that each teacher has a clear and distinct role during instruction. The typical approaches include:

- *One teaching, one assisting:* In this format, one teacher is clearly identified as the "lead" teacher. This professional conducts most of the instruction, leads classroom discussions, and responds to most of the students' questions. The second teacher observes and "drifts" throughout the class during instruction.
- *Station teaching:* This approach typically uses two or more stations at which the students are placed. The coteachers divide the instruction into two segments, with the content presented in separate sites in the classroom.
- *Parallel teaching:* Parallel teaching divides the class in half, with each coteacher responsible for instruction to one half of the class.

- *Alternative teaching:* The alternative settings in this approach usually include one small group and one larger group of students. One group may receive instruction that focuses on reteaching material that may not be mastered by students. The second group, presumably made up of students who have learned the previous skills, may begin to preview the material to be covered during the next class period.
- *Team teaching:* Classroom instruction in the team teaching approach is shared by the coteachers. One teacher often lectures while the second teacher demonstrates the concept being presented.

WHAT ARE SOME WAYS TO FACILITATE LESSON ORGANIZATION?

Lesson plans can be written in such a way that they will cause everyone involved in the process to pound their chests and expound on the virtues of effective lesson planning! But while creating well-written lesson plans is helpful, a plan that does not translate into successful classroom practice is of little value, and the time spent to devise it was essentially wasted. To avoid this frustration, one should take several factors into account when completing and using the lesson plans.

The six-point lesson plan provides the general framework for teachers as they prepare lessons designed to meet the needs of all students. In the development of such a plan, several key elements are particularly important to consider. Jitendra et al. (2002) list four key elements in designing lesson plans that can be used most effectively in the inclusive classroom (see Figure 5.1). Initially, the lesson plan should consider background information. This may include general information about the current topic, specific material that will be considered in the lesson, and a review of material previously learned. The second element is a general goal statement. The goal statement is directly related to the content and serves as a representation of the "big picture" of the lesson's content. Next, Jitendra et al. recommend that attention be given to specific content-learning outcomes. This element of the lesson plan focuses on the knowledge forms (e.g., facts, principles) and intellectual operations (e.g., reiteration, summarization, application) that students will be expected to grasp. Specific attention to these factors helps to ensure student understanding and application of the new information in a variety of settings. Finally, attention is given to learning vocabulary that is crucial to understanding the principles and concepts of the individual lesson. This information is

Figure 5.1   Key Elements in Planning a Lesson

Unit Background:

This is a unit from the Grade 5 social studies curriculum. The previous unit was "Our Colonial Heritage." The current unit (Unit 4, Chapters 7 & 8), "The American Revolution," is a continuation of an exploration of "our great country." In this unit, students will learn about the events that led to the American Revolution and independence from Britain. Review of previously taught information will include the 13 colonies and the impact of the British rule over the colonies from across the ocean.

General Content Goal Statement:

This unit will explore "the struggles of the colonists to gain independence from Britain" (bigger picture).

Specific Content Outcomes:

Students will

- Identify the causes of the American Revolution (summarize a concept)
- Analyze the meaning of "No taxation without representation" (evaluate a principle)
- Compare and contrast the British Army and the Continental Army (evaluate concepts)
- Analyze the impact of religious beliefs on the two parties in the American Revolution (predict a principle)
- Evaluate the contributions to the Patriots' cause by individuals from other countries (evaluate a concept)
- Summarize the contributions of women and minorities in the Revolution (summarize facts)

Unit Vocabulary:

Chapter 7. Parliament, legislature, ally, tax, tariff, representation, treason, petition, liberty, boycott, Congress, repeal, massacre, Committees of Correspondence, blockade

Chapter 8. Olive branch, continental, mercenary, enlist, revolution, independence, allegiance, declaration, grievance, neutral, pacifist, movement, encroach, regiment, siege

SOURCE: Jitendra et al. (2002).

crucial to more advanced learning and provides the coteachers with a clear path in implementing the lesson plan. This lesson plan becomes a significant document in helping the coteachers present material in the classroom setting because it is directly focused on a specific sequence of steps to consider and is designed to guide the coteachers through the entire lesson.

Making the Process as Simple as Possible

For a period of time, the acronym *KISS* was used in education, business, and in just about every other setting imaginable. *KISS* represents the phrase "*Keep It Simple, Stupid.*" While it seems sometimes that education has gone to the other end of the spectrum, there are many occasions in which it is very appropriate to *KISS*! One of these occasions may be the implementation of a lesson plan. While it is important for a lesson to consider the six steps of an effective lesson, it is also appropriate to reduce the paperwork that may be incumbent upon the more detailed lesson plan. For example, Vaughn, Schumm, and Arguelles (1997) developed an effective, thorough, and simple format to enable coteachers to plan and implement lessons on a daily basis. The authors title the form "Coteaching Daily Lesson Plans," and it is an excellent example of how planning can be effectively, clearly, and quickly incorporated into the daily routine of inclusion (see Figure 5.2). The coteachers update the information each day, using whatever language makes sense to them. They can then modify or accommodate the lessons as appropriate and do so with a minimum of busywork. This format is one that we would recommend to teachers in the daily planning process. It may be used along with more formal lesson plans, although it can also stand alone. We sincerely believe that all teachers can and should incorporate techniques that make their professional lives simpler while continuing to focus on the overriding goal of meeting the needs of all students.

Using Data to Make Instructional Decisions

As the lesson plans are implemented in the classroom setting, it is important for the coteachers to use information gained from one lesson to help prepare and implement the following lesson(s). Once again, the

Figure 5.2   Coteaching Daily Lesson Plans

Date	What Are You Going to Teach?	Which Coteaching Techniques Will You Use?	What Are the Specific Tasks of Both Teachers?	What Materials Are Needed?	How Will You Evaluate Learning?	Information About Students Who Need Follow-up Work

SOURCE: Vaughn, Schumm, and Arguelles (1997).

initial step in the lesson plan is some type of review and focusing activity. This step considers the material taught in the previous lesson and uses it as a foundation for the next skill/concept in the SCOS. The consideration of the previous material is extremely beneficial to building new skill or concept knowledge, especially for students with special needs. When students can make a connection between a learned skill and a new skill, the likelihood of learning the new skill is greatly increased. However, the professionals working in the inclusive classroom must exert caution as they proceed to a new lesson. As noted above, on many occasions a student may not have mastered the preskills necessary to progress to the next level of skills. If this is the case, the best review and focus activity in the world will not be sufficient. For this reason, it is extremely beneficial to collect information about the performance of each student in the classroom. This data collection need not be extensive or all encompassing; however, there should be enough information for the team to make decisions as to particular interventions, modifications, or accommodations to be used in the upcoming lessons.

For example, in working with a student (we'll call him Matt) who has not mastered multiplication and subtraction facts, some type of alternative instruction may be appropriate. Rather than beginning instruction on division with and without remainders, the lesson may provide an opportunity for one teacher (likely the special educator) to work individually or in a small group with Matt. This session will focus on either learning the prerequisite skills or introducing or encouraging the student to use a calculator to complete the division items. In this case, the lesson plan will indicate the specific intervention that would be incorporated into the general lesson (ensuring that Matt understands how to enter numbers into the calculator with division items). Upon demonstrating the effective use of the calculator, Matt is brought into the classroom instruction, learning the concept of division that would allow him to use the calculator.

This relatively simple example is provided to show that in many cases a modification or accommodation can be easily implemented in the inclusive classroom. In addition, the example highlights the importance of using information that has been collected on individual students. If the coteachers had not taken the time to review Matt's work, instruction would have focused on division with and without remainders. It is likely that Matt would have experienced little success and a great deal of frustration, especially if he conceptually understood division; Matt might say, "I know it is when we separate items into equal groups even though we make have some left over. I just can't do the multiplying and subtracting under the little division box thing!" Because he *does* understand the concept of division, the use of the calculator enables him to successfully complete division items while he continues to work on the prerequisite skills in other settings (e.g., while doing homework or in a before- or after-school tutoring program). By using the data collected during previous lessons, the coteachers are able to prepare a lesson that is appropriate for Matt and the remainder of the class. Data can be collected by immediately reviewing guided practice activities, by reviewing previous independent practice activities, or by incorporating an alternative method of collecting information. One such method involves the development of a chart that can be used in the classroom setting by coteachers in an elementary school. The chart is simple in its design, which makes it eminently applicable to the classroom setting. Appl, Troha, and Rowell (2001) used the chart to guide discussions about specific teaching concerns, which led them to identify strategies that could be used to remediate the specific concerns. (See Figures 5.3(A) and 5.3(B).)

Figure 5.3(A)   Decision-Making Chart for Remedial Work With Student (General Format)

Child:	Teachers:	Date:

Team members present:

Child's strengths and interests:

Concerns about the child's learning:

Problem statement:

Brainstorming ideas:

Idea(s) selected:

Implementation of the idea:

How/What?	When?	Who?

Time line for implementation:

Evaluation of the intervention:

• Outcomes:

• Future plans:

SOURCE: Appl, Troha, and Rowlee (2001).

Figure 5.3(B) Decision-Making Chart for Remedial Work With Student (Completed Form)

Child: John Doe	Teachers: Smith (Gen. Ed.), Jones (Sp. Ed.)	Date: 3-4-05

Team members present: Jones, Smith, Miller, Cruz

Child's strengths and interests: social skills, athletic ability, symbol-sound relationship in reading, strong sight-word recognition (i.e., mastered 275 of the 300 Fry words); mastered sums and differences to 18, regrouping from ones place to tens place in addition and subtraction.

Concerns about the child's learning: does not generalize skills to higher-level tasks; reading comprehension is far below basic skills in reading; reads slowly and deliberately; complains of difficulty seeing the page; consistent errors with multidigit addition and subtraction.

Problem statement: Team will attempt to identify reason(s) why John is not successful with higher-level skills. The team will review previous individual and group testing information and teacher feedback and records, meet with teachers to find additional information, talk directly to John to determine if his input may be beneficial, and complete a visual screening (with the school nurse) to begin to determine if John's visual acuity may be a factor.

Brainstorming ideas:

- Pair John with a class "buddy."
- Collect additional diagnostic information (e.g., receptive and expressive language with school's speech therapist).
- Increase time in resource room.
- Help secure tutorial support for John in and out of the school setting.
- Provide strategy training for John.
- Provide direct instruction training for John.

Idea(s) selected: Collect additional language data and begin direct instruction program.

Implementation of the idea:

How/what?	When?	Who?
Additional diagnostic data	immediately	Smith, Ms. Davis (Speech Therapist)
Direct instruction in reading	immediately	Jones and Smith

Time line for implementation: schedule diagnostic as soon as possible; begin a 2-week trial period with direct instruction from October 4 to 14.

Evaluation of the intervention:

- Outcomes: John mastered three word family patterns not previously learned.
- Future plans: incorporate language data and recommendations into John's daily academic work; continue direct instruction, monitor progress, and modify accordingly.

SOURCE: Format from Appl, Troha, and Rowlee (2001). See the article for an additional example.

WHERE CAN I FIND RESOURCES OR MORE INFORMATION ON LESSON ORGANIZATION?

Books

Bursuck, W. D., Friend, M., & Best, K. (1999). *Instructor's manual for including students with special needs: A practical guide for classroom teachers* (2nd ed.). Boston: Allyn & Bacon.

Friend, M., & Cook, L. (2000). *Interactions: Collaboration skills for school professionals* (3rd ed.). New York: Longman.

Nolet, V., & McLaughlin, M. J. (2000). *Accessing the general curriculum: Including students with disabilities in standards-based reform.* Thousand Oaks, CA: Corwin.

Walther-Thomas, C., Korinek, L., McLaughlin, V. L., & Williams, B. T. (2000). *Collaboration for inclusive education: Developing successful programs.* Boston: Allyn & Bacon.

Web Sites

The Lesson Plans Page (www.lessonplanspage.com). Contains additional information on lesson planning.

The Master Teacher (www.masterteacher.com). Has materials available online, including *Interactive Lesson Plans and Modifications for Inclusion CD-ROM Planner 1 and 2 Lesson Plans and Modifications for Inclusion and Collaborative Classrooms* (Books 1 and 2).

Organizations

Association for Supervision and Curriculum Development (ASCD)
1250 N. Pitt St.
Alexandria, VA 22314
(703) 549-9110
Web: www.ascd.org/

Council for Exceptional Children
1110 N. Glebe Rd., Suite 300
Arlington, VA 22201
(800) 224-6830
Web: www.cec.sped.org/index.html

National Association of State Boards of Education (NASBE)
1012 Cameron St.
Alexandria, VA 22314
(800) 220-5183
Web: www.nasbe.org/

National Information Center for Children and Youth with Disabilities
   (NICHCY)
P.O. Box 1492
Washington, DC 20013-1492
(800) 695-0285
Web: www.nichcy.org/index.html

The Association for Persons with Severe Handicaps (TASH)
29 W. Susquehanna Avenue
Suite 210
Baltimore, MD 21204
Phone: (410) 828-8274
Fax: (410) 828-6706
Web: www.tash.org/

CHAPTER REFERENCES

Appl, D. J., Troha, C., & Rowell, J. (2001). Reflections of a first-year team: The growth of a collaborative partnership. *Teaching Exceptional Children, 33,* 4–8.

Jitendra, A. K., Edwards, L. L., Choutka, C. M., & Treadway, P. S. (2002). A collaborative approach to planning in the content area for students with learning disabilities: Accessing the general curriculum. *Learning Disabilities Research and Practice, 17,* 252–267.

Maroney, S. A., & Searcy, S. (1996). Real teachers don't plan that way. *Exceptionality, 6,* 197–200.

Murawski, W. W., & Dieker, L. A. (2004). Tips and strategies for co-teaching at the secondary level. *Teaching Exceptional Children, 36,* 52–58.

Vaughn, S., Schumm, J. S., & Arguelles, M. E. (1997). The ABCDEs of co-teaching. *Teaching Exceptional Children, 30,* 4–10.

Welch, M. (1992). The PLEASE strategy: A metacognitive learning strategy for improving the paragraph writing of students with mild learning disabilities. *Learning Disability Quarterly, 15,* 119–128.

What Is Behavior Management and Motivation?

Outline Questions

Why should I use behavior management and motivation in my classroom?

How do I use behavior management and motivation in my classroom?

How do I evaluate how well behavior management and motivation activities work in my classroom?

What are some commonly used behavior management and motivation activities?

Where can I find resources or more information on behavior management and motivation?

WHY SHOULD I USE BEHAVIOR MANAGEMENT AND MOTIVATION IN MY CLASSROOM?

In general, the goals of teaching behavior to students in inclusive classrooms fall into two broad categories: developing social competencies and improving self-concept and attitudes toward school. Students with disabilities often bring a history of failure into any classroom setting.

Repeated failures in academics and/or social interactions create a "failure-filled past." Sadly for the students, their expectations for success become nonexistent, creating a "failure-filled future" as well. The following are common reactions to school failure: refusal to learn, hostility, negative reactions, resistance, dependency, discouragement, distractibility, and withdrawal. Also common in children who have experienced significant and chronic failure are poor judgment, lack of social competence, poor self-concept, difficulties in perceiving how others feel, problems socializing and making friends, and problems in establishing family relationships.

Behavior management techniques are commonly used to address social problems (Lerner, 1997). It is important to manage behaviors in inclusive classrooms because they often represent the main reason teaching some children is more difficult than teaching others. Activities for improving problem behaviors are readily available (see Resources).

HOW DO I USE BEHAVIOR MANAGEMENT AND MOTIVATION IN MY CLASSROOM?

Anyone working in schools will tell you that keeping accurate records is the first step in an effective classroom management program. But evaluation of behavior for management and motivation is challenging because "appropriateness" of behavior can change between settings, situations, and people. Most teachers have high degrees of tolerance for some behaviors and none at all for others. Others are accepting of almost anything that students may do, and still others run a "very tight ship" with strict rules for what is expected. As in any classroom, behavior and motivation problems occur in inclusive classrooms, and there is no list of simple ways to manage all of the possible problems that might occur. The next best alternative is to collect accurate records of the extent to which the behavior occurs and compare them to standards that make sense in the context of the classroom or school.

Tests of intelligence and achievement, classroom observations, and structured and unstructured interviews about an individual's behavior are commonly used to declare students eligible for inclusive services. Performance data on these measures can be found in the school records of virtually every student with disabilities in a special education or general education class. Professionals believe the data are important enough to collect and save because the scores are used to make educational decisions. Performance on tests, observations, and interviews is also used to evaluate an individual's progress in special programs and to evaluate the overall effectiveness of efforts to educate all students. Scores on observations and interviews are frequently used to plan instructional programs for students once specific behavior problems have been identified as the basis for special education interventions.

Using Observations to Plan Interventions

Observations can be completed over several days in different settings by different individuals. Definitions for what is being observed can vary, and the context of the observation can influence the nature of the performance being counted. The observation system can be very simple or very complex.

A five-step process guides the effective use of observations to improve social problems:

1. Define the target behavior.

2. Conduct the observation.

3. Replicate the observation.

4. Evaluate the data produced by the observation.

5. Plan interventions.

What Behavior Is Being Observed?

The first step in doing an observation is defining or describing the problem behaviors that will be observed. Clear statements about the targets of observation are necessary so that procedures used in data collection can be repeated. Precise descriptions of what action(s) will be observed help to maximize the accuracy and reliability of the observations. Actions such as pointing, writing, oral reading, walking, moving, and saying are easily counted.

Operational definitions are useful because they provide a description of "what the problem looks like." Some examples of operationalizations of problems commonly seen in inclusive classrooms are presented in Table 6.1. Each contains a statement of the circumstances under which the problem occurs (i.e., "Given . . .") and a description of the observable nature of the problem (i.e., "the student will . . ."). In their simplest forms, all behavior problems can be described with such operational definitions; the exact nature of the behaviors to be observed for each problem may differ from person to person, since no two people are exactly alike.

Problems may be differentiated along a "continuum of inference" (see Figure 6.1). Those at the low end of the continuum (i.e., low-inference problems) require less interpretation for identification. For example, failure

Table 6.1 Examples of Social Problems of Students in Inclusive Classrooms

Problem	Operational Definition
Low self-concept	Given an activity in which personal performance is expected, the student responds with statements and/or actions that reflect anticipated or actual failure due to perceived personal inadequacies.
Low self-management skills	Given an opportunity to participate in an activity or complete a task, the student responds with statements or actions that reflect limited awareness of expected social behaviors, limited independent functioning, and/or an inability to control impulses that result in inappropriate behavior.
Limited comprehension	Given a situation in which behaviors requested by another individual are to be demonstrated, the student fails to respond or responds with statements or actions that suggest a limited understanding of some aspects of the expected action.
General social withdrawal	Given a situation or activity that requires interaction with others, the student responds with statements or actions that reduce the likelihood of participation.

SOURCE: Algozzine (1998).

Figure 6.1 Inference and Observation Continuum

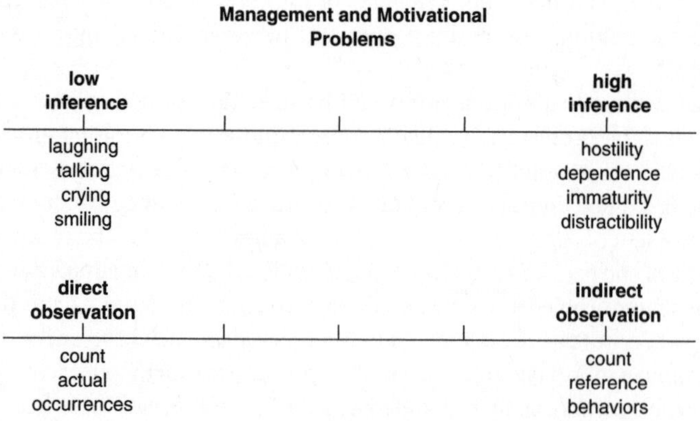

Management and Motivational Problems

low inference	high inference
laughing	hostility
talking	dependence
crying	immaturity
smiling	distractibility

direct observation	indirect observation
count	count
actual	reference
occurrences	behaviors

Table 6.2   Examples of Reference Behaviors for Social Problems of Students
With Learning Disabilities

Problem	Observable Reference Behaviors
Low self-concept	Making statements such as "What do you think I am, a genius or something? I can't do that!" or "I don't know, I'm too dumb for that one."
	Not beginning work because it's "too hard."
	Not answering questions directed to entire class.
Low self-management skills	Making statements such as "Come on, dummy!" or "Don't be so stupid" in reference to work of others during group assignments.
	Frequently fighting to be first in line, first to answer a question, or first to perform a classroom task.
	Messy schoolwork, work areas, or personal appearance.
Limited comprehension	Making statements such as "I don't understand what you want me to do."
	Requesting that instructions be repeated several times and subsequently failing to perform the requested behavior.
General social withdrawal	Sitting alone in the lunchroom or during recess or other activities in which peers are actively involved.
	Failing to be selected by classmates as a team member or group participant.

SOURCE: Algozzine (1998).

to raise one's hand to answer a question in class may be thought of as a low-inference problem; occurrences can be recorded or counted easily by observers with little or no training. High-inference problems, on the other hand, are not as easily observable. They are counted by recording representative reference behaviors. For example, low self-concept is a high-inference social problem; it is observable only through identification and tabulation of observable reference behaviors thought to reflect it (e.g., failure to raise one's hand in response to open questions, negative self-statements, failure to volunteer answers). Targets of observations should be specified using low-inference words and phrases that define an action that can be observed. Examples of low-inference reference behaviors that can be used in identifying social problems of students with learning disabilities are presented in Table 6.2.

How Is Behavior Being Observed?

When observing classroom behavior, one should distinguish the unit being measured (i.e., the problem) and the measurement unit (i.e., the count or occurrence of the problem). Once an observational target has been specified, the unit of measurement is selected and an observation form is developed. The measurement units in assessing management and motivation problems are of varying degrees of precision; simple frequency or duration of occurrence, as well as more elaborate measures, such as inter-response time, may be the "count."

An important aspect of defining behavior problems is the formation of a unit of measurement that is consistent and reliable. *Consistency* refers to the likelihood that the problem will appear the same each time we look at it—that is, the extent to which the problem is recognizable when we try to observe it. *Reliability* of the unit of measurement can be thought of as the extent to which the problem would be similarly counted by different people or by one person on several different occasions. A count of a problem is reliable if we can be reasonably sure that another observer would have recorded the same occurrences. Considering these aspects of defining behavior helps teachers and other professionals develop technically adequate measures of social problems of students with learning disabilities.

Decisions about what to count are made based on the nature of the problem being addressed. One of three types of records is typically used. A written report of behavior as it occurs is called an anecdotal record. Tangible evidence that behavior has occurred is called a permanent product. An observational record of behavior as it occurs is called a behavior count. Anecdotal records, permanent products, and behavior counts are used in social problem data collection procedures for students with learning disabilities.

Anecdotal Records. Anecdotal reports are written to provide a complete as possible description of a student's behavior during a recording period. They typically do not focus on specific behaviors but rather provide contextual information for identifying specific problems in need of behavioral management and intervention. The procedure does not produce counts of problems but instead descriptions of interactions or individuals. Guidelines for writing anecdotal reports include the following:

1. Describe the setting, including people and their relationships to each other as well as activities occurring before and during the recording session.

2. Describe everything the target student says or does.

3. Describe who does what to the target student.

4. Differentiate fact (what actually happens) from impressions and interpretations (what you think about what happens).

5. Differentiate events with passage of time so that duration of responses and interactions can be evaluated.

Anecdotal records provide a basis for determining factors that are controlling appropriate and inappropriate behaviors of students. They are commonly used in planning activities to improve management and motivational problems in inclusive classrooms.

Permanent Products. Records that behavior has occurred are called permanent products. Spelling tests, completed assignments, workbook pages, projects, and other tangible items provide evidence that behavior has occurred. Analysis of these products provides teachers with indications of the quality and quantity of a student's behavior. The following vignette illustrates one use of permanent product recording:

Ms. Jones was concerned about the tidiness of some of her students. She decided to keep track of the number of items that each student misplaced during the school day. Each time she supplied a student with a pencil, piece of paper, or other school supply, she made a note of it on a recording sheet. Each time she picked up a piece of clothing, task sheet, or other item belonging to one of the students, she made a note of it on the recording sheet. At the end of the school day, she checked each student's desk and noted its general appearance and the condition of its contents. She used the results of her permanent product recording to plan an intervention to improve the students' behavior.

Analysis of permanent products is appropriate when a teacher is interested in observing the results of previous behavior and the dimensions of the data collection (i.e., how many products of what type from what sources will be reviewed) can be specified.

Behavior Counts. Whereas permanent product recording provides information about behavior after it has occurred, behavior counts are records of behavior as it is actually occurring. Different types of behavior count recordings are appropriate for different types of behaviors. Event recording is used when the number of times a behavior is occurring is of interest; however, it is generally not the method of choice when a behavior occurs at very high rates or for long periods of time. Interval recording (or time sampling) is used when the proportion of time a behavior is occurring is of interest; it does not provide accurate estimates of the number of times or length of time a behavior occurs, but it provides clear representations of patterns of performance during observation sessions. Duration recording is used when the length of time a behavior is occurring is of interest, and latency recording is used when the length of time it takes before a behavior starts occurring is of interest. Both of these are appropriate when length of time rather than occurrence is the target of observation for a specific behavior. Each type of recording requires a slightly different observation form.

Sometimes it is difficult to observe and record behavior in the classroom due to other classroom activities. Some teachers use tape recorders, video recorders, or other types of technology to record students' behavior. For example, a teacher can videotape a classroom during a period of the day when behavior problems typically occur. Rather than spend teaching time taking observations, he or she will be able to take behavior counts when viewing the videotape later in the day.

Where Is Behavior Being Observed?

Because students act differently at different times during the day when they are with different teachers doing different tasks, observations that are representative are the goal of those who observe to plan instruction. Representativeness can be improved by completing multiple observations.

Observations of randomly selected classroom peers are useful in establishing the importance of the levels of behavior that are observed for targeted students. Knowing that Juan completes 5 reading comprehension items during the same time period that a random peer completes 15 provides a meaningful goal when targeting Juan's academic performance for improvement. Similarly, knowing that Phyllis hits other students every other day but that other students do it less often helps to establish the importance and need of interventions for Phyllis's inappropriate social behavior.

Multiple observations in different settings with different teachers and different instructional lessons can also be of value in explaining a student's social behavior problems. For example, when observations after lunch reveal higher rates of behavior than those taken before lunch, a teacher is provided with a potentially valuable cue for organizing an instructional intervention plan. Similarly, if a student "behaves better" with a colleague, that teacher may provide useful techniques for improving the behavior in another teacher's room.

Whenever possible, you should conduct interobserver agreement sessions and calculate the reliability of their observations. Reliability for observational data can generally be calculated by comparing the number of times the observers agreed to the number of times they agreed and disagreed. For example, if, during the same observational session, one teacher observed 10 negative self-statements and another observed 9 occurrences of the same behavior, the reliability of the observations would be .90 (9 agreements / 9 agreements + 1 disagreement); put another way, there would be 90% agreement during the observational session (i.e., teachers would agree on 9 of 10 of the negative self-statements).

What Do Observations Mean?

Interpretations of observational data are generally aided by tables and graphs. Tables are used to summarize and create numeric representations of the results of observational sessions; graphs provide a visual representation of results. Tabular presentations can be simple or complex; they should be used to compile the results of an observation from numerous recording forms and represent them in an alternate form that is easier to read and evaluate. Table 6.3 shows a sample tabular presentation of observational data on the negative self-statements of two students.

Table 6.3   Sample Tabular Presentation of Observational Data on the Negative Self-Statements of Two Students

	Negative Self-Statements	
Day	(Arvin)	(Fred)
Monday	17	6
Tuesday	32	8
Wednesday	23	6
Thursday	10	11
Friday	25	15
Average	21	9

Data from multiple observation forms are easily represented in a single table that facilitates making judgments about a student's behaviors (e.g., Arvin makes more negative self-statements than a randomly selected peer on most days, his behavior seems worse on Tuesday, and he has days when he acts like a randomly selected peer). These data can also be presented in graphic form.

In a simple line graph, the unit of measure is presented on the vertical axis and the occasion for measurement is presented on the horizontal

axis. Data gathered by observing more than one student can be represented on the same graph to facilitate comparisons and interpretations.
Figure 6.2 is a graphic presentation of the data previously presented in
Table 6.3. While graphing the results of observations does not change the
rates at which problem behaviors occur, it may be easier to see relations
between them when they are graphically presented than when tables are
used to summarize the results of an observation.

Figure 6.2   Sample Graphic Presentation of the Observational Data on
Two Students' Negative Self-Statements Given in Table 6.3

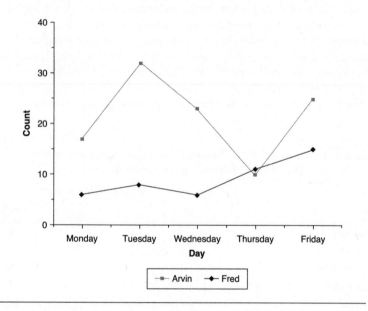

Data are presented independently on a line graph: That is, data from
each observation occasion represent discrete measures of the level of
behavior for a particular observation session. It is also possible to show
the accumulation of behaviors across observations. In cumulative graphs,
data from successive observations are added to amounts accumulated at
previous occasions. Cumulative graphs are useful when a teacher is interested in seeing total amounts of behavior or showing degrees of change in
behaviors over time.

Different types of graphs provide different types of information. Line
graphs are more appropriate when discrete, independent levels of behavior are

the target of interpretation; cumulative graphs are more appropriate when a rate of change or combined levels of behavior are being interpreted.

What Teaching Activities Should Be Planned?

Once observational data descriptive of the levels of a student's problem behaviors are gathered, instructional activities can be planned: That is, a teacher must decide whether to directly or indirectly attack the problem identified as a result of the assessment activities. The types of decisions made relate to the instructional goals of the teacher. For example, producing increases or decreases in deficient or excessive target behaviors is an appropriate behavioral intervention plan (i.e., instructional plan for behaviors) for behaviors that directly interfere with student progress in a content area. Increasing or decreasing alternative behaviors is appropriate when target behaviors are occurring at tolerable rates and other behaviors are easier to modify. After observing the rate at which a student works, talks, or asks questions during a lesson, teachers can decide whether the rate of work should be increased, the rate of talking should be decreased, or the rate and type of questions asked during a lesson should be increased. Having decided on the direction for change within a student's behavior, teachers must decide how to bring about the change. This involves answering questions such as the following: Should I try positive reinforcement? Should I try negative reinforcement? Should I punish inappropriate behaviors? What types of reinforcement can I use? How long should the intervention be used? How will I know if my plans are effective? What alternatives do I have if my first plan doesn't work?

Using Interviews to Plan Interventions

Observational techniques are the most direct way of judging the extent of social problems; however, inventories, checklists, and rating scales are also frequently used to assess behavior (Gresham, Cook, & Crews, 2004; Walker, Ramsay, & Gresham, 2004). Inventories, checklists, and rating scales are all forms of interviews in which opinions about a person's behavior are supplied by the person or other people. Some interviews are open-ended, unstructured samples of questions. In others, standardized items are the basis for the scores obtained by asking questions. The following questions shape a perspective on conducting interviews to more effectively plan instruction:

1. How is information being gathered?

2. What questions are being asked?

3. What happens during the interview?

4. What does the information mean?

5. What teaching activities should be planned?

Who Provides the Information?

It is possible to obtain information by directly asking a student questions or by asking others to supply the information. While parents, peers, and other teachers are generally excellent sources of information about a student's strengths and weaknesses, the information obtained from them is sometimes different from the information students provide about themselves. Similarly, information provided by individuals with particular biases (either favorable or unfavorable) toward the target student may be practically less valid and reliable than that obtained from people with more neutral, general opinions. It is very important to consider the source of any information collected by asking questions, and, whenever possible, efforts should be made to gather evidence from multiple sources for corroboration.

What Information Is Desired?

Information collected from opinions about a learning problem is not the same as information obtained by observing a student. For example, dialogue similar to the following can be heard each day in America's schools:

Teacher: Please open your books to the story starting on page 17.

Student: Oh, good! I can read that! It's easy. Why do I have to do it?

Teacher: You may be able to do it, but I haven't heard you read it.

Student: I told you I can read it. What more do you want?

When conducting interviews, teachers should also evaluate the representativeness of the questions being asked. Just as it is possible for tests with the same names to contain different levels and types of content, it is possible for interviews to vary in content. Teachers who use interviews effectively keep track of the content included in the interview that they are using. By identifying the number and types of questions asked as well as the consistency with which the content is sampled, teachers obtain a clearer picture of what the interview information means. This provides a basis for evaluating the pedagogical validity of the interview: That is, knowledge about the nature of an interview's content provides a basis for evaluating the extent to which the obtained information is appropriate as a measure of content being sampled and taught. For example, if one is planning an instructional unit on communication skills, a teacher-made interview containing criterion-related items that focus on the skills being taught would be a better measure of baseline skills than a standardized, formal interview of attitudes toward school. When one is evaluating the results of an interview, it is also important to keep track of the extent to which the items sampled are actually observable; unfortunately, many questions on commercially available and teacher-made interviews focus on "behaviors" that cannot be observed (e.g., I like school more this year; Learning is fun; I feel good about myself). It is very difficult to develop behavioral intervention plans and evaluate progress using such information.

How Is Information Provided?

The purpose of interviewing a student or others who know him or her is to obtain information for a controlled sample of questions; the outcome of such a procedure is typically represented as a score or set of scores. Such quantitative information is a useful indicator about factors sampled during the interview. Scores reflective of performance are sometimes less valuable when planning instruction than information describing the performance. Qualitative information collected during an interview can be very useful when planning instruction. For example, a student may become distracted after answering several questions in a row; others may show signs of embarrassment when answering items about their families. Some students are very confident when orally responding to questions during an interview; others display a lack of confidence in their replies. Two students may obtain the same overall score on an interview, but their answers may be provided in very different ways that can be useful in planning instruction. Keeping track of qualitative as well as quantitative performance during an interview is a valuable way to use obtained information more effectively.

What Does Information Mean?

When using answers obtained primarily by asking questions, it is important to remember that an interview is a limited, potentially biased sample of the information available about social problems. Interviews provide answers that form the basis for inferential judgments about an individual. Interviews are not observations, and it is generally considered best practice to verify or cross-check the information obtained from them by gathering similar data in a different form. For example, even though administering a behavior rating scale provides a score indicating the extent to which the target student is hyperactive, distractible, or depressed, the relation between that score and the student's actual behavior may be weak. Observing to confirm presence or absence of problems indicated by results of interviews is similar to verifying problems identified using standardized tests by conducting formal or informal follow-up assessments. Once confidence in the results of an interview has been established, the task of using the information for developing behavioral intervention plans remains. Judgments about the levels and types of social problems revealed during an interview and subsequent data-gathering activities are the basis for developing appropriate teaching plans.

What Teaching Activities Should Be Planned?

As stated earlier for observational data, once a teacher has gathered descriptive information about the levels of a student's strengths and weaknesses, he or she must decide whether to directly or indirectly attack problems identified as a result of the assessment activities. The same considerations apply regarding the types of decisions made and the techniques used. Information gathered from several sources (e.g., classmates, parents, other teachers) provides additional targets for classroom and extracurricular interventions.

HOW DO I EVALUATE HOW WELL BEHAVIOR MANAGEMENT AND MOTIVATION ACTIVITIES WORK IN MY CLASSROOM?

Gathering data on behavior is a basis for making judgments not only about levels of current problems but also about progress after intervention and can help the teacher to arrange and manage consequences of behavior.

Graphs and charts are used to illustrate daily levels of problems, and decisions about the effectiveness of interventions are made by comparing levels of performance during baseline (no intervention) and intervention phases of a treatment plan. Typically, the vertical axis of the graph represents the behavior count (e.g., number of times a problem occurs, percentage of appropriate or inappropriate responses) and the horizontal axis represents consecutive times (usually days) that behavior was recorded. Different phases of the treatment plan are illustrated with vertical lines on the graph (see Figure 6.3), and decisions about the effectiveness of interventions are made by comparing levels of performance across these phases.

Figure 6.3   Phases of a Sample Behavior Management Treatment Plan

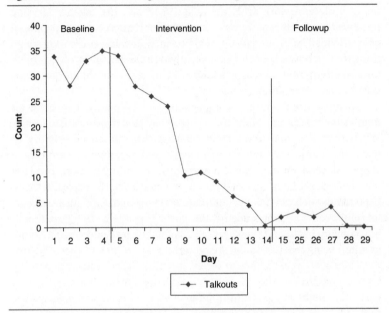

WHAT ARE SOME COMMONLY USED BEHAVIOR MANAGEMENT AND MOTIVATION ACTIVITIES?

The techniques of behavior management can be divided into procedures that increase, maintain, decrease, or shape behavior.

Increasing and Maintaining Behavior

Reinforcement increases the likelihood that behavior will continue to occur in the future. Positive reinforcement is the application of a consequence following a behavior that increases the likelihood that the behavior will continue to occur. Negative reinforcement is the removal of a consequence following a behavior that increases the likelihood that the behavior will continue to occur. A reinforcer is a consequence that increases or maintains a behavior. The effect of applying or removing consequences determines whether reinforcement has occurred.

If John continues to turn in written work that is neat after his teacher praises his efforts, his teacher has used positive reinforcement. If the number of Mike's positive self-statements increases when his teacher places a check on his point card, positive reinforcement is being used.

If Terry's classroom behavior improves when her teacher reduces the number of homework problems assigned to her, her teacher is using negative reinforcement. The key component of reinforcement is increased or maintained behavior; positive reinforcement involves presenting something that increases behavior, and negative reinforcement involves removing something that increases behavior. Reinforcers are things or actions that increase or maintain behavior.

Choosing reinforcers is an important part of planning a behavior management program. Some things have biological importance to people. When they are used to improve behavior, they are called primary or intrinsic reinforcers. Foods are commonly used as primary reinforcers in classroom behavior management programs. Secondary reinforcers do not have biological importance, but they have value because people like them. Expressions such as winking, laughing, nodding, and clapping are powerful reinforcers for some students. Physical contact (e.g., hugging, touching, rubbing back) and privileges (e.g., being line leader, being classroom monitor, being teacher's aide) are powerful reinforcers for other students. Activities such as extra time at recess, listening to rock music, socializing with friends from other classrooms, and not having homework on a particular night are powerful reinforcers for other students. Anything that increases or maintains behavior is a reinforcer. Social problems of students with learning disabilities can be improved by careful application of things students like (positive reinforcement) and/or removal of things that they do not like (negative reinforcement).

A *contract* is a document that places reinforcement contingencies in a written form. Contracts are usually negotiated between a teacher and a student; they usually contain some form of "If . . . then . . ." agreement. The contract should contain precisely written statements describing the expected behavior so that later disagreement about what was really meant will be avoided. The description should include circumstances under which the behavior is to occur and a criterion level for successfully meeting the terms of the contract. A statement about the specifics of reinforcement should also be included.

Contracts add the following advantages to a reinforcement system:

1. A written contract is a permanent product that reflects the conditions of the original contingency for consultation by both teacher and student.

2. The process of negotiation that leads to the contract helps students to see themselves as active participants in their learning as they each take part in setting their own expectations and limitations.

3. The writing of a contract represents individualization of instruction.

4. Contracting provides important documentation that represents current objectives between IEP meetings, and such information may be shared with parents as an important part of a student's inclusive education program.

Examples of some statements used in contracts to improve social problems of students with learning disabilities are provided in Table 6.4.

Tokens are things that can be exchanged for reinforcers; token systems include tokens and backup reinforcers. Tokens are delivered contingently upon targeted behaviors and exchanged later for backup reinforcers. Tokens can be any objects that are portable, durable, and easy to handle. Poker chips, paper clips, button, stars, paper money, or tickets are good tokens. Check marks, punched holes, points, stamps, or any written symbols also work well. Students should be told that they are working for tokens that can be exchanged at a later time for backup reinforcers. The exchange of tokens can take many forms. A common one is the classroom store in which reinforcers are valued (e.g., 50 points) and purchased during exchange periods.

Some teachers use point-based token systems with an entire class. For example, the following system could be used to improve behavior during class discussions: When a discussion is held, points are earned if students listen and contribute three times (4 points), twice (3 points), or once (2 points) or if they just pay attention and listen (1 point). No points are earned if students do not listen to the discussion.

Token systems are easy to develop and implement. Students generally enjoy putting them together and earning points for good behavior. Token systems can be very useful in managing a wide variety of social problems of students with learning disabilities.

The *schedule of reinforcement* is the pattern of timing selected for delivering reinforcers. Reinforcers can be delivered after every occurrence of a target behavior or after some, but not all, appropriate responses. When a student receives reinforcement after every target response, a continuous schedule of reinforcement is being used. When a specified number of responses or a specified time must pass before a student receives reinforcement, an intermittent schedule of reinforcement is being used. Different types of intermittent schedules of reinforcement are presented in Table 6.5. In general, continuous schedules are useful when teaching new behaviors, and intermittent schedules are useful for maintaining behaviors.

Table 6.4   Statements From Contracts for Improving Social Problems of Students in Inclusive Classrooms

Problem	Contract Statement
Low self-concept	I agree to make five positive statements about my oral reading ability each day. If I do this, Ms. Jones will cut at least three pages from my reading homework.
Low self-management skills	If I raise my hand when asking or answering a question during math, then I can have 5 extra minutes of free time.
Limited comprehension	If I line up without pushing or shoving other students for 1 week, I can be line leader for the next week.
General social withdrawal	During the week of November 9–13, I agree to sit with Mary, Joan, and Sally during lunch. If I do, Mr. Rex will buy us each an ice cream on Friday of that week.

Table 6.5   Some Intermittent Schedules of Reinforcement

Type	Characteristics
Fixed-ratio (FR)	Student is reinforced on occurrence of a specified number of responses. For example, on an FR5 schedule, every fifth appropriate response would be reinforced.
Variable-ratio (VR)	Student is reinforced after a variable number of responses; average numbers are used to establish schedules. For example, on a VR10, reinforcement would be delivered on the average of every 10th appropriate response.
Fixed-interval (FI)	Student is reinforced on the first occurrence of a behavior after a specified time has passed. For example, on an FI5, target behavior is reinforced on its first occurrence after each 5-minute time lapse.
Variable-interval (VI)	Student is reinforced on the first occurrence of a behavior after a variable amount of time has passed. For example, on a VI5, target behavior is reinforced on its first occurrence after each time lapse (with time lapses variable but lasting an average of 5 minutes).

Decreasing Behavior

Punishment decreases the likelihood that behavior will continue to occur in the future. Punishment by application is the presentation of a

Table 6.6   Examples of Techniques for Decreasing Behaviors

Technique	Characteristics
Differential reinforcement of lower rates of behavior (DRL)	Reinforcement is provided when rates of inappropriate behavior are below specified levels.
Differential reinforcement of other behaviors (DRO)	Reinforcement is provided when inappropriate target behavior does not occur for a specified period of time.
Differential reinforcement of incompatible behaviors (DRI)	Reinforcement is provided when a behavior that is incompatible with the targeted behavior occurs.
Extinction	Reinforcement maintaining inappropriate behavior is abruptly withdrawn.
Response cost	Inappropriate behavior results in removal of specified amount of reinforcers.
Time out	Opportunity to earn reinforcement is eliminated.
Overcorrection	Inappropriate behavior results in student restoring disrupted environment or people to a state that is better than before the behavior occurred or results in student practicing appropriate behavior at high rates.

consequence following a behavior that decreases the likelihood that the behavior will continue to occur. Punishment by removal is the elimination of a consequence following a behavior that decreases the likelihood that the behavior will continue to occur. The effect of applying or removing consequences determines whether punishment has occurred. A punisher is a consequence that decreases behavior. Sometimes reinforcement is used to bring about reductions in behavior by increasing other behaviors that are occurring at low rates or that are incompatible with inappropriate behaviors targeted for change. Illustrations of techniques for decreasing behavior are presented in Table 6.6.

Shaping Behavior

Sometimes the teacher must use shaping procedures for teaching new social behaviors. When students do not respond with appropriate behavior immediately, it may be necessary to identify and reinforce approximate behaviors. For example, if Jimmy never plays with his peers or plays with them very infrequently, it may take a very long time to reinforce him if we wait for him to make an appropriate response. However, Jimmy can be reinforced for any type of interactive peer response, such as sitting next to one of his classmates. The next step would be to reinforce Jimmy for answering a question of one of his classmates until finally, after many steps, Jimmy is reinforced only for the playing behavior. In shaping procedures, steps and successive approximations of criterion behaviors are reinforced. If Phyllis's teacher wants her to continue working for a 20-minute period, her shaping procedure might include reinforcing Phyllis for staying in her seat for 3 minutes, then 5 minutes, then 12 minutes, then 15 minutes, and then 20 minutes. Shaping procedures use schedules of reinforcement to bring about desired social behaviors in students with learning disabilities.

Management and Motivation in Perspective

Arvin had been characterized as the "brightest" student many teachers had ever worked with in Hemhaw Elementary School. Actually, his intelligence test scores were in the average range and his report cards grades were usually fine except in the areas related to literacy and behavior. At first he received "N's" (Needs improvement) but more recently these had turned to "U's" (Unsatisfactory) each marking period. Typical complaints about his social behavior included "Doesn't follow directions," "verbal disruptiveness," "physical disruptiveness," "can't sit still," "poor peer relations," "name-calling," and "general antisocial behavior." Rather than spoiling or just surviving the school year, Arvin's teacher decided to implement a behavior management program.

First she identified key problems and developed an operational definition for them: "Arvin's main problem is disruptiveness. Given a situation in which others are actively engaged in productive behavior, Arvin demonstrates responses that disturb, distract, or otherwise bother his peers. Specifically, he hits other students during independent work times and causes a general classroom disruption by doing it."

Next, she gathered baseline data on the extent to which Arvin was disruptive. She used this information to evaluate the effectiveness of her management program. She discussed her concerns with Arvin, and they agreed to the following contract terms: "Arvin will not touch another student in the room during regular school hours. Each time he touches another student, he will lose 15 minutes of free time. Every hour of class time that is free from touching will earn one dollar to be used in the school store." After 4 days of implementing the program, Arvin's hitting behaviors decreased completely, and his teacher decided to modify the program to reinforce prosocial behaviors (e.g., hand raising during instructional discussions) that she wanted Arvin to develop.

Like Arvin, many students in inclusive classrooms have problems with behavior. Some of the characteristics of these problems include difficulties judging the feelings of others, difficulties in social interactions, poor self-concepts, and inappropriate social behaviors. Behavior management techniques in which environmental consequences are arranged to produce specific changes in behaviors are commonly used to improve behavior problems. The key concepts of this approach include precisely defining the problem, gathering information on the extent to which it occurs, implementing procedures to increase or decrease behavior, and monitoring levels of behavior before, during, and after trying to change it. Behavioral approaches have been effective in managing a wide variety of management and motivational problems in inclusive classrooms.

WHERE CAN I FIND RESOURCES OR MORE INFORMATION ON BEHAVIOR MANAGEMENT AND MOTIVATION?

Research Articles

Kern, L., Delaney, B., Clarke, S., Dunlap, G., & Childs, K. (2001). Improving the classroom behavior of students with emotional and behavioral disorders using individualized curricular modifications. *Journal of Emotional and Behavioral Disorders, 9,* 239-247.

Descriptive Articles

Fink, J. (2004). Conclusions on inclusion. *Clearing House, 77,* 272–274.
Metzger, M. (2002). Learning to discipline. *Phi Delta Kappan, 84,* 77–84.

Books

Alberto, P. A., & Troutman, A. C. (1986). *Applied behavior analysis for teachers* (2nd ed.). Columbus, OH: Merrill.
Algozzine, B. (1998). *Problem behavior management: Educator's resource service.* Gaithersburg, MD: Aspen.
Algozzine, B., Ysseldyke, J. E., & Elliott, J. (1997). *Strategies and tactics for effective instruction.* Longmont, CO: Sopris West.
Algozzine, B., Ysseldyke, J. E., & Elliott, J. (1997). *Timesavers for educators.* Longmont, CO: Sopris West.
Morgan, D. P., & Jenson, W. R. (1988). *Teaching behaviorally disordered students.* Columbus, OH: Merrill/Macmillan.
Sprick, R., & Howard, L. (1995). *The teacher's encyclopedia of behavior management: 100 problems/500 plans.* Longmont, CO: Sopris West.

Sprick, R., Howard, L., Wise, B. J., Marcum, K., & Haykin, M. (1998). *Administrator's desk reference of behavior management: Leadership guide.* Longmont, CO: Sopris West.

Book Chapters

Algozzine, B., & Algozzine, K. (2005). Building school-wide behavior interventions that really work. In P. Clough, P. Garner, J. T. Pardeck, & F. Yuen (Eds.), *Handbook of emotional and behavioral difficulties* (273–283). Thousand Oaks, CA: Sage.

Web Sites

Positive Behavioral Interventions and Support (www.pbis.org/main.htm). The National Technical Assistance Center on Positive Behavioral Interventions and Supports (PBIS) was established by the U.S. Department of Education's Office of Special Education Programs to give schools capacity-building information and technical assistance for identifying, adapting, and sustaining effective schoolwide disciplinary practices.

CHAPTER REFERENCES

Algozzine, B. (1998). *Problem behavior management: Educator's resource service.* Gaithersburg, MD: Aspen.
Gresham, F. M., Cook, C. R., & Crews, S. D. (2004). Social skills training for children and youth with emotional and behavioral disorders: Validity considerations and future directions. *Behavior Disorders, 30,* 32–46.
Walker, H. M., Ramsay, E., & Gresham, F. M. (2004). *Antisocial behavior in school: Evidence-based practices.* Belmont, CA: Thomson/Wadsworth Learning.

What Works in Teaching Reading?

LuAnn Jordan and Jennifer A. Diliberto

Outline Questions

What works in teaching reading?

What are the basic components of reading?

How can I be sensitive to my students' reading difficulties?

What are reading strategies, and how can I use them in my inclusive classroom?

How do I use content enhancement in my inclusive classroom?

How do I evaluate how well reading strategies work in my inclusive classroom?

Where can I find resources or more information about teaching reading?

O f all the academic problems students face in today's classrooms, poor reading skills are by far the most prevalent. Research from the National Institutes of Child Health and Development (NICHD) indicates that at least 10 million school-age children in the United States are poor readers, a staggering statistic. Although reading difficulties occur as often in girls as in boys, boys are four times more often identified with a learning disability in reading than girls (Shaywitz, Shaywitz, Fletcher, & Escobar, 1990). One way to understand this problem is by looking at fourth-grade students, who (when they enter fourth grade) have spent at least 4 years of school in formal reading instruction. Shaywitz, Fletcher, and Shaywitz (1996) report that 20% of fourth-grade students are considered "dysfunctional" readers. Moreover, approximately 40% of fourth graders read below a basic level of achievement (able to read and complete work at grade level), according to national assessments of reading progress (Fletcher & Lyon, 1998; Orton Dyslexia Society, 1997). For these students, formal instruction in reading will be decreasing, rather than increasing, so their chances of "catching up" are minimal without intervention.

Fletcher and Lyon (1998) describe poor reading as a chronic problem; thus, students who are poor readers in third grade are still poor readers in ninth grade unless they have reading intervention. Students from ethnic minorities experience even greater rates of reading failure (Moats, 2000). Poor reading skills take a toll on individuals and society as a whole; reading failure leads to outcomes such as lower-paying jobs, a greater likelihood of incarceration, a greater likelihood of needing public assistance, and fewer opportunities for personal development in general.

Amidst all this dismal information about reading, there is hope. We know more about teaching reading than ever before, and because of Reading First and Early Reading First initiatives, which are a part of the No Child Left Behind Act of 2001, more attention is being paid to quality reading instruction than ever before. This attention should lead to better reading outcomes for all students.

The principles that "work" for teaching reading are the following:

- Teachers' understanding of the basic components of reading
- Teachers' sensitivity to the presence of reading problems in their students, regardless of age and/or ability level
- Teachers' competence in using reading strategies to help students read better and comprehend essential information that is presented

WHAT ARE THE BASIC COMPONENTS OF READING?

In 2000, the National Reading Panel (NRP) published a series of meta-analyses in the area of reading to assess reading research as well as the effectiveness of various approaches to teaching reading. These meta-analyses encompass effective instructional interventions for each critical reading component:

phonemic awareness, phonics, fluency, vocabulary, and text comprehension. Reading strategies usually address one of these critical components of reading. A brief overview of these components is presented here.

Phonological awareness (PA) is the understanding and demonstration that spoken language can be broken down into smaller units such as words, syllables, and/or phonemes (individual letter sounds). *Phonological awareness* also describes the ability to focus on and manipulate phonemes in spoken words. Strategies in PA involve teaching students to understand differences and similarities in sound and to connect sounds into larger units of sound (such as words).

Phonics—the Alphabetic Principle describes an instructional approach that links the sounds of spoken language to printed letters or graphemes. The National Reading Panel (2000) describes phonics as the method used to teach about letter-sound relations and how to use letter sounds to read or spell. Strategies in phonics involve teaching students to connect the visual prompt of letters with the sound or sounds they represent.

Fluency is defined as the ability to read text quickly, accurately, and with the proper expression. Reading fluency allows the reader to concentrate on understanding the written material because mental energy does not have to be spent on sounding out words. Moreover, fluency is highly correlated with comprehension. Students who comprehend well usually are fluent readers also. Strategies in fluency involve oral reading with students as they gain mastery over sounds, syllables, and words. Fluency strategies also immerse the students in reading connected text in reading passages.

Vocabulary is the study of words and their meanings. Vocabulary contributes to comprehension of connected text as students gain understanding of many words.

Comprehension is understanding what is heard and read. It is the goal of all the reading skill building that we teach. Comprehension strategies can include answering questions based on reading, paraphrasing material, making predictions, and determining the main idea and details. Comprehension of printed material is the true long-term goal of any reading strategy because we can apply what we read only when we comprehend it. However, for many students, especially students with disabilities, strategies in the areas of phonological awareness, phonics, and/or fluency may be needed before significant comprehension is possible.

HOW CAN I BE SENSITIVE TO MY STUDENTS' READING DIFFICULTIES?

Teachers of any grade or course can develop an understanding of their students' reading abilities by providing students with opportunities to demonstrate their reading skills. Such opportunities can include reading and summarizing information, reading and answering questions (e.g., end-of-chapter questions), and oral reading. If students have reading difficulties, they are likely to have problems with one or more of these activities. Further investigation may be warranted to determine a reading disability if the following warning signs are present:

- Students answer questions using few words, either orally or in writing.
- Students have trouble recalling the material they have just read.
- Students give incomplete answers.
- Students are frustrated when they cannot find the exact answer in the book.
- Students refuse to read aloud in class.
- Students act out to avoid reading aloud in class.

WHAT ARE READING STRATEGIES, AND HOW CAN I USE THEM IN MY CLASSROOM?

A three-tiered model of reading intervention can be used to explain the different approaches teachers can take to improve their students' reading skills. A *primary* level of intervention addresses universal instruction for all students to promote reading achievement. All teachers can be involved in this kind of reading instruction. A *secondary* level of intervention includes targeted small group or individual instruction for students who need additional support or assistance to successfully acquire new skills. Although this type of instruction can be implemented in any inclusive classroom, classrooms where team teaching is in place are preferred. Finally, a *tertiary* level of intervention addresses individualized, intense, specialized instruction for individual students who continue to experience marked difficulties in learning to read despite previous instruction and intervention efforts. This type of instruction is usually found in special education settings (Good, Kame'enui, Simmons, & Chard, 2002).

Whether or not you are a reading teacher, you can incorporate good reading strategies into your classroom routine. These strategies will help make information clearer to all of your students, not just your students with disabilities. Reading strategies are important because in any classroom setting there will be students who need to improve their reading skills. Reading strategies can help students get the most from their reading no matter what their reading abilities are.

For reading teachers, choosing and implementing programs, materials, and strategies that address reading difficulties efficiently and directly is critical. Results of the NRP's meta-analyses identified several skills as crucial to success in reading. Students must be able to manipulate phonemes in words, use systematic phonics instruction to decode words, increase fluency through repeated oral reading, increase vocabulary to achieve gains in comprehension, and use cognitive strategies to improve comprehension. The NRP (2000) suggested that reading programs include activities for teaching these skills when providing reading instruction.

For teachers who do not teach reading, increasing vocabulary and comprehension will be the primary concerns. Students who have poor reading skills will need special help in these areas. There are a number of basic reading strategies you can implement in your classroom. Many of these are small things that make a big difference. Basic reading strategies are listed in Table 7.1.

If you are the only teacher in your classroom, your opportunities to teach reading strategies will be limited to strategies that you decide to teach to the whole class and/or your ability to divide your classroom for small group instruction. Team teaching provides more options for delivering strategy instruction in all areas (see Chapter 8 on cognitive strategies), including reading strategies.

Reading strategies can be implemented in powerful ways in team teaching situations. Brief descriptions of five models of team teaching are presented here. See Chapter 4 for more detailed descriptions. In the first three models, teachers group students according to their learning needs. In the next two models, students remain together in heterogeneous groups.

1. *Station Teaching:* Each teacher delivers instruction to one small group at a time while the students are arranged at "stations" around the classroom. In this model, students switch from one station to another. Often one station is set up for independent work (Friend & Cook, 2000).

Table 7.1   Basic Reading Strategies

- Choose reading materials that are interesting to your students and written at their reading ability level.
- Summarize difficult reading material, and provide that information to your students at a level they can understand.
- Preview difficult material with your students; discuss difficult concepts with them to ensure understanding.
- Divide difficult material into smaller chunks of material.
- Highlight important information with a highlighter pen.
- Draw attention to outlines, words in boldface print, and italics.

2. *Parallel Teaching:* The special education teacher instructs a small group of students in a designated area of the general education classroom while the general education teacher instructs the larger group. Each teacher has a group and provides instruction in the same room at the same time. The same topic is addressed by each teacher but in different formats and/or levels (Friend & Cook, 2000).

3. *Alternative Teaching:* Much like parallel teaching, except the roles of the special educator and general educator may switch, with the special educator teaching the large group while the general educator pulls out the smaller group. One teacher will manage the majority of the class while the other teacher pulls a small heterogeneous group aside to preview, review, assess, or provide enrichment. The purpose and membership of the small group are subject to constant change (Friend & Cook, 2000).

4. *Teaching Together:* Two teachers manage and instruct the class at the same time. Flexibility is a must as the two teachers employ various instructional formats such as small group instruction, partner work, or individual instruction (Friend & Cook, 2000). This model allows the general and special education teachers to manage and instruct together.

5. *Coteaching:* The general education teacher and special education teacher cooperatively teach the lesson, going back and forth in presentation, questioning, leading activities, and so forth. This service delivery model exemplifies the height of collaboration, as teachers partner in instruction from beginning to end. The model allows the two teachers to take advantage of each others' strengths as they prepare, teach, and evaluate student learning.

Seven reading strategies and approaches, the critical reading components they address, and the appropriate inclusion models for their use are illustrated in Table 7.2. The reading strategies and approaches will be described next.

Advanced Organizers

Advanced organizers are methods for bridging and linking old information with new learning. Individuals need strategies to be able to learn large amounts of information, and linking information to learning they have mastered is one way to assist that process. Advanced organizers serve three major purposes:

Table 7.2   Reading Strategies, Critical Components, and Suggested Inclusion Models

Reading Strategies	Reading Component(s)	Inclusion Model
Advanced organizers	Comprehension	All types—station teaching, parallel teaching, alternative teaching, teaching together, and coteaching
Multisensory instruction	Phonics, phonological awareness	Station teaching
Peer teaching	Comprehension, fluency	Teaching together, station teaching
Power thinking	Comprehension	All types—station teaching, parallel teaching, alternative teaching, teaching together, and coteaching
Kansas Learning Strategies	Comprehension	All types—station teaching, parallel teaching, alternative teaching, teaching together, and coteaching
Direct instruction programs	Phonics, phonological awareness	Station teaching, parallel teaching, teaching together
Great Leaps in Reading	Fluency	Station teaching, parallel teaching, teaching together

1. They direct attention to what is most important in the material to be presented.

2. They highlight relationships among ideas and concepts that will be presented.

3. They remind students of relevant information they already know.

Here are four examples of advanced organizers:

1. *Expository organizers* describe the new content.

2. *Narrative organizers* present highlights of the new information in a story.

3. *Skimming* shows students how to scan material to familiarize themselves with it before reading.

4. *Graphic organizers* apply visual organization to the content to be read.

Advanced organizers can be used successfully in all types of inclusion models to increase student retention of concepts and skills. Mercer and Mercer (2005) use the mnemonic *LIP* to provide an advance organizer.

L = Link information to prior knowledge.

I = Introduce today's material.

P = Provide a rationale for learning.

Multisensory Reading Instruction

Multisensory reading instruction uses all the learning pathways in the brain—visual/auditory, kinesthetic-tactile (VAKT)—simultaneously to teach letters and words. The theory behind this type of instructional activity is that engaging all the learning channels enhances memory and learning. This type of instruction in reading includes using various manipulative objects such as letter/word tiles, magnets, sandpaper, sand, and shaving cream to teach letter names, letter sounds, and words.

Multisensory reading instruction can be used with inclusion models that allow for small group instruction (parallel and station teaching) as well as inclusion models that allow students to work in peer-tutoring pairs (teaching together). Some specific types of multisensory instruction include the Fernald method (Fernald, 1988), which teaches whole words, and the Gillingham method (Gillingham & Stillman, 1970), which stresses phonics. Each approach is designed to help readers with severe problems.

The Fernald method includes having the student write a target word in crayon and then go back and trace the word while reading it aloud. The student continues to practice the word and expands the activity by writing stories about the word and keeping a word file.

The Gillingham method requires a rigorous instructional period (i.e., five weekly lessons for a minimum of 2 years). Each letter sound is taught using a combination of drill cards, tracing, copying, and other activities.

Peer Teaching

Peer teaching (also known as peer tutoring and classwide peer tutoring) consists of structured activities done in pairs where peers engage in frequent interaction with each other. Activities such as review of previously learned material (sight words, comprehension questions from a story) are appropriate for peer teaching. The peers provide corrective feedback, and the students take turns as tutor and tutee (Fuchs, Fuchs, & Burish, 2000). Peer teaching can be used in any inclusion model where students are paired.

Power Thinking

Power thinking is a hierarchical system for outlining information. For example, the information can be grouped according to main ideas, subtopics, and details. Numbers are used to signify those levels. Power thinking can increase comprehension of students' reading in any inclusion setting, as it can be taught in both small group and large group formats.

Here is how power thinking works:

Power 1: main idea, thesis, or topic

Power 2: subtopic, category of a Power 1, detail of a Power 1

Power 3: detail or subtopic of a Power 2

. . . and so on . . .

And here is an example:

1: TV shows

   2: Dramas

      3: *E.R.*

      3: *7th Heaven*

      3: *Law & Order*

   2: Sitcoms

      3: *Friends*

      3: *Frasier*

      3: *Everybody Loves Raymond*

   2: Soap operas

      3: *All My Children*

      3: *Days of Our Lives*

      3: *Guiding Light*

A social studies example might be:

1: Location

  2: Absolute

    3: Latitude and longitude coordinates

    3: Street address

  2: Relative

    3: In the Atlantic Ocean

    3: West of Madagascar

    3: 30 miles south of Albany

University of Kansas Learning Strategies in Reading Comprehension

Kansas Learning Strategies are designed to teach students with learning problems how to become more active in the learning process. Examples include the paraphrasing strategy, the visual imagery strategy, and the self-questioning strategy.

One visual imagery strategy for reading comprehension is *RIDER:*

R = Read a sentence.

I = Image (make an image).

D = Describe how the new image is different from the last sentence.

E = Evaluate (as you make the image, check to be sure it contains everything necessary).

R = Repeat (as you read the next sentence, repeat the steps to RIDE).

Each letter of *RIDER* is a cue for a specific action that would be appropriate for the student to take in a classroom.

These comprehension strategies can be used with inclusion models that allow for small group instruction (station teaching, parallel teaching, alternative teaching, teaching together). With some logistical preparation for the whole group, comprehension strategies can be implemented classwide.

Direct Instruction Programs

Direct instruction programs in reading are instructional programs that provide explicit instruction in sounds, letters, words, and comprehension.

These programs require some training to implement effectively. Examples include *Reading Mastery, Corrective Reading, Reasoning and Expression,* and *Horizons.* Direct instruction programs in reading can be used in inclusion models that incorporate small group instruction, such as station or parallel teaching.

Great Leaps in Reading is an individualized reading fluency program for kindergarten through adult readers. Instruction is divided into three areas:

1. *Phonics:* develops knowledge of letter sounds

2. *Sight Phrases:* teaches mastery of sight words

3. *Reading Fluency:* uses age-appropriate high-interest stories specifically designed to build reading fluency, motivation, and proper intonation

Great Leaps in Reading works well in station teaching, where students form small groups. This supplementary reading program can also be used where individuals or small groups of students can be pulled out for instruction by assistants or volunteers.

HOW DO I USE CONTENT ENHANCEMENT IN MY INCLUSIVE CLASSROOM?

Another way to improve your students' comprehension is to enhance the way you present information. Content enhancements, developed at the University of Kansas Center for Research on Learning (KU-CRL), assist teachers in organizing their content so that students remember more, understand better, and retain concepts. Schumaker, Deshler, and McKnight (1991) encourage teachers to use the content enhancements to make abstract information more concrete and scaffold new information upon information already learned. The student's active involvement in the use of the content enhancement greatly increases the benefit. The content enhancements developed at the KU-CRL include *routines*, or strategic instructional procedures that assist students in successfully using *devices* (instructional tools that include visual and verbal information). Some examples of routines are the unit organizer routine (Lenz, Bulgren, Schumaker, Deshler, & Boudah, 1994), the concept mastery routine (Bulgren, Deshler, & Schumaker, 1993), and the framing routine (Ellis, 1998).

HOW DO I KNOW IF READING STRATEGIES WORK IN MY CLASSROOM?

You can evaluate the effect of your reading strategy instruction by asking two questions regarding reading skills and achievement in general. First, are your students reading better? Curriculum-based assessment such as fluency measures (ask students to read grade-level passages for 1 minute, measuring the number of words read per minute) and comprehension activities (have students answer questions after reading the text) can reveal whether students are improving in their reading skills. Another question regards your students' performance in the subject area you teach. For example, if you teach science, your intention would be that the reading improvement would generalize to the students' ability to comprehend text, understand directions, and show mastery of science concepts.

There are a few things to consider if you plan to implement a reading strategy in your classroom. First, find out whether the reading approach, program, or strategy has been field-tested. Data that support using the strategy with students similar to yours should strengthen your confidence in using the strategy. Next, consider how much preparation is needed for each teacher in the inclusion setting. Finally, consider the level of administrative support, resources needed, and resources available. Optimum implementation is a result of a good foundation and good support for your specific situation.

Remember that the contributions you make to a person's reading skills are contributions that can truly change a life. Even if you are not a reading teacher, you can make an impact on students in this critical skill area.

WHERE CAN I FIND RESOURCES OR MORE INFORMATION ON READING STRATEGIES?

Research Articles

Baker, S., Gersten, R., Dimino, J. A., & Griffiths, R. (2004). The sustained use of research-based instructional practice. *Remedial and Special Education, 25*, 5–25.

Boudah, D. J., Lenz, B. K., Bulgren, J. A., Schumaker, J. B., & Deshler, D. D. (2000). Content learning through the unit organizer routine. *Teaching Exceptional Children, 32*(3), 48–56.

Bulgren, J. A., Deshler, D. D., & Schumaker, J. B. (1997). Use of a recall enhancement routine and strategies in inclusive secondary classes. *Learning Disabilities Research and Practice, 12*(4), 198–208.

Bulgren, J. A., Deshler, D. D., Schumaker, J. B., & Lenz, B. K. (2000). The use and effectiveness of analogical instruction in diverse secondary content classrooms. *Journal of Educational Psychology, 92*(3), 426–441.

Cho, S., & Ahn, D. (2003). Strategy acquisition and maintenance of gifted and nongifted children. *Exceptional Children, 69,* 497–506.

Dembo, M. H., & Seli, H. P. (2004). Students' resistance to change in learning strategies courses. *Journal of Developmental Education, 27*(3), 2–9.

Deshler, D. D., Schumaker, J. B., & Lenz, B. K. (1984). Academic and cognitive interventions for LD adolescents: Part I. *Journal of Learning Disabilities, 17*(2), 108–117.

Ellis, E. S., & Sabornie, E. J. (1990). Strategy-based adaptive instruction in content-area classes. Social validity of six options. *Teacher Education and Special Education, 13*(2), 133–144.

Fuchs, D., Fuchs, L. S., & Burish, P. (2000). Peer-assisted learning strategies: An evidence-based practice to promote reading achievement. *Learning Disabilities Research and Practice, 15,* 85–91.

Kline, F. M., Schumaker, J. B., & Deshler, D. D. (1991). Development and validation of feedback routines for instructing students with learning disabilities. *Learning Disability Quarterly, 14*(3), 191–207.

Lenz, B. K., Alley, G. R., & Schumaker, J. B. (1987). Activating the inactive learner: Advance organizers in the secondary content classroom. *Learning Disability Quarterly, 10*(1), 53–67.

Palincsar, A. S., & Brown, A. L. (1984). Reciprocal teaching of comprehension-fostering and comprehension-monitoring activities. *Cognition and Instruction, 1*(2), 117–175.

Wehby, J. H., Falk, K. B., Barton-Arwood, S., Lane, K. L., & Cooley, C. (2003). The impact of comprehensive reading instruction on the academic and social behavior of students with emotional and behavioral disorders. *Journal of Emotional and Behavioral Disorders, 11,* 225–230.

Wehmeyer, M. L., Hughes, C., Agran, M., Garner, N., & Yeager, D. (2003). Student-directed learning strategies to promote the progress of students with intellectual disability in inclusive classrooms. *International Journal of Inclusive Education, 7,* 415–429.

Descriptive Articles

Bulgren, J., & Scanlon, D. (1997). Instructional routines and learning strategies that promote understanding of content area concepts. *Journal of Adolescent and Adult Literacy, 41,* 292–302.

Deshler, D. D., & Lenz, B. K. (1989). The strategies instructional approach. *International Journal of Disability, Development and Education, 36,* 203–224.

Deshler, D. D., & Schumaker, J. B. (1986). Learning strategies: An instructional alternative for low-achieving adolescents. *Exceptional Children, 52,* 583–590.

Ehren, B. J. (2002). Vocabulary intervention to improve reading comprehension for students with learning disabilities. *Perspectives on Language and Education, 9*(3), 12–18.

Fuchs, D., Fuchs, L. S., Thompson, A., Svenson, E., Yen, L., Al Otaiba, S., et al. (2001). Peer-assisted learning strategies in reading. *Remedial and Special Education, 22,* 15–21.

Harris, K. R., & Pressley, M. (1991). The nature of cognitive strategy instruction: Interactive strategy construction. *Exceptional Children, 57,* 392–404.

Palincsar, A. S. (1986). Metacognitive strategy instruction. *Exceptional Children, 53,* 118–124.

Swanson, H. L. (1989). Strategy instruction: Overview of principles and procedures for effective use. *Learning Disability Quarterly, 12,* 3–14.

Books

Jones, B. F., Palincsar, A. S., Ogle, D. S., & Carr, E. G. (1987). *Strategic teaching and learning: Cognitive instruction in the content areas.* Alexandria, VA: Association for Supervision and Curriculum Development.

National Reading Panel. (2000). *Report of the National Reading Panel: Teaching children to read: An evidence-based assessment of the scientific research literature on reading and its implications for reading instruction.* Bethesda, MD: National Reading Panel, National Institute of Child Health and Human Development.

Wolfe, P. (2001). *Brain matters: Translating research into classroom practice.* Alexandria, VA: Association for Supervision and Curriculum Development.

Book Chapters

Bulgren, J. A., & Lenz, B. K. (1996). Strategic instruction in the content areas. In D. D. Deshler, E. S. Ellis, & B. K. Lenz (Eds.), *Teaching adolescents with learning disabilities: Strategies and methods* (2nd ed., pp. 409–473). Denver: Love.

Lenz, B. K., Bulgren, J. A., & Hudson, P. (1990). Content enhancement: A model for promoting the acquisition of content by individuals with learning disabilities. In T. E. Scruggs & B. L. Y. Wong (Eds.), *Intervention research in learning disabilities* (pp. 122–165). New York: Springer.

Rosenshine, B. (1997). Advances in research on instruction. In J. W. Lloyd, E. J. Kame'enui, & D. Chard (Eds.), *Issues in educating students with disabilities* (pp. 197–221). Mahwah, NJ: Erlbaum.

Rosenshine, B. (1997, March). *The case for explicit, teacher-led, cognitive strategy instruction.* Paper presented at the annual meeting of the American Educational Research Association, Chicago.

Web Sites

Direct Instruction reading programs:

Association for Direct Instruction (www.adihome.org).

National Institute for Direct Instruction (www.nifdi.org/).

Science Research Associates (SRA) Direct Instruction (www.sraonline.com/index.php/home/curriculumsolutions/di/9).

Graphic Organizers (www.graphic.org). Contains resources you might find useful for writing and using graphic organizers. Especially helpful are the links to articles and books on the Web.

Great Leaps in Reading (www.greatleaps.com/).

Guilford County Schools, North Carolina, "Activity, Curriculum, and Technology: Cognitive Strategies" (http://its.guilford.k12.nc.us/act/strategies/cognitive.htm). This collection of cognitive strategies includes "power notes" and "dump and clump."

LD Online, "Peer Assisted Learning Strategies in Reading" (www.ldonline .org/ld_indepth/reading/peer_assisted.html).

North Central Regional Educational Laboratory (NCREL) (www.ncrel .org). The North Central Regional Educational Laboratory (NCREL) is a not-for-profit organization dedicated to helping schools—and the students they serve—reach their full potential. NCREL specializes in the educational applications of technology. Use the search function on the home page to search the site for useful information on graphic organizers.

ProTeacher (www.proteacher.com). ProTeacher is a professional community for elementary school teachers, specialists, and student teachers in prekindergarten through Grade 8. The open membership includes visitors from across the United States and guests from around the world. The site features over two dozen active discussion boards and an extensive archive and directory of teacher-selected lesson plans, teaching ideas, and resources.

Reading Quest, "Power Thinking" (http://curry.edschool.virginia .edu/go/readquest/strat/pto.html).

Reading Quest, "Strategies for Reading Comprehension" (http://curry.edschool.virginia.edu/go/readquest/strat/). Contains various strategies for reading comprehension.

Teach-nology (http://teachers.teach-nology.com). Make your own graphic organizers on this site by filling out a simple form. The materials are made instantly and can be printed directly from your computer.

University of Kansas Learning Strategies (www.ku-crl.org/).

University of Kansas Center for Research on Learning, "CRL Publications List" (www.ku-crl.org/publications/index.html). Provides an annotated bibliography of research and other publications from the KU-CRL.

CHAPTER REFERENCES

Bulgren, J. A., Deshler, D. D., & Schumaker, J. B. (1993). *The content enhancement series: The concept anchoring routine.* Lawrence, KS: Edge Enterprises.

Ellis, E. (1998). *The content enhancement series: The framing routine.* Lawrence, KS: Edge Enterprises.

Fernald, G. (1988). *Remedial techniques in basic school subjects.* Austin, TX: PRO-ED.

Fletcher, J. M., & Lyon, G. R. (1998). Reading: A research-based approach. In W. M. Evers (Ed.), *What's gone wrong in America's classrooms* (pp. 50–77). Stanford, CA: Hoover Institution Press, Stanford University.

Friend, M., & Cook, L. (2000). *Interactions: Collaboration skills for school professionals.* New York: Longman.

Fuchs, D., Fuchs, L. S., & Burish, P. (2000). Peer-assisted learning strategies: An evidence-based practice to promote reading achievement. *Learning Disabilities Research and Practice, 15,* 85–91.

Gillingham, A., & Stillman, B. (1970). *Remedial training for children with specific disability in reading, spelling, and penmanship* (7th ed.). Cambridge, MA: Educators Publishing Service.

Good, R. H., Kame'enui, E. J., Simmons, D. S., & Chard, D. J. (2002). *Focus and nature of primary, secondary, and tertiary prevention: The CIRCUITS model* (Tech. Rep. No. 1). Eugene: University of Oregon, College of Education, Institute for the Development of Educational Achievement.

Lenz, B. K., Bulgren, J. A., Schumaker, J. B., Deshler, D. D., & Boudah, D. J. (1994). *The content enhancement series: The unit organizer routine.* Lawrence, KS: Edge Enterprises.

Mercer, C. D., & Mercer, A. R. (2005). *Teaching students with learning problems* (7th ed.). Upper Saddle River, NJ: Merrill.

Moats, L. C. (2000). *Speech to print: Language essentials for teachers.* Baltimore: Paul H. Brookes.

National Reading Panel. (2000). *Teaching children to read: An evidence-based assessment of the scientific research literature on reading and its implications for reading instruction* (NIH Pub. No. 00–4754). Washington, DC: National Institute of Child Health and Human Development, National Institutes of Health.

Orton Dyslexia Society. (1997). *Informed instruction for reading success: Foundations for teacher preparation* (A position paper of the Orton Dyslexia Society). Baltimore: Author.

Schumaker, J. B., Deshler, D. D., & McKnight, P. C. (1991). Teaching routines for content areas at the secondary level. In G. Stover, M. R. Shinn, & H. M. Walker (Eds.), *Interventions for achievement and behavior problems* (pp. 473–494). Washington, DC: National Association of School Psychologists.

Shaywitz, S. E., Fletcher, J. M., & Shaywitz, B. A. (1996). A conceptual model and definition of dyslexia: Findings emerging from the Connecticut Longitudinal Study. In J. H. Beitchman, N. Cohen, M. M. Konstantareas, & R. Tannock (Eds.), *Language, learning and behaviour disorders* (pp. 199–223). New York: Cambridge University Press.

Shaywitz, S. E., Shaywitz, B. A., Fletcher, J. M., & Escobar, M. D. (1990). Prevalence of reading disability in boys and girls: Results of the Connecticut Longitudinal Study. *Journal of the American Medical Association, 264,* 998–1002.

What Are Cognitive Strategies?

Outline questions

What do I need to know about cognitive strategies?

Why should I use cognitive strategies in my classroom?

What is content enhancement, and what does it have to do with cognitive strategies?

How do I evaluate how well cognitive strategies work in my classroom?

What are some commonly used cognitive strategies?

Where can I find resources or more information on cognitive strategies?

WHAT DO I NEED TO KNOW ABOUT COGNITIVE STRATEGIES?

Cognitive strategies are useful tools in assisting students with learning problems. The term *cognitive strategies* in its simplest form means the use of the mind (cognition) to solve a problem or complete a task. Cognitive strategies may also be referred to as *procedural facilitators* (Bereiter & Scardamalia, 1987), *procedural prompts* (Rosenshine, 1997), or *scaffolds* (Palincsar & Brown, 1984). A related term is *metacognition*, the self-reflection or "thinking about thinking" necessary for students to learn effectively (Baker, Gersten, & Scanlon, 2002).

Cognitive strategies provide a structure for learning when a task cannot be completed through a series of steps. For example, algorithms in mathematics provide a series of steps to solve a problem. Attention to the steps results in successful completion of the problem. In contrast, reading comprehension, a complex task, is a good example of a task that does not follow a series of steps. Further explanation is provided below.

A cognitive strategy serves to support the learner as he or she develops internal procedures that enable him or her to perform tasks that are complex (Rosenshine, 1997). Reading comprehension is an area where cognitive strategies are important. A self-questioning strategy can help students understand what they read. Rosenshine states that the act of creating questions does not lead directly to comprehension. Instead, students search the text and combine information as they generate questions; then they comprehend what they have read.

WHY SHOULD I USE COGNITIVE STRATEGIES IN MY CLASSROOM?

The use of cognitive strategies can increase the efficiency with which the learner approaches a learning task. These academic tasks can include, but are not limited to, remembering and applying information from course content, constructing sentences and paragraphs, editing written work, paraphrasing, and classifying information to be learned.

Students with disabilities often approach learning tasks with few strategies or, worse yet, incorrect strategies. They may not have a clue about how to start to solve a problem or complete an activity. The explicit teaching of cognitive strategies has been found to help learners with disabilities to more confidently and effectively approach a learning task. Using cognitive strategies they are able to do the following:

- Preview a task
- Decide which actions to take that will enable them to complete the task
- Follow through on those actions
- Evaluate whether they were successful

In a classroom where cognitive strategies are used, the teacher fulfills a pivotal role, bridging the gap between student and content/skill to be learned. This role requires an understanding of the task to be completed, as well as knowledge of an approach (or approaches) to the task that he or she can communicate to the learner.

WHAT IS CONTENT ENHANCEMENT, AND WHAT DOES IT HAVE TO DO WITH COGNITIVE STRATEGIES?

Content enhancement is the teacher's use of cognitive strategies to shape both the task of learning and the student's approach to learning. Bulgren, Deshler, and Schumaker (1997) highlight three important teacher activities in their model of content enhancement:

1. Teachers evaluate the content they cover.

2. Teachers determine the necessary approaches to learning for student success.

3. Teachers teach with routines and instructional supports that assist students as they apply appropriate techniques and strategies.

In this way, the teacher emphasizes *what* the students should learn, or the "product" of learning. In addition, the teacher models the *how* or "process" of learning.

The implementation of cognitive strategies in your inclusive classroom complements your skills as a "master learner." You are considered a master learner because, as the classroom teacher, your students know that you know a lot and that you must be good at learning. By teaching cognitive strategies, you will show your students that learning can be helped along by good strategies. You will also learn some new strategies that you may find useful! We are presenting some practical applications for cognitive strategies in this chapter.

Content Evaluation

When a teacher is comfortable with the content he or she is teaching, he or she knows which parts are the most important, the most interesting, and the easiest (or hardest) to learn. The teacher evaluates the content with various questions in mind:

- How important is this information to my students?
- Is any of this information irrelevant to the point that I can minimize or exclude it?

- How will my students use this information beyond my classroom (in general education classrooms, college and/or career settings, etc.)?
- What parts of this information do I think my students will grasp quickly?
- For what parts of this information do I think my students will need "extras" (more time, more examples, peer help, more explanation, applications, etc.)?
- How should I pace the presentation?
- Which evaluations are going to help me know that my students understand this information?

The more experienced the teacher is with content, the better he or she will be able to plan students' cognitive journey through the information or skills that will be unfamiliar to them.

Determination of Necessary Approaches

Now the teacher's attention turns to his or her knowledge of the students. Student characteristics such as intellectual ability, interest in the subject, and general motivation to learn are considered. The teacher selects learning approaches that complement the learner characteristics while ensuring success with the content. A teacher who teaches cognitive strategies well will connect learner and task. A strategy will be chosen because it is the best strategy for *both* the learner's characteristics and the task and/or content that needs to be mastered.

Routines and Instructional Supports

Once the best strategy or strategies have been selected, the teacher begins the work of teaching the strategy to the student(s). Explicit instruction is used to impart the components or steps of the strategy. Often the strategy will include actions or routines that are repeated each time the strategy is implemented. Practice to mastery of these routines is critical for effective learning of the strategy, especially for learners with disabilities. Additional instructional supports such as guided practice, independent practice, verbal practice, and written or oral tests may also be used.

A Real-Life Example

You can compare the teaching of cognitive strategies to teaching a friend to drive in your hometown. Because you are in your hometown, you know the area, or content, very well. In addition, the person you are teaching to drive is your friend, so you know the learner well. This knowledge can make your teaching more efficient because you have two areas of expertise (the content and the learner) at your disposal. You will use a combination of explicit instructions (turn left on Church Street) and supports (maps, the rule that "all avenues run north-south") to teach your friend how to navigate around town. You may also use verbal directions as opposed to maps, depending on your friend's preferred mode of information.

Just as important, you can avoid situations that could become barriers to learning (and your friendship). For example, if your friend tends to be anxious, you will *not* begin your instruction during rush hour!

HOW DO I KNOW IF COGNITIVE STRATEGIES WORK IN MY CLASSROOM?

Evaluation of cognitive strategies takes place on two levels. First and foremost, the question is whether students of all types of abilities are benefiting from using the strategies. Are grades better? Are student work products of a higher quality? Are the students more confident in performing the target skill? At another level, you can evaluate students' ability to implement the strategy. For example, you would evaluate how well students elaborate on content, or organize tasks, or use imagery to remember essential information. Improved overall performance is the goal, but knowing how well your students use the strategies you teach them is also important.

You may also find that your diverse learners implement their cognitive strategies in a diverse fashion. As long as they are achieving the overall goals, and/or improving skills, give them enough room to individualize the strategies whenever you can.

WHAT ARE SOME COMMONLY USED COGNITIVE STRATEGIES?

Because they are diverse and highly relevant to tasks, the use of cognitive strategies by teachers and students can significantly influence important learning outcomes for students. The use of cognitive strategies can increase the efficiency and confidence with which the learner approaches a learning task, as well as his or her ability to develop a product, retain essential information, or perform a skill. While teaching cognitive strategies requires a high degree of commitment from both the teacher and learners of all kinds of abilities in your classroom, the results are well worth the effort. Table 8.1 presents an overview of cognitive strategies that are widely used.

Table 8.1 Cognitive Strategies Overview

Strategy Type	Brief Description	Examples
Orienting strategies	Students' attention is drawn to a task through teacher input, highlighted material, and/or student self-regulation.	Students learn to cue to teacher's "listen carefully" or to boldface type.
Specific aids for paying attention	Students' attention is maintained by connecting a concrete object or other cue to the task.	A special pencil cues the student to pay special attention to punctuation when he is writing sentences.
Specific aids for problem solving or memorization	Students' problem solving is enhanced by connecting a concrete object or other cue to the task.	Concrete objects are used in solving math problems.
Rehearsal	Students practice (rehearse) target information through verbalization, visual study, or other means.	Students practice vocabulary and definitions through games in which they must orally repeat target information.
Elaboration	Students expand target information by relating other information to it (e.g., creating a phrase, making an analogy).	Students relate the life of an ant colony to their community.
Transformation	Students simplify target information by converting difficult or unfamiliar information into more manageable information.	A poem is transformed into a play or story.
Imagery*	Students transform target information by creating meaningful visual, auditory, or kinesthetic images of the information.	Students visualize a scene described in a passage.
Mnemonics*	Students transform target information by relating a cue word, phrase, or sentence to the target information.	"My Dear Aunt Sally" is used for the order of mathematical operations (multiply, divide, add, subtract).
Organization	Students put in categories, sequence, or otherwise organize information for more efficient recall and use.	Words in lists are placed in categories.

*Imagery and mnemonics can be considered special types of transformational strategies.

SOURCE: Adapted from "How Do Teachers Teach Memory Skills?" by Moely et al., 1986, *Educational Psychology, 21*, pp. 55–57.

Orienting Strategies

An orienting strategy directs a student's learning to a task. The student's attention is drawn to a task through teacher input such as a cue, material that is highlighted, and/or student self-regulation.

How Can Orienting Strategies Help Your Students?

Orienting strategies are helpful to students because they direct attention to important information. As students learn to use their own orienting strategies, they become more independent in their learning.

How Can You Implement Orienting Strategies to Effectively Meet the Diverse Learning Needs of Students?

Orienting strategies are basic to teaching and learning. As you point out significant information to students and then teach the students to determine what information is significant, you address their basic learning question, "Do I need to remember this?"

Using the words "Listen carefully . . ." is a good example. This verbal cue alerts the learner that the information that follows needs to be remembered.

What Are the Different Types of Orienting Strategies?

There are basically three approaches to orienting information, reflecting who or what is doing the orienting: the teacher, the material, and/or the student. When the *teacher* orients the student to something important, he or she cues the student that the information that follows is important and should be remembered. Verbal cues such as "Pay attention to this" or "This is on the test" orient the student to key information. Visual cues such as the teacher writing certain information on the board and/or pointing to information also orient the learner. The *material* can have orienting characteristics that draw attention to certain points. Italics, boldface, and text set apart (such as definitions) are orienting characteristics. Finally, as the *student* learns to self-orient to information, he or she grows in independence as a learner. In the case of printed information, the student self-orients by scanning information to determine what is important to remember and then taking some action such as highlighting, underlining, or taking notes to emphasize important information. In the case of verbal information, the student self-orients by listening to determine what is important to remember (including using "cues" given by the speaker) and then taking some action such as taking notes or using verbal rehearsal to remember important information.

How Do You Decide Which Orienting Strategy to Use?

Consider your students' needs for attending to information and their ability to decide whether information is important. The less able they are to discern important information, the more the teacher needs to orient them.

How Do You Construct Your Own Orienting Strategy?

- Analyze the information to be attended to and determine how your students will best attend. Do you need to do all the work, or can you guide them to find important information themselves? In the beginning of the year, for example, you may spend a lot of time orienting students to important information. As the year progresses, however, you should be able to fade some of your efforts as the students do more orienting for themselves. You may also allow learners who learn the cues quickly to remind the other learners.
- Determine whether you will use verbal cues, visual cues, other cues, or a combination.
- Present information to be attended to and learned.
- Guide students through the orienting process.
- Reinforce (a) the students' learning of the material and (b) their ability to attend based on the cues provided.
- If students are able to self-orient, monitor and reinforce this process and their learning.

Specific Attentional Aids

A specific attentional aid is like an orienting strategy, but the student's attention is maintained by the connection of a physical object or verbal cue to the task. An example of a specific attentional aid is my "ring strategy." I am not usually very aware of the rings I wear, but if one is on the "wrong" finger, I become very aware of it. When I want to remember something for a short period of time (e.g., to pass along a message or to buy a specific item at the grocery store), I move the ring from my ring finger to my index finger while thinking about what I want to remember. Sometimes I use verbal rehearsal also. Putting a ring on a finger that usually does not have one draws my attention to it and cues me to remember why I moved the ring in the first place.

How Can Specific Attentional Aids Help Your Students?

Specific attentional aids can help students remember essential information by connecting that information to something highly accessible: an object, language, or a part of the body. Because the aid is accessible, the student can use specific attentional aids often and easily.

How Can You Implement Specific Attentional Aids to Effectively Meet the Diverse Learning Needs of Students?

Teachers can implement the use of specific attentional aids for the entire classroom, small groups, or individuals. You may begin by teaching specific attentional aids in areas other than academics. For example, you may use a cueing word or phrase to remind students to get into cooperative teams, such as "Go Gators!" (or Pirates, etc.). After students learn the basics, you can apply them to academic areas.

What Are the Different Types of Specific Attentional Aids?

There are various types of specific attentional aids. Three categories can be used to describe them:

- *Objects*—small or large, anything to which you can attach meaning
- *Language*—words, phrases, or sentences, spoken or written
- *Body parts*—Fingers and toes work best

How Do You Decide Which Specific Attentional Aid to Use?

Consider your students' needs for attending. Determination of the best specific attentional aid may be a trial and error process, especially when deciding between language and an object. Allow the students to have input as they connect meaning with the specific attentional aid.

How Do You Construct Your Own Strategy for Using a Specific Attentional Aid?

- Analyze the information to be attended to, and determine how your students will best attend. Are there some objects or language that will provide better cues than others?
- Present information to be attended to and learned.
- Guide students through the selection of the specific attentional aid. Allow students to select their own specific attentional aid when possible.
- Reinforce (a) the students' learning of the material and (b) their ability to attend based on the specific attentional aids.
- If students select their own specific attentional aid, monitor and reinforce this process and their learning.

Specific Aids for Problem Solving or Memorization

A student enhances his or her problem solving or memorization using a specific problem-solving aid by connecting a concrete object or other cue to the task. Counters and other concrete objects used in mathematics are examples of specific aids.

How Can Specific Aids Help Your Students?

Specific aids can help students perform tasks or memorize information by connecting information to something concrete. The presence of the concrete object allows the learner to process information more efficiently. You will not want the student to use the concrete object indefinitely. Counters, for example, serve to support the learner until he or she learns to do mathematics on a more abstract level.

How Can You Implement Specific Aids to Effectively Meet the Diverse Learning Needs of Students?

Teachers can implement the use of specific aids for the entire classroom, small groups, or individuals. You may begin by teaching the use of specific aids in areas where concrete instruction is needed. Math and science are content areas where concrete instruction is prevalent and necessary.

What Are the Different Types of Specific Aids?

Specific aids for problem solving or memorization are produced commercially. Counters, maps, and globes are examples of commercial products. Teachers may also construct their own specific aids that are tailored to specific content.

How Do You Decide Which Specific Aid to Use?

Consider your students' needs for learning. Allow the students to have input as they connect meaning with the specific aid for problem solving or memorization.

How Do You Construct Your Own Strategy for Using a Specific Aid for Problem Solving or Memorization?

- Analyze the information to be attended to, and determine how your students will best attend. Are there some objects or materials that will be more effective than others?
- Present information to be attended to and learned.
- Model the use of the specific aid. Guide students as they use the specific aids.

- Reinforce (a) the students' learning of the material and (b) their ability to attend based on the specific aids.
- If students select or create their own specific aid, monitor and reinforce this process and their learning.

Rehearsal Strategies

A rehearsal strategy involves repeatedly practicing information to learn it. When students are presented with specific information to be learned, such as a list, often they will attempt to memorize the information by repeating it over and over. They may say the words out loud or subvocalize the information (say it to themselves). The repeated practice increases their familiarity with the information. For many people, the learning of their social security number, their telephone number, or the items they want to pick up at the grocery store prompts them to use a rehearsal strategy.

How Can Rehearsal Strategies Help Your Students?

Rehearsal strategies can be used to learn relatively small amounts of information and are good for learning "foundation information." Foundation information is necessary to learn before more complex learning can take place. For example, learning that $a + b = b + a$, or the commutative property of addition, is essential to doing more complex work in algebra.

How Can You Implement Rehearsal Strategies to Effectively Meet the Diverse Learning Needs of Students?

One of the most important concepts you will teach students about rehearsal strategies is how to evaluate when a rehearsal strategy is just right and when a different strategy is needed. For certain information (such as the telephone number we need to memorize until we can write it down or make the call), verbal rehearsal of the numbers is a fine strategy; no more complex approach is necessary. However, memorizing long lists of information may require a different strategy to yield better results. Helping students evaluate whether rehearsal will accomplish the task in the best way will enhance their knowledge of themselves as learners.

Attaching a multisensory experience to the rehearsal may also assist the learners. For example, many children can only "say" their alphabet when they sing the ABC song. You may find that some learners do better with rehearsal strategies when they can attach sound or movement to the items to be learned.

Learners may also become attached to the sequence of their learning. For example, when I'm doing business over the phone, I'm often asked for the last four digits of my social security number. I have to start reciting at the beginning of my social security number because that is the sequence in which I learned it. Understanding that your students may have different approaches and preferences (some may prefer to practice in quiet, others with noise; some students will want the written information nearby) will allow you to provide a supportive environment for their diverse needs.

If you are using rehearsal to teach information that contributes to a larger concept or skill, keep in mind that lots of practice may be required for the students to learn the information to a level of automaticity. After initial learning takes place, you will need to review at times to ensure that the students have retained the information. We have all memorized information that we have promptly forgotten when we stopped rehearsing.

How Do You Decide Which Rehearsal Strategy to Use?

Consider your students' preferences for rehearsing information, and allow for as much variety as possible. Encourage students to create songs or dances to go with the information to be learned.

Making a game out of the rehearsal work is helpful also. Some ideas include the following:

- *Bean Bag Toss*—Students recite information when the bean bag gets tossed to them. Then they toss to another student or back to the teacher.
- *Choral Response*—Students respond as a group with rehearsed information (especially helpful in the early stages of rehearsal).
- *Team Competition*—Teacher asks questions requiring rehearsed information, students answer individually to gain points for their team. Teams can consult with each other in early stages of learning; later competitions may require individual responses.

How Do You Construct Your Own Rehearsal Strategy?

- Analyze the information to be taught, and determine whether rehearsal is the best approach.
- If it is, decide whether you want the students to rehearse individually, in pairs or groups, as a whole classroom, or a combination of these. If information is important to the whole group, and/or if it contributes to a larger concept or strategy, then group rehearsal should be included.
- Arrange information in the best order you can devise. This helps makes the information easier to memorize. If students need to rearrange information, be willing to consider that also, but do not

compromise the learning. For example, rehearsing the seasons out of order may be easier for some students, but is the resulting learning as good?
- Remember to think about student abilities so that the format for the rehearsal (games, songs, dances, etc.) facilitates understanding rather than confusion.
- Present information to be attended to and learned.
- Guide students through the rehearsal process.
- Reinforce (a) the students' learning of the material and (b) their ability to use rehearsal.

Elaboration Strategies

An elaboration strategy involves using elements of what is to be learned and expanding them. The student expands the target information by relating other information to it (e.g., creating a phrase, making an analogy).

How Can Elaboration Strategies Help Your Students?

Elaboration strategies connect information to be learned with information that students already know. This connecting takes stress off working memory because connections create efficiency of learning and memory.

How Can You Implement Elaboration Strategies to Effectively Meet the Diverse Learning Needs of Students?

Because elaboration strategies create connections, or bridges, to information to be learned, they can be powerful instructional tools for a classroom. The confidence that students have in already knowing the connected information can support their learning of new information.

What are some different types of elaboration strategies? There are various approaches to elaborating upon information:

A phrase or sentence may be applied to the information:

The World Trade Center was attacked on September 11, 2001. The date "9/11" also refers to an emergency situation. The attack on the WTO certainly constituted an emergency situation.

An analogy may be applied to the information:

An election campaign is like a battle. One side "fires" by saying something against the other side, and then the other side retaliates by doing the same thing.

A relationship may be drawn (based on specific characteristics found in the stimulus material):

Photosynthesis is a process where plants take in carbon dioxide from the air and produce oxygen. That works just the opposite of me (a human), because I take in oxygen and produce carbon dioxide. This creates a fine balance!

How Do You Decide Which Elaboration Strategy to Use?

Consider the information to be elaborated upon and the needs and abilities of your learners. Analogies, for example, are rather complex ways of connecting information. Enlist student ideas and discussion to help you develop the best elaboration strategy.

How Do You Construct Your Own Elaboration Strategy?

- Analyze the information to be elaborated upon, and consider learner needs and abilities. Also consider the information that students already know.
- Present information to be attended to and elaborated upon.
- Guide discussion about the information to formulate effective elaboration (e.g., phrases, sentences, analogies, relationships).
- Provide sample elaborations.
- Reinforce (a) the students' comprehension and recall of the material and (b) their ability to elaborate.

Transformational Strategies

Transformation means "change." Students use a transformational strategy when they convert difficult or unfamiliar information into more manageable information. The simpler or more familiar information is learned efficiently. Here is an example of how readers transform written information, such as a short story. When students read the story, they can do a variety of things to change the information. They can embellish it, enhance it, or elaborate upon it, adding other information to the existing information. In the other direction, they can distill it, reduce it, or condense it, thus narrowing the information down to its basic concepts. They use a transformational strategy to change the information into another format. Paraphrasing is an example of a transformational strategy. Learners begin with another person's written (or spoken) information and transform that information into something else without losing the meaning of the original.

How Can Transformational Strategies Help Your Students?

Transformational strategies are helpful when students have some grasp of the information, at least enough to be able to transform it. Moreover, transformational strategies are helpful when students need to show that they have a deep understanding of the material. By demonstrating an ability to transform the information into their own words while maintaining the intent of the original information, they show that they have gone beyond a surface understanding and are beginning to "own" the material.

How Can You Implement Transformational Strategies to Effectively Meet the Diverse Learning Needs of Students?

A challenge of using transformational strategies is that they require students to manipulate information without changing the basic concepts of it. Extra effort is involved, and often students do not know where to begin. You may recall questions that are usually given at the end of chapters in content textbooks such as social studies. Questions that begin with "On what date did . . ." are usually (and understandably) preferred over questions that begin, "Compare and contrast the causes of . . ." When information is transformed rather than just reported, as in paraphrasing, a series of decisions must be made regarding the material. Questions such as the following arise:

- Is this part essential or can I leave that out?
- How can I say that in my own words without changing the meaning?
- How much context do I need to describe here?
- I wonder what's for lunch? ;)

Students with learning problems can get stalled dealing with these questions before any visible work begins. One of the most important skills you will teach students about transformational strategies is how to process the information they are to transform. An approach to paraphrasing could look like this:

1. Read the entire passage to be paraphrased. (If there is too much information, break the passage down into smaller chunks.)

2. Record a key word that relates to the concept of the paragraph.

3. Develop a main idea sentence from the key word.

4. Record two detail sentences that support the main idea and reflect information from the passage.

Be prepared with a variety of written and spoken materials as you sharpen transformational strategy skills. Materials that are highly motivating to students will make both the teacher's and the students' jobs easier.

Opportunities for practice can include formal activities such as using higher-order thinking skills (e.g., summarize, evaluate, compare and contrast) to address written or spoken materials. Informal activities such as describing the highlights of a movie also involve transformational strategies. As you provide frequent formal and informal opportunities for practice, reinforce both the learners' comprehension of the material and their ability to use transformational strategies.

What Are the Different Types of Transformational Strategies?

There are various approaches to transforming information. The goal is to take something difficult and makes it simpler. For example, if you have difficulty reading maps, a transformational strategy you might use is to visit mapquest.com to get verbal directions. The content area of math is full of transformational strategies. Rules, formulas, and properties transform information for processing and computation. One transformational strategy that students learn when computing fractions is to "simplify" the fraction, or transform it to its lowest terms.

In the area of reading comprehension, transformational strategies lead to a deep understanding of the text. Some students learn to paraphrase very well, pulling out main ideas and details. Others may do well with developing questions about the information, answering the questions, and then using the answers to interpret the information. Imagery and mnemonics are powerful transformational strategies and will be addressed in separate sections.

How Do You Decide Which Transformational Strategy to Use?

Consider your students' strengths for transforming information, and capitalize on these as much as possible. For example, learners who naturally ask a lot of questions may do well with questioning strategies. Think about your favorite approaches for transforming information, and prepare to teach them as examples to your students.

How Do You Construct Your Own Transformational Strategy?

Analyze the information to be transformed, and determine how you would best transform it. If we use self-questioning as an example, then you would do the following:

- Develop some example questions to show students.
- Present information to be attended to and transformed.
- Involve students in developing more questions.
- As students get stronger in developing questions, fade your involvement in question development.
- Reinforce (a) the students' comprehension of the material and (b) their ability to develop and answer questions.

Imagery Strategies

Imagery strategies involve activating the memory by taking the information to be learned and creating meaningful visual, auditory, or kinesthetic images of it.

How Can Imagery Strategies Help Your Students?

Imagery strategies are helpful when a student has some grasp of the information to be learned. Creating images of the information allows for efficient access and personalizes the learning for the student.

How Can You Implement Imagery Strategies to Effectively Meet the Diverse Learning Needs of Students?

Imagery is a highly effective strategy for increasing comprehension.

An advantage of imagery is that the learner can use it in a highly individualized manner. Some students will develop imagery strategies on their own. For many students, however, specific instruction on how to develop images will be needed. A visual imagery strategy for reading comprehension is *SCENE* (Schumaker, Deshler, Zemitzsch, & Warner, 1993):

S = Search for the picture words as you read.

C = Create or change the scene.

E = Enter lots of details.

N = Name the parts.

E = Evaluate your picture.

Each letter of *SCENE* is a cue for a specific action that would be appropriate for the student to take in a classroom.

How Do You Decide Which Imagery Strategy to Use?

Consider your students' strengths for making images from information, and capitalize on these as much as possible. Visual learners will probably experience the greatest success.

How Do You Construct Your Own Imagery Strategy?

- Analyze the information where you will apply imagery.
- Consider whether learning the imagery will make your students' learning more efficient.
- Determine whether you will use visual, auditory, or tactile imagery or a combination of senses.
- Ensure that the imagery can address a significant amount of information to be learned.
- Ensure that the imagery relates well to the task.
- Present information where imagery will be used.
- Guide students through making the imagery.
- Reinforce (a) the students' learning of the material and (b) their ability to use imagery.

Mnemonic Strategies

Mnemonic strategies can be described as transformational strategies (described above). Students use a transformational strategy when they convert difficult or unfamiliar information into more manageable information. The simpler or more familiar information is learned efficiently.

A mnemonic is a device, such as a formula or rhyme, used as an aid in remembering. Mnemonic strategies are a special kind of transformational strategy because they apply specific language to learning and connect information to be learned with key words or letters.

How Can Mnemonic Strategies
Help Your Students?

Mnemonic strategies are helpful when a student has some grasp of the information to be learned, and needs to order it for efficient access. The order that the mnemonic applies allows the learner to retrieve information quickly.

How Can You Implement Mnemonic Strategies to
Effectively Meet the Diverse Learning Needs of Students?

A warning about mnemonics: They should make learning *easier, not harder.* I have seen students struggle to learn complicated mnemonics that someone else made up when it would have been easier for them to learn the information outright. Mastropieri and Scruggs (1998) define mnemonics as a systematic procedure for enhancing memory. They caution that mnemonics are not a comprehensive teaching method. Moreover, mnemonics are memory strategies, not comprehension strategies.

When mnemonics are used correctly, they can streamline the learning process, giving students access to broad amounts of information. Because they create "bridges" to other information, less working memory is required. An advantage of mnemonics is that they can be applied to a multitude of content information, from behavior to academics to careers to hobbies. An Internet search of "mnemonics" yielded 41,460 hits. Web sites addressing medical mnemonics, boating mnemonics, spelling mnemonics, and bird song (yes, even warbling) mnemonics were included. So, for whatever you want to teach, there is probably a mnemonic for it.

A mnemonic for appropriate behavior during a class lecture is *SLANT*:

S = Sit up.

L = Lean forward.

A = Ask questions.

N = Nod your head.

T = Track the teacher.

Each letter of *SLANT* is a cue for a specific action that would be appropriate for the student to take in a classroom. Moreover, the word *slant* indicates the position of the body in the classroom, where the student is slanting forward and showing interest in what is going on.

What Are the Different Types of Mnemonic Strategies?

Two types of mnemonic strategies will be discussed here. Students use *key word mnemonics* when they learn to associate unfamiliar words to be learned with words that are familiar and that may rhyme or have some physical resemblance to the target word(s). The following example comes from the Web site www.bucks.edu/~specpop/mnemonics.htm:

In Spanish, the word *cabina* means "phone booth". Invent an image of a cab trying to fit in a phone booth. When you see the word *cabina*, you should be able to recall this image and thereby retrieve the meaning "phone booth."

Students use *first-letter mnemonics* when they take the first letters in each item in a list and form a word that relates to the main idea of the list. An example is *PENS* (Schumaker & Sheldon, 1999):

P = Pick a formula.

E = Explore words to fit the formula.

N = Note the words.

S = Search for subject and verb.

Other mnemonics may include pictures or rhymes.

How Do You Decide Which Mnemonic Strategy to Use?

Consider your students' strengths for transforming information, and capitalize on these as much as possible. Mnemonics that relate well to your students' preferred methods of learning will be most successful. Finally, think about your favorite approaches for developing mnemonics, and prepare to teach those as examples to your students.

How Do You Construct Your Own Mnemonic Strategy?

- Analyze the information where you will apply a mnemonic.
- Consider whether learning the mnemonic will make your students' learning more efficient.
- Ensure that the mnemonic that you have developed or will develop with your students is relevant to the information to be learned.
- Ensure that the mnemonic has a minimum number of steps to learn.
- Present information to be attended to and learned.
- Then teach the mnemonic, using *LIP* (a mnemonic for introducing a lesson, or "give it some lip"):

L = Link the new information to information the students already know (e.g., "Today we're going to learn a series of actions that will help you write a sentence. What do you know already about writing sentences?")

I = Introduce the new information to the students (as in the example of *PENS* above).

P = Provide a rationale for learning the mnemonic. ("Why do you want to write good sentences?")

- Reinforce (a) the students' learning of the material and (b) their ability to learn the mnemonic(s).

You may also consider teaching your students to develop their own mnemonics. The University of Kansas (Ellis, 1992) has published a strategy for developing mnemonics. As you might suspect, that strategy also has a mnemonic as part of the instruction, or *LINCS*.

L = List the parts.

I = Indicate a reminding word.

N = Note a LINCing story.

C = Construct a LINCing picture.

S = Self-test.

Organizational Strategies

An organizational strategy is like a transformational strategy in that it allows the learner to manipulate information. Students manipulate, integrate, and/or otherwise interact with the information so that it is more easily learned and remembered.

How Can Organizational Strategies Help Your Students?

Organizational strategies are most helpful to students who have some grasp of the information but are aware that restructuring the information will help them learn it better or more efficiently. Organizational strategies also reach beyond academics into areas such as preparation for class and care of possessions. For example, students could be asked to list their activities that they participate in after school. Chores, clubs, sports, and individual activities could be included. Next, students could organize their activities by classifications such as "high priority," "medium priority," and "low priority." Finally, students could organize the activities by category.

How Can You Implement Organizational Strategies to Effectively Meet the Diverse Learning Needs of Students?

Because organizational strategies are so versatile, they are powerful instructional tools for a classroom. You may begin by teaching basic concepts of organizational strategies in areas other than academics; after students learn the basics, you can apply them to academic areas. Prioritizing is a good example. You can teach students concepts about prioritizing by discussing elements of their day: responsibilities at school, responsibilities at home, spending time with friends, spending time on homework, and so on. Then you can use that exercise to help students prioritize information to be learned.

What Are the Different Types of Organizational Strategies?

There are various approaches to organizing information. *Prioritizing* is a cognitive strategy students need in many settings, especially as they reach middle school age. *Clustering* requires the student to divide information into small, more accessible "chunks" to facilitate acquisition and then storage of information in memory. *Categorizing* requires the student to rearrange information by identifying relationships between items in lists. Memory is enhanced by the links created by connecting the information.

How Do You Decide Which Organizational Strategy to Use?

Consider your students' needs for organizing information. A number of organizational strategies may need to be employed. Applying organizational strategies to areas other than academics may be highly motivating and can lead to successful organization of other types of information.

How Do You Construct Your Own Organizational Strategy?

- Analyze the information to be organized, and determine how you would best organize it. Keep in mind that your organization approaches may not be the same as those of your students.
- Show students various approaches to organize information, and then reorganize the information.
- Provide information that your students need to reorganize.
- Guide students through the organization process.
- Reinforce (a) the students' comprehension of the material and (b) their ability to organize.
- If students are able to organize on their own, monitor and reinforce this process and their learning.

WHERE CAN I FIND RESOURCES OR MORE INFORMATION ON COGNITIVE STRATEGIES?

Research Articles

Baker, S., Gersten, R., Dimino, J. A., & Griffiths, R. (2004). The sustained use of research-based instructional practice. *Remedial and Special Education, 25,* 5–25.

Boudah, D. J., Lenz, B. K., Bulgren, J. A., Schumaker, J. B., & Deshler, D. D. (2000). Content learning through the unit organizer routine. *Teaching Exceptional Children, 32*(3), 48–56.

Bulgren, J. A., Deshler, D. D., & Schumaker, J. B. (1997). Use of a recall enhancement routine and strategies in inclusive secondary classes. *Learning Disabilities Research and Practice, 12*(4), 198–208.

Bulgren, J. A., Deshler, D. D., Schumaker, J. B., & Lenz, B. K. (2000). The use and effectiveness of analogical instruction in diverse secondary content classrooms. *Journal of Educational Psychology, 92*(3), 426–441.

Calhoon, M. B., & Fuchs, L. S. (2003). The effects of peer-assisted learning strategies and curriculum-based measurement on the mathematics performance of secondary students with disabilities. *Remedial and Special Education, 24,* 235–246.

Cho, S., & Ahn, D. (2003). Strategy acquisition and maintenance of gifted and nongifted children. *Exceptional Children, 69,* 497–506.

Dembo, M. H., & Seli, H. P. (2004). Students' resistance to change in learning strategies courses. *Journal of Developmental Education, 27*(3), 2–9.

Deshler, D. D., Schumaker, J. B., & Lenz, B. K. (1984). Academic and cognitive interventions for LD adolescents: Part I. *Journal of Learning Disabilities, 17*(2), 108–117.

Ee, J., Moore, P. J., & Atputhasamy, L. (2003). High-achieving students: Their motivational goals, self-regulation and achievement and relationships to their teachers' goals and strategy-based instruction. *High Ability Studies, 14*(1), 23–40.

Ellis, E. S., & Sabornie, E. J. (1990). Strategy-based adaptive instruction in content-area classes. Social validity of six options. *Teacher Education and Special Education, 13*(2) 133–144.

Evans, C. J., Kirby, J. R., & Fabrigar, L. R. (2004). Approaches to learning, need for cognition, and strategic flexibility among university students. *British Journal of Educational Psychology, 74,* 507–529.

Fuchs, D., Fuchs, L. S., & Burish, P. (2000). Peer-assisted learning stra'egies: An evidence-based practice to promote reading achievement. *Learning Disabilities Research and Practice, 15,* 85–91.

Fuchs, L. S., Fuchs, D., Prentice, K., Burch, M., Hamlett, C. L., Owen, R., & Schroeter, K. (2003). Enhancing third-grade students' mathematical problem solving with self-regulated learning strategies. *Journal of Educational Psychology, 95,* 306–316.

Housman, D., & Porter, M. (2003). Proof schemes and learning strategies of above-average mathematics students. *Educational Studies in Mathematics, 53,* 139–159.

Kline, F. M., Schumaker, J. B., & Deshler, D. D. (1991). Development and validation of feedback routines for instructing students with learning disabilities. *Learning Disability Quarterly, 14*(3), 191–207.

Lenz, B. K., Alley, G. R., & Schumaker, J. B. (1987). Activating the inactive learner: Advance organizers in the secondary content classroom. *Learning Disability Quarterly, 10*(1), 53–67.

Lenz, B. K., & Scanlon, D. (1998). Smarter teaching: Developing accommodations to reduce cognitive barriers to learning for individuals with learning disabilities. *Perspectives, 24*(3) 16–19.

Mastropieri, M. A., & Scruggs, T. E. (1998). Enhancing school success with mnemonic strategies. *Intervention in School and Clinic, 33*(4), 201–208.

Meltzer, L., Reddy, R., Pollica, L. S., Roditi, B., Sayer, J., & Theokas, C. (2004). Positive and negative self-perceptions: Is there a cyclical relationship between teachers' and students' perceptions of effort, strategy use, and academic performance? *Learning Disabilities Research and Practice, 19,* 33–45.

Palincsar, A. S., & Brown, A. L. (1984). Reciprocal teaching of comprehension-fostering and comprehension-monitoring activities. *Cognition and Instruction, 1*(2), 117–175.

Putnam, M. L. (1992). The testing practices of mainstream secondary classroom teachers. *Remedial and Special Education, 13*(5), 11–21.

Schumaker, J. B., & Clark, F. L. (1990). Achieving implementation of strategy instruction through effective inservice education. *Teacher Education and Special Education, 13*(2), 105–116.

Sperling, R. A., Howard, B. C., Staley, R., & DuBois, N. (2004). Metacognition and self-regulated learning constructs. *Educational Research and Evaluation, 10,* 117–140.

Wehby, J. H., Falk, K. B., Barton-Arwood, S., Lane, K. L., & Cooley, C. (2003). The impact of comprehensive reading instruction on the academic and social behavior of students with emotional and behavioral disorders. *Journal of Emotional and Behavioral Disorders, 11,* 225–230.

Wehmeyer, M. L., Hughes, C., Agran, M., Garner, N., & Yeager, D. (2003). Student-directed learning strategies to promote the progress of students with intellectual disability in inclusive classrooms. *International Journal of Inclusive Education, 7,* 415–429.

Descriptive Articles

Baker, S., Gersten, R., & Scanlon, D. (2002). Procedural facilitators and cognitive strategies: Tools for unraveling the mysteries of comprehension and the writing process, and for providing meaningful access to the general curriculum. *Learning Disabilities Practice, 17,* 65–77.

Bulgren, J., & Scanlon, D. (1997). Instructional routines and learning strategies that promote understanding of content area concepts. *Journal of Adolescent and Adult Literacy, 41,* 292–302.

Deshler, D. D., & Lenz, B. K. (1989). The strategies instructional approach. *International Journal of Disability, Development and Education, 36,* 203–224.

Deshler, D. D., & Schumaker, J. B. (1986). Learning strategies: An instructional alternative for low-achieving adolescents. *Exceptional Children, 52,* 583–590.

Deshler, D. D., Schumaker, J. B., Alley, G. R., Warner, M. M., & Clark, F. L. (1982). Learning disabilities in adolescent and young adult populations: Research implications. *Focus on Exceptional Children, 15*(1), 1–12.

Ehren, B. J. (2002). Vocabulary intervention to improve reading comprehension for students with learning disabilities. *Perspectives on Language and Education, 9*(3), 12–18.

Fuchs, D., Fuchs, L. S., Thompson, A., Svenson, E., Yen, L., Al Otaiba, S., et al. (2001). Peer-assisted learning strategies in reading. *Remedial and Special Education, 22,* 15–21.

Harris, K. R., & Pressley, M. (1991). The nature of cognitive strategy instruction: Interactive strategy construction. *Exceptional Children, 57,* 392–404.

Lenz, B. K., & Deshler, D. D. (1990). Principles of strategies instruction as the basis of effective preservice teacher education. *Teacher Education and Special Education, 13*(2), 82–95.

Palincsar, A. S. (1986). Metacognitive strategy instruction. *Exceptional Children, 53,* 118–124.

Schumaker, J. B., & Deshler, D. D. (2003). Can students with LD become competent writers? *Learning Disability Quarterly, 26,* 129–142.

Swanson, H. L. (1989). Strategy instruction: Overview of principles and procedures for effective use. *Learning Disability Quarterly, 12,* 3–14.

Walker, S. E. (2003). Active learning strategies to promote critical thinking. *Journal of Athletic Training, 38,* 263–268.

Books

Bereiter, C., & Scardamalia, M. (1987). *The psychology of written composition.* New York: Lawrence Erlbaum.

Jones, B. F., Palincsar, A. S., Ogle, D. S., & Carr, E. G. (1987). *Strategic teaching and learning: Cognitive instruction in the content areas.* Alexandria, VA: Association for Supervision and Curriculum Development.

Wolfe, P. (2001). *Brain matters: Translating research into classroom practice.* Alexandria, VA: Association for Supervision and Curriculum Development.

Book Chapters

Bulgren, J. A., & Lenz, B. K. (1996). Strategic instruction in the content areas. In D. D. Deshler, E. S. Ellis, & B. K. Lenz (Eds.), *Teaching adolescents with learning disabilities: Strategies and methods* (2nd ed., pp. 409–473). Denver: Love.

Lenz, B. K., Bulgren, J. A., & Hudson, P. (1990). Content enhancement: A model for promoting the acquisition of content by individuals with learning disabilities. In T. E. Scruggs & B. L. Y. Wong (Eds.), *Intervention research in learning disabilities* (pp. 122–165). New York: Springer.

Rosenshine, B. (1997). Advances in research on instruction. In J. W. Lloyd, E. J. Kameanui, & D. Chard (Eds.), *Issues in educating students with disabilities* (pp. 197–221). Mahwah, NJ: Lawrence Erlbaum.

Rosenshine, B. (1997, March). *The case for explicit, teacher-led, cognitive strategy instruction.* Paper presented at the annual meeting of the American Educational Research Association, Chicago.

Swanson, H. L., & Cooney, J. B. (1991). Learning disabilities and memory. In B. L. Wong (Ed.), *Learning about learning disabilities* (pp. 103–127). New York: Academic Press.

Web Sites

Bucks County Community College, "Mnemonics—Memory Techniques" (www.bucks.edu/~specpop/mnemonics.htm). Includes mnemonics by category.

Graphic Organizers (www.graphic.org). Contains resources you might find useful for writing and using graphic organizers. Especially helpful are the links to articles and books on the Web.

Guilford County Schools, North Carolina, "Activity, Curriculum, and Technology: Cognitive Strategies" (http://its.guilford.k12.nc.us/

act/strategies/cognitive.htm). This collection of cognitive strategies includes "power notes" and "dump and clump."

North Central Regional Educational Laboratory (NCREL) (www .ncrel.org). The North Central Regional Educational Laboratory (NCREL) is a not-for-profit organization dedicated to helping schools—and the students they serve—reach their full potential. NCREL specializes in the educational applications of technology. Use the search function on the home page to search the site for useful information on graphic organizers.

ProTeacher (www.proteacher.com). ProTeacher is a professional community for elementary school teachers, specialists, and student teachers in prekindergarten through Grade 8. The open membership includes visitors from across the United States and guests from around the world. The site features over two dozen active discussion boards and an extensive archive and directory of teacher-selected lesson plans, teaching ideas, and resources.

Reading Quest, "Strategies for Reading Comprehension" (http://curry .edschool.virginia.edu/go/readquest/strat/).

Teach-nology (http://teachers.teach-nology.com). Make your own graphic organizers on this site by filling out a simple form. The materials are made instantly and can be printed directly from your computer.

University of Kansas Center for Research on Learning, "CRL Publications List" (www.ku-crl.org/publications/index.html). Provides an annotated bibliography of research and other publications from the KU-CRL.

University of Texas, "Cognitivism" (http://uts.cc.utexas.edu/~best/html/ learning.htm). Eight areas of cognitive strategies are addressed.

CHAPTER REFERENCES

Baker, S., Gersten, R., & Scanlon, D. (2002). Procedural facilitators and cognitive strategies: Tools for unraveling the mysteries of comprehension and the writing process, and for providing meaningful access to the general curriculum. *Learning Disabilities Research and Practice, 17*(1), 65–78.

Bereiter, C., & Scardamalia, M. (1987). *The psychology of written composition.* New York: Lawrence Erlbaum.

Bulgren, J. A., Deshler, D. D., & Schumaker, J. B. (1997). Use of a recall enhancement routine and strategies in inclusive secondary classes. *Learning Disabilities Research and Practice, 12*(4), 198–208.

Ellis, E. (1992). *The LINCS strategy.* Lawrence: Edge Enterprise.

Mastropieri, M. A., & Scruggs, T. E. (1998). Enhancing school success with mnemonic strategies. *Intervention in School and Clinic, 33*(4), 201–208.

Moely, B. E., Hart, S. S., Santulli, K., Leal, L., Johnson, T., & Rao, N. (1986). How do teachers teach memory skills? *Educational Psychology, 21*, 55–57.

Palincsar, A. S., & Brown, A. L. (1984). Reciprocal teaching of comprehension-fostering and comprehension-monitoring activities. *Cognition and Instruction, 1*(2), 117–175.

Rosenshine, B. (1997). Advances in research on instruction. In J. W. Lloyd, E. J. Kameanui, & D. Chard (Eds.), *Issues in educating students with disabilities* (pp. 197–221). Mahwah, NJ: Erlbaum.

Schumaker, J. B., Deshler, D. D., Zemitzsch, A., & Warner, M. M. (1993). *The visual imagery strategy.* Lawrence: University of Kansas.

Schumaker, J. B., & Sheldon, J. B. (1999). *Proficiency in the sentence writing strategy.* Lawrence: University of Kansas.

Swanson, H. L., & Cooney, J. B. (1991). Learning disabilities and memory. In B. Y. L. Wong (ed.), *Learning about learning disabilities.* New York: Academic Press.

What Are Effective Accommodations and Modifications?

Outline Questions

What do I need to know about accommodations and modifications?

Why should I use accommodations and modifications in my classroom?

What are some commonly used accommodations, and how do I use them in my classroom?

What are some commonly used modifications, and how do I use them in my classroom?

Where can I find resources or more information on accommodations and modifications?

WHAT DO I NEED TO KNOW ABOUT ACCOMMODATIONS AND MODIFICATIONS?

Attempts have likely been made to provide appropriate assessment and instructional considerations for students with disabilities since the passage of the Individuals with Disabilities Education Act (IDEA, P.L. 94–142, 1975). However, recent updates of IDEA continue to provide greater legal impetus to meet the needs of these students. IDEA mandates that students with disabilities be served in the general classroom setting to the maximum degree possible. In fact, if services are provided outside the general classroom, the IEP must provide a rationale and explanation for the placement to occur. These students are to be involved in and provided the opportunity to "make progress in the general curriculum . . . and (provide) a statement of the program *modifications* or supports for school personnel that will be provided for the child" (IDEA, 614(d)(1)(A)(i); emphasis added). IDEA further mandates that students with disabilities be included "in all general State and district-wide assessment programs, with appropriate *accommodations*, where necessary" (612(a) (16) (A); emphasis added).

It is unfortunate that it is often necessary to legally mandate the application of appropriate accommodations and modifications for students with or without disabilities. Accommodating the unique learning needs of students with disabilities and modifying the assessment and instructional material used with all students in the general classroom setting are essential components of effective instruction. This is true regardless of the legal mandates established. Nonetheless, it is often necessary to provide legal mandates to re-emphasize the importance of such considerations. The intent of this chapter is to provide an understanding of the meaning of accommodations and modifications as they pertain to students with disabilities. In addition, specific techniques will be discussed that provide teachers, test administrators, school administration, and parents greater insight and access to meeting the unique needs of these students.

WHY SHOULD I USE ACCOMMODATIONS AND MODIFICATIONS IN MY CLASSROOM?

Assessment measures and instructional materials can be altered through the introduction of accommodations or modifications. Generally, an accommodation is the action taken to make something more suitable by adjusting to the individual circumstances of each situation. A modification, on the other hand, is the act of making something different. Recently, a professional golfer named Casey Martin was given the opportunity to compete against his fellow professionals in spite of his physical disability. His physical disability was accommodated by providing him the opportunity to ride in a golf cart even though his peers were required to walk. The act of adjusting to the circumstances of Casey Martin's disability (i.e., accommodating to his unique needs) provided him with the chance to compete with other professional golfers. It is still necessary for him to hit his shots from the same place as the other golfers, he must continue to use equipment that is approved by the Professional Golfers Association (PGA), and he must adhere to the myriad of rules that govern professional golf. In other words, the use of the golf cart "levels the playing field" for Casey Martin as he competes against his peers. The cart provides Casey Martin the opportunity to compare his golf skills to those of his peers while considering his unique needs in the process. However, Casey Martin is not provided with additional modifications to the game of golf, as they would conceivably provide him with an unfair advantage. For example, if he were allowed to tee off 50 yards closer to the hole than the rest of his peers, Casey Martin would unfairly benefit from this modification to the game. Making the total distance of the hole different (i.e., shorter) for Casey Martin would clearly give him an unfair advantage over his peers. In an effort to level the playing field for Casey Martin, the rule changes would effectively "un-level" the field for everyone else. This is the basic and crucial difference between an accommodation and a modification.

Accommodations and modifications are designed to provide all students equal access to information both taught and evaluated in our schools. That is, school personnel can accommodate the assessment process as well as the instructional practices that teachers use in the classroom. As evidenced in the example of Casey Martin, *accommodations* and *modifications* are not synonymous terms. The following sections will describe the appropriate application of accommodations and modifications to assessment and instruction of students with disabilities.

Accommodations

Accommodations are adjustments to the assessment tools being used or the instructional material implemented in the general classroom setting that attempt to level the playing field by removing the barriers to performance created by a disability (Fuchs & Fuchs, 2001). They are intended to provide students with disabilities with an opportunity to access the curriculum or test material to ultimately demonstrate what has been learned (Nolet & McLaughlin, 2000). Consequently, accommodations generally do not provide for adjustments to the specific content being taught and/or tested. This suggests that students with disabilities are exposed to content material that is similar to the material presented to students without disabilities. Likewise, in-class testing or high-stakes testing (e.g., competency tests or end-of-course tests) reflects the content to which *all* students have been exposed. In addition, accommodations typically do not reduce the quantity of material for which students with disabilities are responsible. A geometry curriculum, for example, may require students to learn 14 theorems and 2 postulates when studying parallel lines and planes.

Classroom instruction would focus on these 16 rules. Classroom tests as well as the high-stakes test that might occur at the end of the year would also concentrate on the body of knowledge encompassed by the 14 theorems and 2 postulates. All students who participated in the geometry class would be responsible for this body of knowledge and required to demonstrate their knowledge on the specific assessment measure. However, students with disabilities might require specific accommodations to their work that would enable them to effectively access and demonstrate their understanding of the material.

Regardless of the nature or the number of accommodations being used, the accommodations must always be included in the student's IEP. As such, accommodations may vary from student to student. In addition, as the curricula used may vary from state to state, the specific accommodations used may vary relative to the state's curricular focus. Certain states may also indicate that specific accommodations may not be implemented during the state high-stakes testing program. This raises questions as to the effectiveness of the implementation of the specific accommodations in the classroom setting. It is often recommended that the accommodations used in the classroom should be consistent with the accommodations available to the student during testing situations (Washburn-Moses, 2003). In fact, if accommodations are not available to the student on a day-to-day basis, they are not available to the student during testing situations (see Box 9.1). It does not seem to be appropriate or fair to a student to provide specific accommodations during the school year only to disallow the use of these accommodations during high-stakes testing. The use of accommodations that are not permitted during high-stakes testing is also likely to result in the elimination of the individual student's test scores used to determine statewide accountability (Washburn-Moses, 2003). This clearly reduces the impact of the accommodations regardless of the individual success experienced by students with disabilities. Logically, it is crucial to carefully plan and consider the most appropriate and effective accommodations so that all students are provided with the greatest opportunity to perform to the maximum of their ability and achievement level.

Modifications

Modifications are essentially changes or adjustments to the content material that enable students to gain access to instruction in the general classroom setting (Haigh, 1999). The appropriate implementation of modifications must be completed on an individual basis. Clearly, not all students

---

Box 9.1 Accommodations on the SAT

One of the authors maintains a private practice in addition to his faculty position at the university. Recently, two high school juniors have made appointments for a complete psycho-educational evaluation. During the initial interview process, the students and their parents were asked why they were seeking an outside evaluation. The response of both the students and parents was that they wanted to be able to take the SAT in an extended time format and in a quiet setting. It was difficult to burst the bubble of these students and their parents, but it was necessary to tell them that they couldn't get an evaluation and then apply for nonstandard test administration accommodations on the SAT. When they were told that the accommodations would have to be in place during the school day as well, they were surprised. Interestingly, they both did not wish to go forward with the evaluation. When asked why, the students said that the accommodations weren't necessary during the school day but that they would be very helpful when taking the SAT.

---

need modifications. Similarly, not all students with disabilities require modifications in all academic content areas. This is a critical point, as these modifications often result in significant changes to the content or performance expectations for an individual student (Jitendra, Edwards, Choutka, & Treadway, 2002). Students who receive the modified material are often expected to learn something other than what the rest of the class is learning. They may be expected to learn less material or different material altogether (Jitendra et al., 2002). Such considerations often present a Catch-22 for educators; although the intent of modifying instruction is to provide students with disabilities with access to the general curriculum, the modifications themselves often rule out the possibility of such access. If less material is presented to students with disabilities, it may be impossible to "keep up" with the remainder of the class as new, more detailed content is presented. The very act of modifying instruction may increase the gap between the students with and without disabilities (Jitendra et al., 2002). The frustration is exacerbated because the increasing size of the learning gap may not be exclusively due to an individual student's learning difficulty but instead to the student's not being exposed to the material. A simple example of this is presented in Box 9.2.

Box 9.2 Modifications That Increase the Learning Gap

A first-grade classroom teacher taught her class how to complete sums to 9 in arithmetic. She did an excellent job of using manipulative materials, relating and extending the students' understanding to instruction at the representational level, and ultimately introducing more abstract, paper-and-pencil activities involving the addition of numbers with sums to 9. As she corrected and analyzed her students' work, however, she made an error that had a significant impact on one of her students. One student (we'll call him Matt) consistently produced a response that she did not score as correct. A representative sample of the items that Matt completed follows, along with his teacher's feedback:

3	5	7	8	1	2
+3	+4	+1	+1	+5	+4
℮	9	8	9	℮	℮

As she graded Matt's work, the teacher was expecting to see a "6" for items 1, 5, and 6. When she didn't see the "normal" 6, she considered the items to be incorrect. Then, in an effort to help Matt learn his math facts, she gave him several practice sheets to do for homework. The next day in class, Matt presented his homework to the teacher with similar results. Matt's teacher said, "I'm sorry, Matt. You don't seem to be ready to move on. Here are some more 'sums to 9' sheets to practice." Matt continued to complete the sheets but really didn't know why. He knew that 3 + 3 = 6; he just had difficulty writing the 6 correctly. Matt got further behind because he was practicing a skill he had mastered and was not getting practice on a skill with which he needed help and support.

As professional educators, our goal is to maximize the ability and skills of each student placed in our classrooms. Modifications should be designed to help reach this goal. The primary purpose of modifying instruction should be to enhance student learning and to facilitate growth in all students (Haigh, 1999). With this purpose in mind, educators work to identify and implement techniques that modify the content or the assessment tool in such a way that students with special needs have access to the same material as their peers. Techniques that diminish the opportunity for students with special needs to "keep up" with the remainder of the class should be used when it is apparent that individual students will not benefit from exposure to the same material as the students without special needs.

WHAT ARE SOME COMMONLY USED ACCOMMODATIONS, AND HOW DO I USE THEM IN MY CLASSROOM?

The overriding principle that must be considered when implementing any type of accommodation is that the intent is to provide students with disabilities access to the same content as their nondisabled peers. The goal is to accurately reflect the academic growth of the students with disabilities in relation to their peers.

Accommodations to the assessment process or to daily instructional practices generally fall into one of several categories: accommodations to the (a) setting, (b) scheduling, (c) presentation, (d) responses, and/or (e) equipment or technological assistance used (Haigh, 1999; Washburn-Moses, 2003). Not all accommodations will work with all students. The selection of appropriate accommodations should be made through the careful consideration of the individual student's unique needs.

Setting

The setting may be changed so that students with disabilities may complete their work in a setting that reduces the possible distracters that might be present in a typical classroom or test setting. Adjustments to the setting may be effective with instruction and assessment. For example, students may be seated in a study carrel or in a room separate from the general classroom during everyday classroom activities as well as testing situations. In the classroom setting, students may simply be placed in a preferential seating arrangement; this may be in the front of the room, away from windows or doors, or in small group arrangements. Testing may require the student to be placed outside the classroom to facilitate performance. Students who are not easily distracted by normal environmental stimuli may not require adjustments to their setting. Simply placing students in a less distractible setting does not ensure better performance; however, students who consistently experience difficulty focusing on the target material because of the distractions in the environment will likely benefit from changes in their setting.

Scheduling

Accommodations to the student's schedule may allow him or her to complete the test or assignment in an extended time format. This may include time before or after school to complete a test, extended deadlines for papers or projects, or simply frequent breaks during the class or test. Once again, the scheduling accommodation may be extremely beneficial to a number of students with and without disabilities. However, if a student has not learned or been exposed to the content, changes in the time allocated to complete the task are likely to have little impact on the student's understanding or performance. For example, a high school sophomore may be expected to complete the algebra end-of-course test to meet the requirements for graduation with a standard diploma. However, if the student has mastered only addition and subtraction skills, it is unlikely that he or she will be successful with the content on the algebra test. He or she could receive as much time as was possible but still not pass the test because of the lack of necessary exposure or knowledge.

Presentation

The purpose of presenting information to a class is to convey the meaning of the content. Similarly, the intent of any test is to determine what a student knows about the material being evaluated. In an effort to accurately and effectively complete these tasks, it is often helpful to alter the manner in which content or test material is presented. If test directions are presented orally, for example, it may be beneficial for specific students to have the directions in a print format or on an audiocassette tape to ensure their maximum understanding. The use of an overhead projector or white board during class presentations will also increase the opportunity for students to access the content material. The key to presentation accommodations is that each student receives information that is essential to success. Without the accommodations mentioned above, students may not understand the content of the lecture because they do not process information presented in an auditory manner. Their test performance may reflect, not their knowledge, but rather a lack of understanding of the specific demands of the test. These simple accommodations provide *all* students with the opportunity to succeed to the maximum level of ability and skill.

Responses

When we collect work from students, we logically assess their knowledge level on the basis of their completed products. A student's responses to a multiple-choice test typically indicate student understanding and/or the level of preparation for the test. However, in many circumstances the results of students' performance may not reflect their knowledge or degree of preparation. Teachers often grade students' notebooks, looking for neatness and accuracy of information. Students with special needs are often unsuccessful in keeping a notebook neat and accurate due to disorders with attention or difficulty writing for an entire class period. Consequently, students find holes in their notes because they were unable to keep up with the class pace. The use of a note taker often provides a student with special needs with the opportunity to "fill in the blanks" while maintaining expectations that are appropriate to the entire class. Next, a test is administered in U.S. history and asks the students to write an essay describing the differences between the Allied and Axis powers in World War II. The intent is to determine what the students know about the Allied and Axis powers; however, students with an expressive language disorder or some physical disability that makes writing difficult may not produce a response reflective of their understanding. The response may be short or incomplete due to skill deficits in written language and not to a lack of understanding. An alternative response (e.g., taping the response for later transcription) will more likely be a measure of student understanding with little impact on the remainder of the class.

Equipment or Technological Assistance

Efforts to effectively present material to students and to collect information that reflects student understanding can be greatly enhanced by incorporating available equipment and technology. Teachers gladly accommodate their instruction to include the use of Braille material with students with visual impairments. Similarly, class quizzes and high-stakes tests are made available in Braille. Calculators in math provide all students the opportunity to evidence their problem-solving skills with reduced emphasis on basic computational skills. Using a computer equipped with a word-processing program enables students to produce a product that reflects their content knowledge while initially reducing the emphasis on spelling and punctuation. These are simple, easily adapted tasks typically used by many professionals in day-to-day classroom activities. Given the relative ease with which these considerations are applied to the classroom setting, we have often observed them being overlooked or underused. Because it is assumed that the students will incorporate these tools into their classroom or homework activities, teachers tell us that they often fail to check to ensure that the students are actually using the appropriate accommodation. As we work to build independence, it may be very beneficial to ensure that students do indeed take advantage of the accommodations afforded them.

WHAT ARE SOME COMMONLY USED MODIFICATIONS, AND HOW DO I USE THEM IN MY CLASSROOM?

The introduction of accommodations to instruction or assessment of students with disabilities is often reasonably straightforward. A blind student, for example, needs to have Braille text materials or books on tape to have access to content material that is similar to that of the nondisabled students in the general classroom setting. The accommodations do not alter the content of the material but provide access to the material. However, when modifications to instruction or assessment are considered, questions are frequently raised regarding the potential impact of modifying instruction and/or the assessment device used.

Modifying Assessment

Modifications to assessment often change how a test is administered, how it is completed, or what is being measured (Tindal, Hollenbeck, Heath, & Almond, 1997, cited in Jitendra et al., 2002). Test modifications may increase the possibility of misinterpreting an individual's performance on a specific test used by a school, district, or state (Haigh, 1999). Consequently, it is recommended that modifications to tests should be used when the accommodations fail to level the playing field for students with special needs. Earlier in this chapter, for example, taping a response to an essay question was presented as a possible accommodation. If the student(s) was not successful with this and other accommodations, modifications to the test might be considered. The student with special needs might complete a multiple-choice test rather than the essay. Although the multiple-choice test measures similar material, the nature of the test changes the depth and breadth of the understanding necessary to perform well. This modification expects all students to know the material but changes the response required. Multiple-choice questions require students to *select* an answer, while essay questions require the students to *generate* their own response. While this modification collects data about student knowledge, the way of doing it is different from that employed with the remainder of the class. It may be difficult to interpret student performance on the test, raising questions as to the validity of the results; the modifications may artificially elevate the scores of the students with special needs.

Hopefully you are asking yourself, "They are still learning the material. What's wrong with that?" If you did ask this question, congratulations; you see the importance of making adjustments to curricular materials. However, the goal of leveling the playing field must not result in tilting the field in the opposite direction. For this reason, modifications that change the purpose or focus of the assessment device should be used only when existing accommodations or modifications have been implemented with limited success. Any modification that is introduced must provide access to similar material as well as a test format that ensures that the performance of students with special needs is comparable to the performance of their peers. While this may sound illogical for advocates to suggest, it is crucial to recognize that students with special needs are often successful when appropriate and meaningful modifications to instruction are available.

Modifying Instruction

Teachers modify various fundamental principles of classroom instruction to provide access to classroom activities to as many students as possible. General modifications to these fundamental principles are presented here.

Instructional Delivery

Modifying the delivery of instruction may involve presenting material with attention to the learning styles of all students in the classroom. Instruction that includes a verbal description accompanied by some visual stimulus is far more effective than a presentation with only one style considered. Including hands-on/manipulative materials further increases the likelihood of meeting the needs of most students in your classroom. Teachers can also modify their instructional delivery by utilizing appropriate technology whenever possible. Computer software enables students to independently practice skills, thereby allowing the teacher to work directly with struggling students. Teachers also effectively modify their delivery by forming smaller groups to facilitate more explicit instruction for some students while providing other students the opportunity to expand their knowledge through independent learning activities.

Specific Instructional Considerations

The use of learning strategies (i.e., Kansas Learning Strategies), mnemonics (*HOMES* to represent the Great Lakes), semantic mapping, thematic units, and integrated lessons all provide specific and effective learning tools for students. These instructional techniques provide students with a consistent framework upon which to build learning. As these techniques are learned, students can successfully use them in most content area classes. Mapping, for example, can be used in writing essays or term papers, organizing reading material, learning math fact families, or classifying animals in science.

Length of Time

Instruction may be modified by giving students with special needs additional time to complete tests, classroom activities, or long-term assignments. The adjustment of time should be considered when a student demonstrates an understanding or mastery of the target skill but cannot complete the tasks within a set time constraint.

Different Responses

Mrs. Smith, a fourth-grade teacher, has taught her students about the different regions of their state. She then asks the class to write a paragraph describing the differences between the mountain region and the coastal plain region of the state. Most students immediately begin their work; however, one student has difficulty with the assignment because he has a disability in written expression. Another student has recently moved to this state from Vietnam and, although she is developing verbal language, she has had little experience with written language. As a result, these students are likely to fail to demonstrate their understanding of the regional differences in the state. Modifications to the students' responses might include taping the oral answer, using a computer with spell check and grammar check, or asking the students to draw a picture showing the differences.

Increased Opportunity for Access to Material

Students with special needs often do not benefit from curricular material presented in the same format as their peers without special needs. Reading disorders, slow rates of reading, short attention spans, and visual or hearing impairments are a few reasons why students with special needs are often unsuccessful in their attempts to use traditional classroom materials. Modifying instruction might involve requiring these students with special needs to read fewer pages of printed text, but, as supplementation, to listen to books on tape or to a peer reading the remaining text material. Teachers also report that using high-interest, low-demand materials provides the content that is important in a format that more accurately matches the skills of individual students.

Different Expectations

This general modification does not intend to suggest that teachers routinely lower their expectations of students' performance. However, on some occasions it is appropriate to select material that is crucial for all students to know while identifying other information that may be less appropriate for certain class members. Schumm, Vaughn, and Leavell (1994) suggest using a "planning pyramid" in which material is presented that (a) all students should learn, (b) many students should learn, and (c) few students should learn. The premise behind the planning pyramid is that while *all* students are capable of learning, not all students will learn nor need to learn all the information presented in a lesson (Schumm et al., 1994). It is crucial that when teachers are planning to incorporate this type of modification they continue to challenge all students to reach the maximum of their ability while considering the unique needs of individual students.

Level of Involvement

The goal of modifying instruction is to maximize each student's exposure to the curriculum content. It is likely that some students in classes will be unsuccessful with higher-level academic tasks. Jitendra et al. (2002) distinguish between selection and production activities. Classroom tasks that require selection include tasks in which students must choose from a list that has been provided by the teacher. While knowledge or understanding is required for the successful completion of this type of task, the demands are less than those placed on students who must produce the information themselves without specific prompting. All students are exposed to similar material but at a level of involvement that meets each student's needs. Another example of this modification was recently observed in a fifth-grade classroom. The class was working on map skills. The majority of students were asked to find and record the map coordinates for various cities throughout North and South America. As these students were working on this specific map skill, a student with Down syndrome was using a map of Charlotte, North Carolina (her hometown) to find and highlight specific key locations in the city. For example, she was asked to find her house, her school, and the local YMCA where she took swimming lessons. In both examples, the instructional focus was similar, although varying the level of involvement allowed *all* students to benefit from the activity.

Support

Students with special needs often require many practice opportunities to learn and master specific skills. The irony is that these same students often have difficulty maintaining their attention for sustained periods of time or would benefit from changes to their learning environment. Given this paradox, using paraprofessionals, peer tutoring, "reading buddies" from higher grades, or outside volunteers often provides the classroom teacher with the support necessary to provide these practice opportunities. Teachers have been most effective at using these support resources when the support personnel are provided with specific training regarding the tasks to be completed with the students. This training has been provided through a mini-grant program or parent-teacher organization funds. Unfortunately, such training often occurs during the summer or after school hours, requiring more time and energy of all the people involved.

Physical Setting

Modifying the physical environment of the classroom may seem relatively simple and straightforward. Ensuring that the aisles remain clear so that students with physical disabilities or visual impairments may move freely throughout the room is an obvious consideration. However, other considerations provide many other students with the opportunity to perform to the maximum of their ability. Study carrels reduce the visual and auditory distractions that often negatively affect students' classroom performance. Teachers also establish sections of the room in which music can be played (with headphones), where bean bag chairs or other "nontraditional" seating (e.g., large floor pillows, "papa-san" chairs, old bathtubs filled with pillows) is available, or where students can simply lie on the floor to complete their work. Still other classrooms have parts of the room that are warmer (e.g., near the window or the heating vent) or cooler (e.g., near the air-conditioning vent or a fan) in which students may work according o their individual needs or preferences. Not all students will avail themselves of these classroom settings; however, many students will "try out" certain modifications because they appear to be fun or cool. Once they determine that the modification does not help them, these students usually return to a setting that is most appropriate to them.

Modifications for Difficulties in Specific Skill Areas

Additional modifications for difficulties in specific skill areas are provided in Figures 9.1 through 9.4. These activities assume that additional, appropriate considerations will also be in place. For example, a student with a reading disorder may require extended time to complete tasks in addition to specific instructional modifications; the specific modifications are addressed in Figure 9.1. While these are clearly not all-inclusive, they provide a significant number of considerations that have been effective in various classroom settings. We hope that you will use these and other techniques that provide all students with the opportunity to learn, grow, and achieve to the greatest possible extent.

Figure 9.1 Modifications for Reading Difficulties

- Use books-on-tape when available.
- Incorporate high-interest, low-demand materials whenever possible.
- Provide outlines for specific reading assignments.
- Teach students to "chunk" reading material into smaller segments rather that reading an entire section.
- Emphasize the importance of identifying key elements of the "chunked" material before proceeding to additional sections.
- Preteach new or complex vocabulary.
- Incorporate advance and graphic organizers.
- Use story-mapping activities to enhance comprehension.
- Teach and use highlighting strategies.
- Introduce learning strategy techniques.
- Use large-print material.
- Read key directions aloud for all students.
- Allow students to record assignments for use in the home environment.
- Provide written directions prior to the specific task (especially helpful with tests).
- Introduce "what you need to know" charts to students to help them focus on key factors in the text.

Figure 9.2 Modifications for Mathematics Difficulties

- Introduce new concepts using manipulative materials, especially with younger students.
- Help students understand the relationship between the concrete and abstract levels of understanding by emphasizing instruction at the representational level.
- Reduce the number of items to be completed.
- Provide fewer number of items on a single page.
- Use graph paper to help students maintain place value.
- Teach students how to use calculators, and encourage them to do so whenever appropriate.
- Use number lines to help students understand various math concepts.
- Use their experiences to help them learn specific concepts (e.g., teaching negative numbers to some students can be facilitated by using the results of carrying a football—"lost 2 yards, lost 3 yards, gained 8 yards. What is the total yardage?")
- Highlight operation signs to help students complete tasks accurately.
- Introduce students to alternative algorithms, and encourage their use as appropriate.
- Game activities are fun and excellent opportunities to practice math skills.
- Teach and practice specific rules in math such as the multiplicative properties of 1 and 0.
- Provide mixed practice to help ensure that students maintain previously learned skills.
- Introduce visual prompts whenever appropriate; use a green dot with an arrow above the ones place number to help students remember that math goes from right to left.
- Use appropriate technology (e.g., computer software, Web sites) to reinforce skills.

Figure 9.3 Modifications for Written Language Difficulties

- Provide story frames as students begin to expand their written products.
- Incorporate guided notes into the classroom structure to facilitate note taking.
- Allow students to use laptops or other technologies as appropriate to the classroom setting.
- Provide different grades for content and grammar/spelling.
- Enable students to use scribes or tape recorders to indicate their knowledge of the content material.
- Reduce the amount of writing required if this does not interfere with the learning experience; use outlines to indicate understanding.
- Provide story starters as students learn to expand their written work.
- Use content/story maps to help students formulate ideas about writing.
- Teach students to brainstorm as a class, in small groups, and finally individually.
- Use specific learning strategy techniques that allow students to write in a variety of settings (e.g., Kansas Learning Strategies).

Figure 9.4 Modifications for Organizational Difficulties

- Students often don't realize that they are disorganized; help them understand what they do that causes organizational problems.
- Explicitly teach organizational skills, and reward them when they are successful.
- Post agenda items in a conspicuous location in the classroom, and do not remove until students have left for the day.
- Post long-term deadlines in the classroom as well as on an appropriate Web site, enabling parents to have access to the information as well as the students.
- Provide explicit instruction in using and maintaining agendas and notebooks.
- Develop regular routines to help students complete daily tasks; always turn in homework at a specific time of the day/class, and place it in the same place every day.
- Do not assume that students know "how to" do anything; teach them to write their name and date on each page, how to space their work, or how many lines to skip.
- Use color to help differentiate specific content material.
- Endeavor to be as consistent as possible regarding the expectations you have for organizational tasks.
- Teach students to self-question: Did I bring my math book? Do I have my agenda?
- Keep a supply of materials available for the times when you believe it is appropriate to provide them for students.
- Sign homework agenda items to ensure that students have the correct information; while you should try to wean students from this, it is helpful to do this initially.
- Help parents with ideas and strategies that will increase the likelihood of students arriving at school with the correct materials.
  - Check the homework Web site (if available).
  - Post schedules and routines in conspicuous places in the house.
  - Make the child get clothes ready the night before (no changes allowed!).
  - Place all material to go to school in front of the door at night.
  - Be consistent with all that is done with the child (i.e., bedtime, time to awaken, homework time in relation to other factors involved).

WHERE CAN I FIND RESOURCES OR MORE INFORMATION ON ACCOMMODATIONS AND MODIFICATIONS?

Descriptive Articles

Baker, S., Gersten, R., & Scanlon, D. (2002). Procedural facilitators and cognitive strategies: Tools for unraveling the mysteries of comprehension and the writing process, and for providing meaningful access to the general curriculum. *Learning Disabilities Practice, 17,* 65–77.

Web Sites

Reading Quest, "Strategies for Reading Comprehension" (http://curry .edschool.virginia.edu/go/readquest/strat/).

CHAPTER REFERENCES

Fuchs, L. S., & Fuchs, D. (2001). Helping teachers formulate sound test accommodation decisions for students with learning disabilities. *Learning Disabilities Research and Practice, 16,* 174–181.

Haigh, J. (1999). *Accommodations, modifications, and alternates for instruction and assessment* (State Assessment Series, Maryland Report No. 5). Baltimore: Maryland State Department of Education.

Jitendra, A. K., Edwards, L. L., Choutka, C. M., & Treadway, P. S. (2002). A collaborative approach to planning in the content area for students with learning disabilities: Accessing the general curriculum. *Learning Disabilities Research & Practice, 17,* 252–267.

Nolet, V., & McLaughlin, M. J. (2000). *Accessing the general curriculum: Including students with disabilities in standards-based reform.* Thousand Oaks, CA: Corwin Press.

Schumm, J. C., Vaughn, S., & Leavell, A. G. (1994). Planning pyramid: A framework for planning for diverse students' needs during content area instruction. *Reading Teacher, 47,* 608–615.

Washburn-Moses, L. (2003). What every special educator should know about high-stakes testing. *Teaching Exceptional Children, 35,* 12–15.

10

What Works for Ongoing Assessment, Data Collection, and Grading?

Outline Questions

What do I need to know about assessment, data collection, and grading?

What are the purposes of assessment?

What are the legal considerations involved in assessment?

How do I collect assessment data?

What are the considerations involved in grading in an inclusive setting?

Where can I find resources or more information on assessment, data collection, and grading?

WHAT DO I NEED TO KNOW ABOUT ASSESSMENT, DATA COLLECTION, AND GRADING?

Assessment is the process of collecting information to use in making decisions about individual students or groups of students. Teachers use assessment activities to determine areas such as the level of mathematics skills demonstrated by an individual student, the instructional levels appropriate with this student, and the time the student spends completing independent seatwork. Teachers collect this type of information every day in their work with the students in their classroom.

As in other professions, decisions made on the basis of information are generally better than those made in the absence of appropriate data or in spite of it. Different kinds of information collected by teachers are indications of the skills, abilities, or characteristics of their students. Analysis of this information provides answers to questions asked by teachers making decisions about the students. Skills, abilities, and characteristics are assessed when one is deciding if a student is eligible for special education services, deciding what to teach, or deciding whether a special program is being or has been effective.

Skills are behaviors that can be performed, such as running, drawing lines, reading numbers or letters, writing in cursive, adding fractions and columns of numbers, or speaking foreign languages. They are assessed by having students run, draw lines, read groups of numbers or letters, write messages using cursive, add sets of fractions and columns of numbers, or speak words, phrases, and sentences in a foreign language. Such skills are assessed by formally or informally watching students do them and/or by asking parents, teachers, and the students themselves about the extent to which the skills are done at different times and in settings other than school.

Abilities cannot be seen and cannot be performed. Commonly assessed abilities are intelligence, memory, perception, and learning style. Assessing intelligence, memory, perception, or a style of learning involves inference (Salvia & Ysseldyke, 2003). Teachers infer intelligence when a student acts in ways that are believed to reflect this ability. For example, when repeating sets of digits forward and backward is believed to be an indicator of intelligence, a person who repeats more digits forward and backward than his peers is thought to be more intelligent. Similarly, when a fine-motor task such as writing is assumed to be a good measure of perception, judgments about the writing are assumed to be good indicators of perceptual abilities. Generally, levels of ability are assessed by having students perform tasks that are representative of the ability being considered.

Characteristics cannot be performed and include information such as age, race, sex, hair color, and physical stature. Educators identify characteristics by looking at students and examining records compiled about them. Teachers ask questions about characteristics for different reasons; the reasons are generally linked to the kinds of decisions that will ultimately be made. Characteristics are seldom instructional targets but are often used in explaining students' behavior on many skills (e.g., Fred is too young to complete that assignment; Sandy is too short to complete this task).

PURPOSES OF ASSESSMENT

Assessment information is gathered for several reasons. Most teachers collect assessment information simply to track their students' skills or behavior. Some teachers assess because they believe their students have strengths or weaknesses that require attention. Most professionals agree that there are six purposes of assessment in special education: screening or referral, diagnosis, classification or placement, instructional planning, individual progress evaluation, and program evaluation. When assessment information is used to make screening or referral decisions, global measurement of strengths and weaknesses is considered sufficient. At this level of decision making, teachers are interested in generally sorting individuals, and broad descriptive indicators of success or failure on general measures are appropriate. Teachers are also called upon to make instructional planning and evaluation decisions; they use this information to decide what and how to teach and to evaluate an individual student's progress in their classroom instructional program or to evaluate the effectiveness of particular interventions or their overall instructional program.

Teachers and other professionals often make diagnostic decisions that result in the placement or classification of students into groups. Because these decisions are made with reference to predetermined, defined criteria, the assessment data used to make them require more precision and technical adequacy than those used to make screening decisions. For example, students are classified as learning disabled if their scores on an achievement test are significantly below their scores on measures of their ability. Since discrepancies between ability and achievement are central to diagnostic decisions in the area of learning disabilities, we will address specific ability and achievement measures in detail in this chapter. (For more information regarding a comprehensive evaluation, see Box 10.1, on IDEA's mandates on evaluation and their translation into everyday practice, and Table 10.1, which provides a selective list of tests commonly used in identifying students with disabilities, most notably students suspected of having learning disabilities and/or attention disorders.) Before doing that, however, we briefly review legal considerations that influence assessment and decision making in the area of learning disabilities.

Box 10.1 Comprehensive Evaluation

Section 1414 of IDEA 2004 mandates that an evaluation must "(A) use a variety of assessment tools and strategies . . . that may assist in determining—(i) whether the child is a child with a disability; and (ii) the content of the child's individualized education program, including information related to enabling the child to be involved in and progress in the general education curriculum, . . . (B) not use any single measure or assessment as the sole criterion for determining whether a child is a child with a disability or determining an appropriate educational program for the child; and (C) use technically sound instruments that may assess the relative contribution of cognitive and behavioral factors, in addition to physical or developmental factors." Further legislative attention is given to the selection of tests, assuring that the tests "are provided and administered in the language and form most likely to yield accurate information on what the child knows and can do academically, developmentally, and functionally . . . " (Section 1414, (b), (3, A, ii).

This is translated to everyday practice by ensuring that students are administered a battery of tests designed to measure their cognitive ability, academic achievement, and behavior. In addition, assessment tools designed to measure attention, language, the ability to process auditory or visual information, and/or motor skill development may also be used as deemed appropriate by the teachers, school psychologist, and/or parents. The comprehensive evaluation is designed to determine the possible classification of a child as a student with disabilities (e.g., learning disabilities or attention deficit/hyperactive disorder), as well as general or specific intervention strategies that may enhance the likelihood of the student's success.

LEGAL CONSIDERATIONS AND ASSESSMENT

Every student with special needs is guaranteed the opportunity for a free and appropriate public education under the mandates of the Individuals with Disabilities Education Act (IDEA). School personnel must prepare an Individualized Education Program (IEP) for every student who qualifies for services in a special education program. This means that teachers must have clearly documented plans for how instructional time will be spent. Completing the formal document (i.e., the IEP) involves determining annual goals for the student, the kinds of services to be provided, the

Table 10.1   Tests Commonly Used in Identifying Students With Disabilities

Areas Measured	Examples of Commonly Used Tests
Cognitive ability	Wechsler Intelligence Scale for Children–Fourth Edition (WISC–IV); Stanford-Binet Intelligence Scale; Kaufman Assessment Battery for Children (K-ABC); Woodcock-Johnson Tests of Cognitive Ability–III
Academic achievement	
General achievement measures	Woodcock-Johnson Test of Academic Achievement–III; Wechsler Individual Achievement Test–Second Edition; Diagnostic Achievement
Specific achievement measures	Battery–Third Edition
Reading	Woodcock Reading Mastery; Gray Oral Reading Tests; Test of Reading Comprehension
Math	Key Math; Stanford Diagnostic Mathematics Test; Test of Mathematical Abilities
Behavior	Behavior Rating Profile–Second Edition; Behavior Assessment System for Children–Second Edition; Behavior Evaluation Scale–Third Edition
Attention disorders	Conners' Rating Scale–Revised; Copeland Symptom Checklist for Attention Deficit Disorders; Attention Deficit Disorders Evaluation Scale
Language	
Oral language	Test of Language Development–3 Primary and Intermediate Levels; Peabody Picture Vocabulary Test–Third Edition; Expressive Vocabulary Test; Test for Auditory Comprehension of Language–Third Edition
Written language/ expression	Test of Written Language–Third Edition; Woodcock Language Proficiency Battery–Revised; Test of Early Written Language
Motor skills	Developmental Test of Visual-Motor Integration– Fourth Edition; Test of Gross Motor Development–2

personnel who will deliver the services, and a plan for evaluating the student's progress (see Chapter 3 and Table 10.2 for more information).

By law, students with special needs must be educated in the least restrictive environment. This means that the education of students with learning disabilities must be as much as possible like the education of students without special needs. In fact, IDEA and the No Child Left Behind

Table 10.2   Legal Elements of Assessment: Considerations Mandated by IDEA

---

1. Parental Consent
   - The parent or guardian must be fully informed of all educational activities to which he or she is being asked to consent.
   - Parents must be notified of any evaluation and placement the school proposes to conduct and must be informed in his or her native language (including consent forms and parents' rights booklets).
   - Parents must receive a copy of procedural safeguards.
   - Parent permission must be obtained if information is requested by a third party.
   - Developmental information obtained in an assessment must be obtained from the parent/guardian.

2. Nondiscriminatory Assessment
   - Assessment cannot discriminate on racial or cultural basis.
   - Assessment must be administered in the child's native language or other modes of communication.

3. Access to Records
   - Parents have access to any assessment data collected on their child.

4. Conduct of Evaluation
   - *Assessment* is conducted versus merely tests. It must include parent input, must include functional information, and must be related to educational needs.
   - A single test cannot be used for determining criteria for eligibility and placement.
   - The purpose of evaluation is focused on IEP development, with eligibility a secondary purpose (how student will succeed in regular education and needed supports).
   - All tests must be technically sound.
   - All tests must be valid for use.
   - All tests must be administered by trained and knowledgeable personnel.
   - All tests must be administered according to instructions.
   - Assessment must be conducted in all areas of suspected disability.
   - Assessment tools and strategies must provide relevant information to determine educational needs.
   - All assessment information must be reviewed to determine if additional information must be obtained for eligibility and placement.

5. Multidisciplinary Decision Making
   - Must have parents, at least one regular education teacher, at least one special education teacher, a representative of the LEA, an individual who can interpret the instructional implications of evaluation results, other as determined by parents, the child when appropriate.
   - General education teacher requirements: participate in development of IEP, including positive behavioral interventions, supplementary aids and services, program modifications, and support for school personnel; participate in the review and the revision of the IEP.
   - Reevaluation conducted only if conditions warrant reevaluation (determined by the team) and if the parent or teacher requests reevaluation.

Act (NCLB) indicate that placement in the general education classroom is expected and that if such placement does not occur there must be a clearly stated rationale as to why. Many students with special needs are enrolled full time in general education classes and receive services from the special education personnel in the general classroom setting. Other students with special needs leave their general education classes periodically to go to other classes for special education services. Still others are enrolled primarily in special education classes but, to the maximum extent possible, attend general education classes for part of the school day for certain kinds of instruction. For example, a student might be enrolled in a special class but attend a general education class for instruction in math, music, art, or physical education.

By law, students with special needs and their families are guaranteed rights of due process. This means that these students and their families have the same rights under the law as any other people. Educational placements of students with learning disabilities cannot be changed without the informed consent (e.g., written permission) of the student's parent(s) or guardian(s). Parents are also entitled to independent assessments and impartial hearings when decisions about their children are being made.

Students with special needs and their families are entitled to protection in evaluation activities that are part of the educational experience. This means that students cannot be placed in special programs in an arbitrary and capricious manner. Students with handicaps and their families are entitled to have decisions made about them using individually administered tests. It is assumed that the instruments used to make these decisions are appropriate for use with students with handicaps and that the decisions will be made by groups of individuals in an unbiased fashion (e.g., without regard to ethnic, cultural, or racial characteristics). It is expected that students with special needs will participate in statewide assessment programs and that states offer alternative assessment procedures to ensure this participation (more about statewide assessment will follow).

Rules and regulations established by education laws greatly influence what goes on in special education. This is partially due to the dissatisfaction many parents and professionals experienced with early special education practices. For example, there was a time when placement in a special class meant the end of a student's general education experience. Students in special classes lost contact with their general education peers and often remained in special education for their entire school careers. There was a time when students were placed in special classes on the recommendations of one teacher or on the results obtained on one test. Such ill-founded decision making produced special class enrollments in which minority students were overrepresented. There was a time when being in special education meant being different and when being different meant being segregated in an institution or special school. The treatment that people received in these settings was generally harsh and seldom educational. In all these instances, parents and professionals argued that this was not sound educational policy, and legal action was required to ensure that practices changed.

The impact of collecting assessment data has escalated since 2001 when NCLB was passed. NCLB reinforces the assessment components of IDEA by requiring students with disabilities/special needs to participate in general assessments at the state and local level in an effort to maximize their access to the same curriculum as their peers without special needs. States must create rigorous academic content standards in mathematics and reading/language arts. The curricular expectations resulting from the rigorous standards also require that states develop an assessment program that reflects the growth of all students. The assessment tools used by individual states must be aligned to the NCLB standards at one elementary, one middle school, and one high school grade (Roeber, 2002). Academic performance standards must indicate student performance at the advanced, proficient, and partially proficient levels. Further, all states are required to expand the assessments to Grades 3–8, plus one high school grade by the 2005–06 academic year. Between the academic years 2001–02 and 2013–14, states must identify the "proficient" achievement level as a means to determine "adequate yearly progress." In other words, a school's "adequate yearly progress" (AYP) will be determined by the number of students at the "proficient" achievement level relative to their performance on previous schoolwide assessments. Once the designated "proficient" achievement level is identified, each school must ensure that at least that percentage of students is "proficient" in subsequent years. However, beginning with the 2013–14 academic year, each school must have 100% of all students assessed at the "proficient" level.

The implications for all students, parents, and educators are far-reaching and significant, particularly for all involved in an inclusive classroom, as NCLB specifically identifies four groups of students who are likely to be served in this setting. The performance of students with limited English proficiency, students with disabilities, students who are economically disadvantaged, and students from racial-ethnic minorities will be included in the data used to determine AYP along with the total school scores.

COLLECTING ASSESSMENT DATA

Teachers and other professionals involved in the assessment process (e.g., school psychologists, special education teachers) gather assessment data/information using tests, observations, and interviews. A *test* is a set of questions designed to provide information about an individual's knowledge and skill in a content area. An *observation* is a record of an individual's performance of a specified target behavior or behaviors. An *interview* is a set of questions designed to provide information about an individual's history, characteristics, or ability to perform. Tests provide information that cannot easily be gathered by observations and interviews. Observing and interviewing provide unique opportunities for gathering other information as well.

Tests are samples of behavior; testing is the process of exposing an individual to a set of items primarily to obtain a score reflective of the accuracy of the performance (Salvia & Ysseldyke, 2003). Tests vary by administration, content, and form.

Tests can be administered to groups of students or to individual students within a group. They can also be administered using computer programs in formal or informal settings. Some students perform better on formal, individually administered tests; others thrive on opportunities to respond to group-administered formal tests.

Tests vary by the content being measured; achievement tests are different from aptitude tests, which are different from personality tests or tests of perceptual abilities. Content variation is also evident in the types of information gathered (i.e., what skills are assessed) and the representativeness of the content that is sampled. For example, a math test containing 50 items requiring performance of a single arithmetic skill (e.g., adding numbers with sums less than 100) is different from one containing 50 items sampling adding, subtracting, multiplying, and dividing skills.

There are many forms of tests. For example, a test can be administered in a multiple-choice, matching, fill-in, open-ended, essay, or activity format. Tests can also be presented in oral or written form, and student responses can be gathered in oral, written, or active form. Those who develop tests often characterize their measures as norm referenced or criterion referenced. Norm-referenced tests are used to compare a student's performance to that of his or her peers; scores on this type of test are reported as an indication of the number of items that were answered correctly so that age- and grade-level peer comparisons can be completed (see Table 10.3). Criterion-referenced tests are used to identify an individual's performance within a set of content-specific items; scores on this type of test are indications of mastery levels of skill performance (e.g., Mary answered 80% of the items measuring writing skills correctly). Although most tests are developed in specific forms, norm-referenced tests can be interpreted in a criterion-referenced manner and criterion-referenced tests can be interpreted in a norm-referenced manner.

Table 10.3   Types of Instruments Used in Large-Scale Assessment

Assessment Instruments	Advantages	Challenges
Multiple-choice items	Quick to administer Easy to score	Harder to write May not tap higher-order skills
Constructed response items	Tap student thinking/reasoning	More time-consuming/expensive to score
Performance items	Directly assess student behavior	Expensive to administer and to score
Portfolios	Collect data over extended periods of time	Nonstandard Teacher or student assessed?
Criterion-referenced tests	Assess important content standards Demonstrate what students can and cannot do More students with disabilities may be accommodated and therefore participate	Custom-developed programs may be more expensive to develop Lack of comparative data with other students/systems
Norm-referenced tests	Show student performance relative to a norm group Best for selection needs, e.g., selecting students for special programs	Being above average does not mean students have learned skills Fewer students with disabilities participate due to exclusion from norm samples Fewer accommodations permitted

Observations are samples of behavior; observing is the process of watching an individual perform a set of behaviors to determine the frequency, duration, or rate at which each occurs. Observations vary by form, content, and count.

Observations are considered active when ongoing actions are being counted, recorded, and evaluated. When a teacher counts the number of times a student asks permission to go to the restroom or blurts out an answer during language class, an active observational record is being compiled. Observations are considered passive when products of previous actions are being counted, recorded, and evaluated. For example, reviewing completion rates of previous assignments or calculating a grade point average for a specified period of time is a passive observational activity.

Observations differ on the basis of the types of actions or products that are being observed. For example, different observational activities would result when the length of a student argument or the number of words a student read in a minute was observed. Similarly, records of errors made during math recitation would look different from records of oral reading errors.

Observations also differ on the basis of the nature of the actions that are being counted. For example, when doing interval recordings, one records the number of time intervals during which the targeted behavior was observed. Time sampling recording produces a record of the number of times that the targeted behavior was observed after a predetermined period of time. Event recordings produce records of the number of times specified behaviors are observed during an observation period, and duration recordings produce records of the length of time behavior continues. It is also possible to observe the length of time between a request for behavior and its actual occurrence; such latency recording is used when other measures of behavior are considered inappropriate.

Interviews are samples of behavior; interviewing is the process of asking an individual a set of questions about past life experiences, current performance, or future plans. Interviews vary by administration, content, and form.

Interviews can be administered to groups of people, individuals, or third-party representatives. Teachers sometimes ask their students to complete general attitude questionnaires, reinforcement surveys, needs assessment instruments, or oral reports during class periods. They also individually interview students to gather information about them, their families, and their attitudes about school. Sometimes, parents, teachers, friends, classmates, or other individuals provide answers to interview questions about a particular student's likes and dislikes or strengths and weaknesses in areas of concern.

Differences in the purpose and imagination of the interviewer create differences in the content of interviews. For example, interviews about afterschool activities, favorite movies, life at home, parents, sports, and leisure reading will provide different information from interviews about classroom behavior, personality problems, and early development.

Questions within an interview can be presented in structured or unstructured formats. In a structured interview, the order of questions is predetermined and it is assumed that repetitions of the interview will occur in the same order. Unstructured interviews are free of form, and while two unstructured interviews may be similar, it is not necessary that they be so. Responses during interviews can be obtained in written, oral, or checklist forms.

Much of the assessment data that has been collected for each student with special needs will have little direct impact on the day-to-day functioning of the general educator and special educator in the inclusive classroom. That is because students with special needs who are placed in the inclusive setting have already received the norm-referenced testing that resulted in their identification. Consequently, the coteachers may never see the test protocol sheets or even the specific test results. In addition, norm-referenced testing data is of limited value in relation to assessing students' abilities to profit from instruction and in making day-to-day instructional decisions (Salvia & Ysseldyke, 2003). However, the general and special educator can use additional assessment methodology to collect information that is directly applicable to classroom instruction.

Criterion-Referenced Assessment

While norm-referenced testing, by design, compares one student with his or her peers, criterion-referenced assessment considers the individual student in relationship to a specific established set of criteria that focuses on instructional requirements. Various means of testing are used, including oral and written performance measures and comprehensive measures. Two kinds of information are typically assessed: knowledge and performance. Knowledge tests help teachers determine if students have learned targeted information (e.g., science content or literacy lessons). Performance tests reflect competence in areas other than simple recall of knowledge.

The focus of criterion-referenced assessment is performance that can be systematically analyzed to identify an individual's strengths and weaknesses without comparing that individual to others. The benefit with this type of assessment is the opportunity to identify specific skills that a student has or has not learned and then relate the skills to the curricular content. Criterion-referenced assessment is tied more closely to instructional objectives and mastery of specific outcomes than norm-referenced assessment (Salvia & Ysseldyke, 2003).

Comparing an individual's performance to a list of curriculum objectives has benefits for coteachers. A criterion-referenced assessment may be used to assess *only* addition of whole numbers, with several items for each type of problem. Each item is directly related to a specific objective, and performance on these items represents a basis for instructional planning (i.e., if a specific set of items is missed, instruction should focus on these items). The results of criterion-referenced assessment serve as the basis for planning and delivering instruction.

Portfolio assessment provides students with the opportunity to collect and display work that reflects their efforts relative to a specific set of instructional objectives. The purposes of using portfolios include showing growth over time, showing process as well as product, communicating with the student's subsequent teachers, creating a collection of favorite work, reviewing instruction for program evaluation, and aiding in parent conferences. Portfolios should consider the general curricular focus and major instructional goals. In addition, although portfolios can be structured or unstructured, a structured portfolio is driven by a list of requirements developed by the teacher. This structure will be extremely helpful to students with special learning needs in the inclusive classroom. Before implementing a portfolio system, the coteachers need to establish clear purposes and standards to document portfolio reliability. To establish validity, coteachers can combine curriculum-based measurement with the use of portfolios.

Curriculum-Based Measurement

Curriculum-based assessment (CBA) is measurement that uses direct observation of a student's performance as well as the recording of that performance. The assessment is based on the school curriculum in an attempt to make sound instructional decisions. It typically focuses on the core elements of education (e.g., reading, writing, math). CBA refers to any technique that uses direct observation of a skill and recording the results of that observation. Specific academic skills such as words read correctly per minute, numbers written per minute, or words written correctly per minute are typically measured with CBA techniques.

Effective CBA uses repeated measures and consequently takes place over an extended period. A significant advantage to using CBA is that it is easy to administer and score. After the data have been collected, the coteachers and/or the students use graphing to record and exhibit the results. Because the CBA data are collected on a consistent basis, they can be easily analyzed daily, which helps teachers make instructional decisions.

Curriculum-based measurement (CBM) is an alternative approach to academic assessment that allows teachers to closely monitor the rate of student educational progress. Educational researchers have devised CBM as a simple, statistically reliable, and practical means of measuring student skills in basic subject areas such as reading, writing, and arithmetic. In this approach, the student is given brief, timed exercises to complete, using materials drawn directly from the student's academic program.

During the problem identification step of CBM, observations and performance records are gathered in educationally relevant domains (e.g., literacy books, math textbooks). Deciding if discrepancies between expected and actual performance are important enough to require additional instructional support is central to the problem definition step. During problem exploration, treatment alternatives, probable performance improvements, and costs associated with them are identified. Deciding if attempted interventions should be continued or modified is central to the solution implementation step. During the problem resolution step, differences between expected and actual performance are evaluated and decisions are made related to continuing an intervention program.

CBM offers a number of advantages over traditional psychometric practices. First, gathering assessment data in classroom-based curriculum materials and comparing them to similar scores obtained by local peers clearly goes a long way in making diagnostic evaluations relevant for instructional planning and intervention. Too often, items on standardized tests and performances related to them bear little relation to the curricula guiding daily classroom activities. Similarly, CBM can provide simple, reliable, and understandable procedures for making diagnostic decisions. This methodology is empirically sound and provides information directly related to the acquisition and mastery of academic skills.

GRADING IN THE INCLUSIVE SETTING

Providing grades is seemingly a simple activity. Compile all the scores earned by each student on classroom assignments, compute these scores, and produce an overall grade for students' performance. But this simple process is made more complicated in the inclusion classroom by the potential for differentiated instruction, accommodations, or modifications to the work completed by students with and without special needs. Grades become a somewhat sticky topic (Murawski & Dieker, 2004), particularly at the high school level. It is important to remember that grades really do "count" in high school: Grade point averages, class rank, honors, and awards are all contingent upon grades earned in high school classes. In fact, Salend (2005) notes that grading is an issue that has been considered by the Office of Civil Rights (OCR). Given the basic premise of equal opportunity and access, the OCR emphasizes that grades must be assigned in a manner that enables all students to be treated similarly. If modified grading is to be implemented, the grading modifications must be available to all students. Salend (2005) notes that grading students with special needs in the inclusive classroom is challenging in that it is necessary to consider the impact of differentiated instruction and accommodations available to certain students, the roles of the coteachers in the grading process, and issues of equity and fairness. These challenges can be overcome, and grading can occur such that each student receives a grade that reflects his or her effort, mastery, and consistency. However, just as with most elements of coteaching, the presentation of grades must be carefully and conscientiously reviewed by the coteachers.

Several approaches to grading can be incorporated into the inclusive classroom setting. Norm-referenced grading systems (Salend, 2005) assign grades based on preestablished difficulty levels of skills. For example, a student whose grade is 80 on skills that are judged to be grade appropriate (i.e., average) might use a multiplier of 1, which reflects the average level of difficulty of the academic task. Another student who is completing work at a much higher level and similarly scores 80 would receive a higher overall score, as the multiplier for the more difficult skill would likewise be higher than the easier skill. For the sake of convenience, let's assume that the multiplier is 1.1; this student's score would be 88, reflecting the difficulty of the skill. Salend also describes a criterion-referenced grading scale that is directed to the mastery of a specific curricular skill. This grading system is used with curricular items pulled directly from the existing curriculum in the classroom/school. Students are graded relative to the number of items completed (e.g., Matt writes 45 digits per minute), the level of difficulty of the skill (e.g., Erika completed three proofs in geometry using the SAS postulate), or areas that consider behavior (e.g., Davis got out of his chair five times during lunch). Grades can also be assigned with a notation regarding the level of the material being completed. Some schools have specific marks placed on the report card that indicate that the material being considered was below the level in which the student is placed. Others use a notation indicating the grade given as well as the grade level of the material. For example, Matt got a C3, indicating that his performance warranted a C but that the material being evaluated was at the third-grade level. Regardless of the specific technique used to report grades for all students in the inclusive classroom, the overriding principle of fairness and equity must guide the process.

WHERE CAN I FIND RESOURCES OR MORE INFORMATION ON ASSESSMENT, DATA COLLECTION, AND GRADING?

Books

McLoughlin, J. A., & Lewis, R. B. (2005). *Assessing students with special needs* (6th ed.). Upper Saddle River, NJ: Merrill.
Salvia, J., & Ysseldyke, J. E. (2003). *Assessment in special and inclusive education* (9th ed.). Boston: Houghton Mifflin.

Organizations

American Psychiatric Association
1000 Wilson Boulevard, Suite 1825
Arlington, VA 22209-3901
(703) 907-7300
Web: www.psych.org/
E-mail: apa@psych.org

Council for Exceptional Children
1110 N. Glebe Rd., Suite 300
Arlington, VA 22201
(800) 224-6830
Web: www.cec.sped.org/index.html

National Information Center for Children and Youth
   with Disabilities (NICHCY)
P.O. Box 1492
Washington, DC 20013-1492
(800) 695-0285
Web: www.nichcy.org/index.html

Web Sites

MiddleWeb, "Grades, Tests and Assessments" (www.middleweb.com/Grading.html). Contains resources that can help new and experienced teachers refine their grading practices.

University of Washington, "Developing a Personal Grading Plan" (www.depts.washington.edu/grading/plan/frisbie1.htm). The purpose of this instructional module is to assist teachers in developing defensible grading practices that effectively and fairly communicate students' achievement status.

CHAPTER REFERENCES

Murawski, W. W., & Dieker, L. A. (2004). Tips and strategies for co-teaching at the secondary level. *Teaching Exceptional Children, 36,* 52–58.
Roeber, E. D. (2002). *Appropriate inclusion of students with disabilities in state accountability systems.* Denver, CO: Education Commission of the States.
Salend, S. J. (2005). *Creating inclusive classrooms: Effective and reflective practices for all students* (9th ed.). Upper Saddle River, NJ: Merrill.
Salvia, J., & Ysseldyke, J. E. (2003). *Assessment in special and inclusive education* (9th ed.). Boston: Houghton Mifflin.

What Assistance Do Parents and Families Need?

Outline Questions

What do I need to know about parents?

How do I work with parents to maximize their involvement?

What are some approaches that work effectively with parents?

Where can I find resources or more information on parents?

WHAT DO I NEED TO KNOW ABOUT PARENTS?

This is conceivably a simple question to answer; generally speaking, parents of students with special needs are not all that different than parents of students without special needs. Parents are almost always primarily concerned about *their* child. They may respect the need to treat all students fairly, and they may even accept the fact that their child is not perfect. However, when it comes down to it, parents want to know about their child. What did my child do well today? What did she have trouble with today? Why did she have this trouble? What are you going to do about it? And, "Oh yeah, what about the other students in her class?"

Essentially, parents of students with and without special needs want to know the progress their child is making and what can be done in and out of the classroom to make it better.

Given the basic premise that parents are primarily concerned about their own child, it is important for professionals to remember that parents can be the biggest allies in your classroom or your worst possible "enemies." Our belief is that it is in your best interest to have parents as your allies as much as you possibly can. This does not suggest that you have to bend over backwards to satisfy parents, nor does it mean that teachers always have to agree with parents. The most effective strategy for making parents your allies is to listen to their input, try to understand their joys and frustrations, provide useful suggestions as to how they can help their child at home, and treat them and their children with respect. While this may seem a somewhat simplistic perspective, it is nonetheless a good overview of what educators need to remember about parents. As this information is presented to individual parents, it is critical for educators to continue to focus on the main objective of everything that they do with children: The focus must always be on what is best for *all* children in the classroom. Adjusting what happens in the classroom to meet the needs of a child takes precedence over adjusting to meet the needs of the parents. Hopefully, the parents' needs will also be directed to the child's educational and personal well-being. However, educators should never jeopardize the integrity and quality of their classroom activities to satisfy a parent. In an effort to satisfy the parents, focus on the work necessary to satisfy the needs of the students in your classroom. While this won't please all of the people all of the time, it will go a long way to ensuring that you are doing the right thing in your classroom. In efforts to enlist parents as allies, educators must consider several key factors that affect parents and cause them to react and respond as they do.

From the Parents' Point of View

There is some evidence that parents go through a type of grieving process when their child is suspected of having some type of disability or when the child is actually identified as a student with special needs (Falik, 1995). However, it is unclear how parents progress from the initial identification of a problem to the point where the problem has been identified and specific intervention strategies have been implemented. The key factor for educators to remember is that the parents of students with special needs are likely to react in some way. Parents often fail to accept that there is "something wrong" with their child. If and when they do acknowledge the presence of some type of difficulty, parents often begin to try to find solutions to the problem. It is our experience that, as parents try to find solutions to their concerns, they often discover techniques that are not based on sound educational research or expertise. For example, several years ago, medication used for motion sickness was recommended as a cure for learning disabilities. These medications are clearly effective in treating many cases of motion sickness; however, there is no reason, logical or empirical, to suggest that these medications would benefit students with learning disabilities. Nonetheless, if parents are looking for a solution to their child's problem, no stone will be left unturned. As professionals, it is important to be aware of parents' needs and the lengths to which they will go for some satisfaction in their quest to find "something to help our child." After searching for an answer, regardless of the success experienced, parents will typically turn to school personnel to help the child. It is the responsibility of school personnel, to the best of their ability, to provide answers to the questions raised by parents.

Problems Parents May Experience

Parents of Students With Special Needs

Parents of children with special needs often recognize the needs of their children before anyone else. However, they are often hesitant to bring such information to light because they lack the confidence to explain what they experience at home. Parents report that they have made endless trips to professionals, searching for answers to questions that they often can't formulate. "I know there is something wrong, but it is really hard to put into words" is often heard in conversations with parents of students with special needs. The frustration they experience is heightened when they go to the family doctor or a counselor who says to them, "I understand your concern, but some children just develop differently" (M. Ellis, personal communication, 2004). Consequently, parents often experience frustration caused by an inability to provide any specific explanation for the behaviors they observe. This is exacerbated by the time and energy they expend in their efforts to identify the problem and/or solution to their child's behavior (Dyson, 1996). It is important for educators to be aware that, in most circumstances, parents do not just dump a problem in our laps and say, "Fix it!" They look to us to work with them as they try to determine solutions to the problems that have been identified. More importantly, they look to us to listen to what they have experienced and to accept that they are primarily interested in finding ideas and strategies to help their child (M. Ellis, personal communication, 2004).

While most parents accept their *child* with special needs, they often struggle to accept the disability itself. Parents who were successful academically do not understand why their child is not experiencing similar success. As one parent commented to us, "I just don't get it. I did great in school, and my wife made straight A's. Why would our child have so much trouble with school?" The first response was, "Oh, how I wish I could answer that question!" While this response doesn't satisfy parents, it is nonetheless accurate. "Why would our child have so much trouble with school?" is impossible to answer with complete confidence that the response is accurate. Often there is no identifiable cause for high-incidence disabilities. If a cause can be identified, it often occurs at a point when nothing can be done to alter the impact of the cause. One of the authors has a learning disability. When he was very young he was in an incubator; however, the hose that pumped the oxygen into the incubator was inadvertently dislodged, causing him to be somewhat oxygen deprived for a period of time. The impact of this incident surely resulted in the presence of the learning disability due to the insult to the brain. Knowledge of this cause is interesting but of little value beyond that; it is impossible to change the loss of oxygen that occurred. The inability to identify and/or change the cause of the disability often results in a struggle as the parents try to accept the disability. It is less "real" to them because they are unable to manage or control the cause, unable to help their child in a direct, tangible manner. For many parents, this often results in their being less accepting of the disability. Once again, as professionals we must be sensitive to these potential issues, yet remain focused on helping the student work to his or her potential through whatever means necessary (see Box 11.1).

The degree to which parents understand and accept the disability and their child with a disability is a crucial component in understanding the parental responses to the difficulties experienced at school. However, it is professionally critical that we do not overlook the impact the disability may have on the *entire family.* Just as children with special needs differ from other children with special needs, siblings of these children often react differently as well. Siblings often are frustrated and somewhat jealous of the time directed to working with the child with special needs (M. Ellis, personal communication, 2004). The siblings observe the time their parents spend with their brother or sister as taking away from their own time with their parents. They may also feel that the money directed at helping their brother or sister will reduce the opportunity for them to buy the new dress or bike they wanted. However, over time, the siblings of children with special needs come to appreciate their brother or sister and often become integral players in helping them with homework or generally understanding an academic concept presented in school.

Box 11.1 Talking With Parents About Their Attempts to Identify Causes of a Disorder

In explaining the potential inability to identify the cause(s) of a particular disorder, we have found it useful to help parents understand by relating the process to the medical model. If you hurt your shoulder and went to see your doctor, he or she would run a series of tests to see what was medically wrong with your shoulder. He or she would likely begin by asking you questions to try to determine the possible cause of the injury: When did you notice that your shoulder was injured? Do you remember doing anything that might have caused your shoulder to hurt? Does it hurt when you do this or that? While there may be certain cases in which you would remember exactly what happened, there would be other circumstances in which you would not be able to identify the cause. In those cases, the doctor would run a series of tests to rule out certain possibilities, eventually arriving at an accurate diagnosis. It really wouldn't matter what you did to cause the shoulder to be injured; what would be important would be that the doctor identified what was wrong with the shoulder and prescribed medication and/or treatment to help repair your shoulder. This is the fact that we must emphasize with parents. Even though we may be unable to identify a specific cause, we will build a program that is designed to meet the needs of your child.

Parents of Students Without Special Needs

Much of the literature regarding parents and inclusion focuses on the parents of students with special needs. This is somewhat shortsighted in that there is another set of parents that are equally important to the success of any inclusion program. Parents of students without special needs are likely to have no idea about inclusive classrooms, the rationale for the existence of these classrooms, or the impact this option may have on the students placed in the classroom. Educators are often reactive rather than proactive in their approach to circumstances that present themselves in our schools today. We tend to "react" to new methods or materials or new discipline strategies only after a problem has been identified or specific questions are raised. Rather than being proactive and considering the potential implications of the "new" approach, we tend to develop an attitude of "Let's wait and see if we have any questions before we say anything.

Maybe we won't have to even deal with it." While this "wait and see" attitude may often result in positive outcomes, it can also create unnecessary problems. Human nature is such that we feel that we are being duped if we don't find out about something until it is too late to do anything about it. Consequently, we often perceive the event more negatively, even though it may be in our best interests (see Box 11.2). Such is the case with inclusion. Parents report that when they were not informed that their children would be placed in an inclusion classroom until after the school year began, they felt frustrated and somewhat betrayed. However, these parents indicated that they would have reacted positively to the placement option had they known about the choice before the academic year began. Once again, by being "kept in the dark" about the program, parents felt that the school was trying to slip something by them, which obviously creates negative feelings and concerns about the efficacy of any such program. Proactive communication often results in a favorable reaction or at least reduces the potential questions and concerns raised later. Parents of students with and without special needs should be made aware of the potential implementation of the inclusion model before the school year begins. This enables the parents to ask questions about the program, clarify certain issues important to them (see below), and achieve a greater understanding of the program, all of which lead to a smoother transition to the inclusion model.

As the inclusive model is initiated in an individual school, the parents of students without special needs are undoubtedly hopeful that all students in the classroom will receive instruction that is beneficial and appropriate. Having been informed of the implementation of the inclusion model in their school, all parents hopefully begin the school year with a positive, farsighted perspective to the new classroom option. However, the parents of students without special needs, just like the parents of students with special needs, are ultimately concerned about what is best for their child. These parents report that they are perfectly comfortable with the inclusion classroom if they receive an appropriate answer to two questions. The first question is, "Will my child's learning suffer due to the placement of students with special needs in my child's classroom?" Similarly, the second question asks, "Will my child receive less attention due to the placement of students with special needs in my child's classroom?" If the answer is "No" to both of these questions, the parents of students without special needs, like parents of students with special needs, are comfortable with the inclusive setting and often provide very positive feedback about the program.

The positive feedback exists, not only because the parents realize that their child is receiving the attention necessary to ensure academic

Box 11.2 The Issue of Trust Between Educators and Parents

The city of Washington, D.C., was recently granted a professional baseball franchise. When the city agreed to this deal, a specific arrangement was understood to be in effect regarding the cost of a new stadium that was to be built. The baseball owners voted to approve the move of the Montreal Expos to Washington for the 2005 baseball season. As the deadline neared, the Washington, D.C., City Council made a statement that went against the previously negotiated deal: The commission wanted to change the deal by ensuring that at least one half of the cost of the new stadium would be privately paid, eliminating the need to raise taxes or to find alternative methods to raise the stadium money.

Though there can be no question as to why the city council wanted to avoid raising taxes for a baseball stadium, the commission's timing was met with frustration and ire from professional baseball. The commission "reacted" after a deal had essentially been agreed upon; if the issue of funding had been raised prior to the agreement, alternatives would have been more easily negotiated with the best interests of both parties (i.e., professional baseball and the city of Washington, D.C.) in mind.

This story is reminiscent of how educators often work with parents. If educators continue to try to "sneak" items or changes by parents without their input, it is logical to assume that the parents will lose trust in the schools and begin to scrutinize every move made by the schools. While we would hope that the reason to keep parents informed is for the benefit of the students, we recognize that often a more concrete, basic reason is needed. Avoiding future hardships and hassles with parents is likely to be the outcome of being up-front and open about changes. We strongly suggest this up-front approach when introducing inclusion (or any other new and innovative program) to the school(s).

growth, but also because students without special needs have been found to continue to achieve academically at or above the achievement level in a noninclusive classroom setting (Manset & Semmel, 1997; Peltier, 1997). Parents also note that they are encouraged by the inclusion classroom placement option because there are two teachers in the room, a feature that reduces the likelihood of discipline problems created by their child or other children in the classroom. Finally, parents of students without special needs report that because their children are exposed to children with special needs the children establish an appreciation for diversity and disability that was not present before being placed in the inclusive setting (Gerber & Popp, 1999).

HOW DO I WORK WITH PARENTS TO MAXIMIZE THEIR INVOLVEMENT?

After ensuring that they are aware of the rationale and nature of inclusive classrooms, school personnel must endeavor to enlist the support of all parents as the inclusion model is initiated in the individual school. Each school is likely to identify specific strategies that will facilitate the acceptance and success of the inclusion model. However, several considerations should be taken into account as the program is initiated.

Communication and Collaboration Between Home and School

Effective home-school communication is emphasized from the beginning of undergraduate education programs through doctoral work to the implementation on a day-to-day basis. This occurs because of the importance of this communication but also because the lines of communication may not be fully utilized. For a long time in education, both general and special, teachers often made significant efforts to avoid communicating at all with parents. The mentality was "The less they know, the better." It is now clear that this approach to parents is ineffective and often leads to a far less successful classroom experience for the students, teachers, and parents. The technology available affords parents an opportunity to access essentially any and all information about an individual school or district. Not only do parents know more than ever before about the education of their children, they often know more about what should happen than the educators providing the specific service. With the increasing number of parent organizations and support groups, parents are often well informed about their rights and their child's individual needs. The days of keeping parents "in the dark" are, thankfully, over. Teachers and schools must strive to work closely with parents in any academic setting. This appears to be especially true when students are served in an inclusion setting.

Communication with parents provides educators with an opportunity to identify information about the family, the family structure, and the student that might otherwise be overlooked. Recently, a mother expressed her frustration that she and her husband had never been involved in a conference about her child and didn't know the child was having difficulty in school until report cards came out. The classroom teacher responded by reminding the mother that attempts had been made to set up conferences and that each time neither the mother nor the father had attended the conference. The mother was frustrated and eventually blurted out that the reason they had been unable to attend the conferences was that the meetings were scheduled during work hours. Due to financial difficulties, the father was unable to miss work. The family simply could not afford the loss of income that would have occurred if the father had attended the meeting. The mother was unable to find someone to watch the children because of the financial difficulties faced by the family. The mother said this difficulty had not been previously mentioned because she and her husband had been embarrassed to acknowledge it. This example shows that parents who may be perceived as not caring about their child may in fact care deeply but be unable to attend meetings or complete other tasks for logical reasons about which the teacher/school has no knowledge. Professional educators must strive to ensure maximum parental involvement. While it is impossible to ensure that all parents will be involved in their child's education, professional educators must make every possible effort to ensure that parents have the opportunity to participate to the degree possible.

Parents, regardless of their natural biases, know more about their children than any other individual. They live with the child and have learned over time what the child likes to do, eat, watch, or hear. This information can be invaluable to the classroom teacher as he or she begins to develop lessons or identify reward systems for the classroom. Cook and Swain (2001) emphasize that parents have much information about their child that would be helpful to the teacher and the school. A third-grade student with special needs was struggling with written expression. The teacher scored the boy's work but provided little feedback to the parents until the report card was sent home. When the boy's mother looked at the low grade, she called the teacher and asked why the child's struggles had not been previously mentioned. The teacher said that the youngster was doing "the best that he could" and there was no reason to make the parents upset about the difficulty. Regardless of how inappropriate and ineffective the teacher's feedback was, a more important piece of information was not identified: The 8-year-old boy had previously been in a school setting that did not emphasize writing. The student had not been exposed to writing in his previous educational experience. Once the mother was aware of the written expression expectations of third graders, she sought support from an in-school tutorial program. After five one-on-one sessions with the in-school tutor, the student understood the elements of writing and was able to consistently meet the classroom demands and increase his skills throughout the remainder of the year. Had the communication between the school and home been more effective, the student would likely have received help sooner, thereby reducing the frustration of the student, parent, and teacher. Although this situation is true, it may be a best-case scenario example; nonetheless, communication often helps teachers approach students in ways that might not otherwise be apparent.

Working Collaboratively With Parents

A potentially infinite number of factors can cause conflict between the school and the family. These factors may play a significant role in undermining the effective collaboration between parents and school personnel. Lake and Billingsley (2000) suggest eight specific issues that escalate or de-escalate conflict (Table 11.1). One of the most significant causes of conflict is a discrepant view of the student. Parents of students with special needs report that schools often do not consider the unique needs of

Table 11.1 Factors That Escalate or De-escalate Conflict Between Parents and School Personnel

1. Discrepant views of a child or the child's needs.

2. Schools' or parents' lack of knowledge to solve problems or to identify strategies for communication.

3. Service delivery.

4. Constraints: Both parents and school personnel acknowledge that time, money, personnel, and material constraints have a dramatic and often negative impact on what happens in schools.

5. Valuation: Whether parents feel that they are perceived by school personnel as valued participants in the education of their child.

6. Reciprocal power: Parents and school personnel sometimes use whatever means are in their power to establish their ability to secure the desired changes or to maintain status quo. They may, for example, use advocates, anger, or tenacity to endeavor to establish their power in their efforts to secure the most appropriate placement for students.

7. Communication: While communication is a positive factor in de-escalating conflict, lack of communication, infrequent communication, lack of follow-up, or misunderstood communication are likely to increase the conflict between parents and schools.

8. Trust: Parents who trust the school personnel are less likely to create conflict with the school.

SOURCE: Adapted from Lake and Billingsley (2000).

their child but rather view the child according to a deficit model. That is, the school focuses on the areas with which the child has difficulty, with little attention to the areas in which the child experiences success. The school, on the other hand, suggests that parents will often identify one specific event or behavior in which the student was successful without seeing the larger number of skills that have not been mastered.

Another key issue that often results in conflict is what Lake and Billingsley refer to as "valuation." Valuation is the "who or what" people care for or about. Human nature is such that we all have a need to feel valued to some degree. Being perceived as a valuable player in the home-school communication model is important for parents. Parents often report that they have received misleading or blatantly false information from the school. This indicates the school's lack of trust in them and clearly has a negative impact on future communication and collaboration between the home and school.

Parents and school personnel are keenly aware of and sensitive to the service delivery provided for students with special needs. Unfortunately, the specific service delivery choice made may result in conflict between the parents and the school personnel. Lake and Billingsley report that parents may become suspicious of the specific placement of their child if the school is unable to substantiate and appropriately answer questions about how the services are being delivered to their child. Parents consider the lack of appropriate responses as a sign of something wrong with the services and begin to raise even more questions.

In many circumstances, parents have needs that far exceed the roles and responsibilities of school personnel. However, in many cases, parents and family members merely need someone to listen to what they have to say and gain some understanding of their specific situations. Even if there is no solution to a particular problem, parents appreciate the attempts made. While the effort to help a family, in and of itself, may be sufficient reason for attempting to help parents, there is often a side benefit to teachers. It seems that parents are more likely to devote their time and energy to their child's educational needs if they themselves receive support for their personal and family needs (Jephson, Russell, & Youngblood, 2001). Consequently, if we make the effort to help the family, parents may be more involved in seeing that homework is completed, that materials are brought to and returned from the home, or simply that the child attends school on a regular basis. The more the parents are involved, the greater the likelihood of student involvement in school tasks. In efforts to secure and maintain parental involvement, school personnel should begin by listening to what parents say about their expectations of the school.

While there are exceptions, parents typically don't ask schools to provide them with anything that is impossible or prohibitive for the school. Like most of us, parents want to be treated with respect, to be provided with information about their child in relation to the day-to-day and long-term activities in the inclusion classroom, and to be kept abreast of their child's progress on a consistent basis. As stated earlier, parents ultimately want what is best for their child. In achieving this, parents look for teachers, counselors, and/or administrators to be personable, honest, excited, and optimistic (Davern, 2004). Parents also indicate that they want teachers to be sensitive to the unique needs of their child and to communicate effectively with them about those needs. Specifically, parents want the teacher to communicate with them in a manner that is respectful, ongoing, and leading to improvements in their child's educational experiences (Davern, 2004).

A parent of a student with learning disabilities discussed his goals in working with the schools with one of the authors. These goals revolved around three broad topics: self-worth, interaction, and independence.

In considering his self-worth as a person who happened to also be a parent of a student with special needs, this father asked that the teacher approach any communicative act with sensitivity and compassion but without becoming overly sorrowful or full of pity. The goal is not to "feel sorry" for the parent but instead to provide information in a manner that takes into consideration the difficulty likely experienced by the parents in their efforts to raise their child appropriately and effectively. Parents also look for the teacher to identify the child's strengths along with the areas that are in need of remediation. In other words, this father sought feedback from the school that would be encouraging and lead to future changes.

During parent-teacher interactions, parents want assurance that the teacher is knowledgeable about their child and the child's individual needs. They want teachers to be interested in their child and family situation without becoming overly inquisitive. As professionals, we must establish and maintain the rights of the parent and avoid the tendency to seek information that is not germane to the goal of meeting the needs of the child. Appropriate and targeted interest leads the teacher to be responsive to the requests or questions raised without being artificial. Parents are very aware of "canned" responses and are sensitive to their use when the discussion focuses on their child. The father who spoke with us noted that the meetings he had attended were often very somber, almost depressing, events. He indicated that parents appreciate the injection of humor into the meetings as long as the attempts at humor do not "make fun of" their child. Sometimes an anecdote about a specific incident can help put everyone at ease and lead to a more successful conference.

Finally, parents strive for independence, for themselves as well as their child. As such, parents look for the teacher to provide information about the individual goals that have been established for their child. In striving to meet these goals, parents expect the classroom work to be challenging and not coddling. Ultimately, parents of students with special needs and, in fact, parents of all students look for the teacher and school to be future oriented without dwelling on the past or present. If there are problems, parents ask for them to be identified and remediated to the maximum degree possible so that the child can move forward in working toward his or her independence.

The desires of parents and the need for school personnel to work closely with the parents in an effort to maximize the learning and social development of all children is well established. However, often little attention is given to how to help parents in their attempts to provide the support, structure, and feedback their children need in the home setting. Some specific examples are provided below.

WHAT ARE SOME APPROACHES THAT WORK EFFECTIVELY WITH PARENTS?

Television has instituted a phenomenon in our country that is almost epidemic. "Reality TV" has taken over the airwaves. We are not making any value judgment as to the overall quality of these programs, but a few are at least interesting. One show in particular may help educators recognize the needs of parents in working with their children. This program involves the wives of two families switching places for a 2-week period. During the first week the wives must adhere to the lifestyle already in place in the "new home." The second week provides the wives with an opportunity to take control of the house and impose their standards and expectations on the family. The show is a fascinating example of differences in approaches to raising children. One family may be so permissive that the children basically govern the home life; another family has a dictatorial structure that provides the children with no input or opportunity to express their feelings about anything that happens in the home. Almost without exception, both families change after the 2-week swap occurs. In most cases, the mother and father each acknowledge the need for a change and also realize that they are often not even aware of the circumstances that existed in the house. The daily routine was established and judged to be effective. Consequently, there was no need to fix what wasn't broken. The point of this little television program review is not to encourage you to watch the program (if you don't already do so!) but to suggest that parents of students with special needs often do not "know what they don't know." As parents, we all can benefit from objective, targeted information focusing on strategies, ideas, and activities that might be implemented on a day-to-day basis in the home. The following information, though clearly not all-inclusive, has been useful to us and other professionals and is provided in light of the concerns and problems identified earlier in the chapter. The format initially identifies or restates a concern or problem and then lists some recommendations to achieve some resolution to the concern or problem.

Family Issues

- Parents' difficulty explaining their observations of their child
  - Provide parents with specific examples of behaviors that have occurred with other students.
  - Encourage parents to closely observe the behavior by looking for an antecedent and consequent; this often helps parents describe the behavior more clearly and effectively.
  - Also encourage the parents to determine if the behavior occurs at a certain time of the day or during certain events (e.g., dinner or bath time).
- Lack of a specific cause of the special need
  - The most important fact for educators to stress with parents is that there is nothing that can be done about the cause regardless; therefore, it is crucial to focus energies elsewhere.
  - Help parents work toward identifying techniques that will enhance the remediation of the deficit.
  - Provide the names of organizations or individuals with whom parents can speak about their frustration.
- Impact on the siblings
  - As in other circumstances, talk with the siblings about their sister or brother.
  - Provide special days or events for the siblings to make them feel "special" too.
  - Encourage and reinforce the siblings to work with their sister or brother.

School's View of Students and Parents

- The need for school personnel to focus on positive factors
  - Teachers should try to place "good news" phone calls; provide parents with positive feedback whenever possible.
  - In conferences or any other type of communication, begin with positive information.

- Ensure that you reward success in school and that the student tells his or her parents.
- Value parental involvement
  - Listen to parents; treat them as you would expect to be treated by your peers.
  - Act upon the requests parents make.
  - Invite and encourage parents' involvement.
- Personable, honest, ongoing communication, with respect
  - Begin conferences with some general conversation to help parents feel comfortable.
  - Always provide some positive information about the child.
  - Endeavor to communicate with all families via newsletters, e-mails (where and when appropriate), or phone calls.
  - Acknowledge the difficulty of parenting without telling parents that you "know how they must feel"; chances are you don't have any idea how they feel, and parents are aware of this.
- Knowledge of student and family
  - Find out as much as possible about the students in your classroom. A second-grade teacher recently had a student who was out of school for 9 days due to illness; the teacher *knew* the child liked to play video games, so the teacher bought the child a gift card at a local video store. By finding out about her students, she had made a child feel great, which would likely carry over into the classroom.
  - When meeting with parents, ensure that you appear (and hopefully are) interested in their child and family in general.
  - Don't be afraid to say, "I don't know. I will find out the answer and get back to you." It is okay that you don't have all the answers, but to say you do and have the parents find out that you really didn't know the answer can be disastrous.

Parents of Students Without Special Needs

- Not being informed about the initiation of an inclusion program
  - Meet with all classroom parents before school begins to discuss inclusion and other key issues.
  - Involve the parents of children without special needs as much as possible in the school or classroom activities that either directly or indirectly involve students with special needs.
  - Invite parents to observe the classroom after school has been in session for a period of time; this will give all the students a chance to acclimate to the new program.
  - Provide consistent feedback about *their* child.

- Home-school communication
  - Complete a parent survey at the beginning of the year in an effort to identify any potential issues that might be present that might affect school-home communication (e.g., work schedules).
  - Provide alternative meeting times if necessary and appropriate.
  - Try to make "good news" phone calls to facilitate communication with parents and to make the "bad news" calls a little easier for parents to bear.
  - Use e-mail whenever possible; clearly, some parents will not have access to this technology, but the effort will be well accepted.

WHERE CAN I FIND RESOURCES OR MORE INFORMATION ON PARENTS?

Books

Cooper, C., Frattura, E., & Keyes, M. W. (2000). *Meeting the needs of students of ALL abilities: How leaders go beyond inclusion.* Thousand Oaks, CA: Corwin.

Jorgensen, C. M. (1998). *Restructuring high school for all students: Taking inclusion to the next level.* Baltimore: Paul H. Brookes.

Kalyanpur, M., & Harry, B. (1999). *Culture in special education: Building a posture of reciprocity in parent-professional relationships.* Baltimore: Paul H. Brookes.

Moore, L. O. (2000). *Inclusion: A practical guide for parents—Tools to enhance your child's learning.* Minnetonka, MN: Peytral.

Reyler, A. B., & Buswell, B. E. (2001). *Individual education plan: Involved effective parents.* Colorado Springs: PEAK Parent Center.

Articles

Davern, L. (2004). School-to-home notebooks: What parents have to say. *Teaching Exceptional Children, 36,* 22–27.

Organizations

Exceptional Children's Assistance Center
P.O. Box 16
Davidson, NC 28036
Web: www.ecac-parentcenter.org

Learning Disabilities Association
4156 Library Road
Pittsburgh, PA 15234
Web: www.ldanatl.org

National Parent Network on Disabilities
1600 Prince St. Suite 115
Alexandria, VA 22314
Web: www.npdn.org

Web Resources

Gruskin, S., & Silverman, K. (1997, April). *Including your child.* Washington, DC: U.S. Department of Education, Office of Educational Research and Improvement. Retrieved October 4, 2005, from www.ed.gov/pubs/parents/ Including

PACER Center, Inc. (1999). *Understanding the special education process: An overview for parents.* Minneapolis: Author. Retrieved October 4, 2005, from www.fape .org/pubs/ (also available in Spanish, Somali, and Hmong).

CHAPTER REFERENCES

Cook, T., & Swain, J. (2001). Parents' perspectives on the closure of a special school: Towards inclusion in partnership. *Educational Review, 53,* 191–198.

Davern, L. (2004). School-to-home notebooks: What parents have to say. *Teaching Exceptional Children, 36,* 22–27.

Dyson, L. L. (1996). The experiences of families of children with learning disabilities: Parental stress, family functioning, and sibling self-concept. *Journal of Learning Disabilities, 29*(3), 281–287.

Falik, L. H. (1995). Family patterns of reaction to a child with a learning disability: A mediational perspective. *Journal of Learning Disabilities, 28,* 335–341.

Gerber, P. J., & Popp, P. A. (1999). Consumer perspectives on the collaborative teaching model: Views of students with and without LD and their parents. *Remedial and Special Education, 20,* 288–296.

Jephson, M. B., Russell, K. P., & Youngblood, L. A. (2001). Families and early intervention professionals in rural areas: Unique challenges. *Rural Special Education Quarterly, 20*(3), 20–23.

Lake, J. F., & Billingsley, B. S. (2000). An analysis of factors that contribute to parent-school conflict in special education. *Remedial and Special Education, 21,* 240–251.

Manset, G., & Semmel, M. I. (1997). Are inclusive programs for students with mild disabilities effective? *Journal of Special Education, 31,* 155–180.

Peltier, G. L. (1997). The effect of inclusion on non-disabled children: A review of the research. *Contemporary Education, 68,* 234–238.

What Works for Communicating, Consulting, and Collaborating With Other Professionals?

Outline Questions

What do I need to know about communicating, consulting, and collaborating?

Why should I communicate, consult, and collaborate with other professionals?

How do I communicate, consult, and collaborate effectively with other professionals in my classroom?

What are some approaches that are used to communicate, consult, and collaborate with other professionals?

Where can I find resources or more information on communicating, consulting, and collaborating?

WHAT DO I NEED TO KNOW ABOUT COMMUNICATING, CONSULTING, AND COLLABORATING?

Meeting the needs of all students in an inclusive general education class-room involves a number of professionals with varied backgrounds, per-sonalities, goals, expectations, training, and beliefs about the students with whom they will be working. The collaborative relationship will thrive or flounder depending on the degree to which the participating profes-sionals work together as a unit focused on the individual needs of all students. Collaboration potentially involves parents, general education teachers, special education teachers, speech/language pathologists, coun-selors, administration, and related service personnel (e.g., occupational therapists, physical therapists, music teachers, and art teachers). With such a potentially diverse group of professionals involved in meeting the needs of students, communication is an incredibly important factor in helping to ensure success. Collaboration, like any relationship, relies on effective communication. In fact, collaboration has often been compared to marriage. Many marriages struggle simply because the spouses do not take the time to communicate. One spouse will often say that he or she wasn't aware of the existence of a problem; the other spouse states that he or she said nothing on the assumption that the problem or concern was obvious. Without communication between spouses, a small problem can become a major concern. Effective communication is at the heart of any successful relationship, including successful collaborative relationships.

When a school implements an inclusion program, it must begin with effective communication. Initially, the teachers must understand what inclusion is and is not. All participating personnel must also be aware of the rationale for beginning an inclusion program, the way the program will be instituted in the school, those who will be involved, how those involved will be selected for participation, and the school's goals for the inclusion program. This involves communication. Recently, we had the opportunity to work with a small school district that was implementing an inclusion program during the upcoming school year. The first training session was held in mid-August, when the teachers had returned for their planning days before the beginning of school. Once everyone was seated, a district representative stood in front of the amassed teachers and announced that the district had decided to institute inclusion in several schools. Unfortunately, this was the first time that the teachers had heard of this, and they were, to say the least, shocked. Even more unfortunately for us, this was also the first time we had heard that the teachers were not aware that inclusion would be taking place. Suffice it to say that it was a rather rocky academic year. The gross lack of communication clearly undermined the potential success of the inclusion program.

While not all inclusion programs begin with such glaringly unprofessional actions, the lack of effective communication can have results as disastrous as this. If administration fails to communicate the goals and objectives of the inclusion program, little success can be expected. Teachers, regardless of their efforts and interest in the program, will struggle to meet the expectations for a successful program if these expectations are not clearly identified and communicated. If the goals and objectives are clearly delineated but the participating teachers fail to communicate among themselves, inclusion often resembles a pull-out program simply moved to a general education classroom. The special educator works one on one or in small groups with the identified exceptional children, while the general educator works with the remainder of the class. Finally, if the students, those with and without disabilities, do not communicate with their peers and teachers, little success is likely. Communication is crucial throughout the life of the inclusion program. Without effective communication, the "inclusion marriage" will most likely end in an "inclusion divorce."

WHY SHOULD I COMMUNICATE, CONSULT, AND COLLABORATE WITH OTHER PROFESSIONALS?

The verb *collaborate* is defined in two different and very interesting ways. According to the first definition, collaborating is working jointly with others. According to the second definition, it involves working with an enemy force that is occupying one's country. Both of these definitions may be applied when collaboration methods are implemented in schools. The goal of collaboration in schools is to have teachers work jointly in an effort to meet the needs of all students in the general education classroom. In fact, educators look at collaboration as the tool that facilitates an effective inclusion program (Gable, Korinek, & McLaughlin, 1997). However, teachers often view collaboration as an attempt by the "enemy force" (i.e., special educators or other professionals) to occupy their country (i.e., their classroom). Some teachers may build walls to protect themselves and their classrooms from the "enemy force" of collaboration, with the likely result that they will experience less success and satisfaction in a collaborative setting. Clearly, the goal is for general education and special education teachers to perceive and believe that collaboration will foster an environment in which teachers can work jointly to plan and implement ideas that will meet the needs of all the students in the classroom setting.

HOW DO I COMMUNICATE, CONSULT, AND COLLABORATE EFFECTIVELY WITH OTHER PROFESSIONALS?

Table 12.1 lists characteristics of effective collaboration in the inclusive classroom. These are adapted from several resources (Gable et al., 1997; Friend & Cook, 2000) as well as our own professional and personal experience. Each characteristic is discussed in greater detail below.

Any attempt at effective collaboration must establish and *focus on the individual needs of all students* placed in the general classroom setting. If one student or a group of students are not receiving the instruction that is most appropriate to their needs, it is important to identify why this is occurring. If an analysis points to the collaboration in the classroom, the collaborative methods used must be carefully examined. If the method or approach to collaboration is the instructional element that is causing students to achieve less than would be expected, a change in method is warranted. However, if other factors exist (e.g., a student's behavior) that preclude successful collaboration, the inclusion classroom may not be the least restrictive placement for the individual student. Each of these possible factors must be explored to foster the success of each student placed in the inclusion setting.

Educators must choose to participate in an inclusion classroom and be given the opportunity to decline. If teachers are told that they will participate in inclusion and have no input into that decision, they will likely, and logically, not be enthusiastic participants in the process. The teachers in the school district mentioned above were not actively engaged in inclusion

Table 12.1   Characteristics of Effective Collaboration

1. The focus always remains on the individual needs of all students.

2. Educators must choose to participate in an inclusion program.

3. Leadership must be fair and ethical.

4. Common goals must be established and shared by all involved.

5. The team must have the power to make decisions regarding instruction in the inclusion classroom.

6. Communication must be open and welcomed by all members of the team.

7. Team members must be equal partners in the collaborative process.

8. Team members must establish and maintain a sense of mutual trust and respect.

and failed to collaborate consistently and effectively with their colleagues. Even today, several years after the fiasco, it is best not to use the word *inclusion* with many of these teachers, and if the word is used it should be in a whisper! Teachers who have chosen to engage in inclusion should understand that under those circumstances professional collaboration is mandatory. Their choice then enhances the likelihood of successful collaboration, resulting in an effective learning experience for all students.

The leaders of the movement to implement collaboration in their schools must do so in a *fair, ethical manner.* Clearly, the behavior in the example above was neither fair nor ethical. District-level administrators as well as building-level administration must work toward ensuring that several groups of individuals are considered in the decision-making process. The first and most important group is the students. If the students' needs are not met through collaborative methods, it is crucial that alternatives be available. Families are also extremely important in consideration of a collaborative model. Finally, as implied above, the teachers must "buy into" collaboration for success to be possible. Educational leaders must be sensitive to each of these groups as a school moves toward collaboration in the inclusion classroom.

As teachers identify their interest in participating and the educational leaders have paved the way for inclusion, the participants must evidence *common goals* as the collaborative model is implemented. Although it is not necessary for all participating teachers to agree with all the goals of collaboration, it is crucial that they share some goals that foster the successful implementation of collaboration. One such goal is certainly to provide instructional support that focuses on the strengths and needs of the students in the classroom. Additional goals may include increased social interaction between students with and without diverse needs, increased knowledge and acceptance of diversity, more effective use of resources, and improved academic skills.

On several occasions teachers have reported to us that they become frustrated when they do not believe that they have *the power to make decisions* and implement them in the classroom. These teachers present their requests to the school administrators and are told, "It can't be done" for a myriad of reasons. Their frustration comes not so much from the statement that it can't be done as from their having been originally told that the school would adhere to their reasonable decisions. In other words, teachers did not experience the power to implement their plans after being assured of this "power" from the beginning. Although there is no way to predict the future in a school, much less the entire district, when inclusion is planned, administrators must constantly and consistently try to ensure that the efforts of the collaboration team will be implemented. If inevitable changes occur during the process, administrators and team members must meet to discuss the specific and direct impact on the collaboration efforts.

Although discussed at the beginning of this chapter, the crucial role of *communication* in collaborative teams is important to revisit. All team members must feel free to express their opinions without fear of retribution. This is often difficult in group settings, especially if there is a difference of experience among the members. We have all heard statements such as "She's only been teaching for 2 years—I have 20 years of experience" or "That old battleaxe has been around so long she doesn't have any idea what is going on anymore." Whatever the validity of these types of statements, collaborative teams must work to overcome these differences. Inevitably, many teachers question the knowledge or expertise of their peers in some circumstances. However, this questioning must not be allowed to undermine the goal of collaborative inclusion classrooms, which is always meeting the individual needs of all students. Keeping this goal in mind enables team members to feel comfortable in expressing their thoughts, however extreme they may be. The team members must also recognize that the rest of the team may not value their ideas as much as they do.

Collaborative teams must also be designed so that all members are viewed as *equal partners* in the process of providing educational services to students. While some type of "pecking order" may well be established, this hierarchy exists only to facilitate the work of the team. One member may be charged with ensuring that meetings run smoothly and do not turn into gripe sessions where individual members preach their doctrines of teaching. This "facilitator," however, maintains his or her role as an individual member of the team. His or her vote is as important as any other member's but not more so. Meetings should thus provide equal opportunity to the members to express their position and receive feedback from the remaining team members. In any group or team setting, it is crucial to listen to all the ideas presented. Clearly, not all of the ideas will be implemented at the time of the meeting; however, many ideas that may not be applicable at one point during a school year may be more appropriate later. Consideration of all input helps ensure that all members will continue to participate. Effective collaboration teams try to provide each member with responsibilities appropriate to his or her position, experience, and skills. This fosters the implementation of strategies and materials provided by all team members. One final element of team equality is that all members share in the success or struggles experienced by the students in the inclusion classrooms. Statements such as "This thing worked only because I was able to get them to do it my way" or "If she would have listened to me, everything would have been okay" are simply not allowed; if such beliefs are held, they must be considered during the developmental process of establishing collaborative teams. If individual teachers are not comfortable with accepting equal responsibility for all that happens in the classroom, it may be most appropriate to exclude them from involvement in the collaborative process. Instructional decisions are made by the entire team and not by individuals; the entire team must then share the "glory or blame."

Finally, effective collaboration is characterized by *mutual trust and respect.* As in any other situation, trust and respect must be earned. Members must work to ensure that their roles and responsibilities are accomplished to the extent that the team will be successful in achieving the overriding goal of meeting the individual needs of all students. As long as the team and its individual members continue to maintain this focus, trust and respect will exist. Mutual trust and respect enable members to express their differences of opinion with the confidence that these differences will be viewed as one's perspective and nothing more. Working with other people almost always leads to the identification of some differences. These differences should be welcomed and looked upon as an opportunity to improve classroom instruction. No single technique or activity works for all students. Different approaches and ideas make the collaborative team more effective in helping all the students in the classroom. Trust and respect for team members allow the team to make decisions based on the overall good of the team and not the advancement of a single member. Establishing and maintaining trust and respect for the team and all individual members is more easily accomplished if the focus always remains on (can you guess this one?) the individual needs of all students. The focus on the students enables the team to move forward, to overcome many trivial differences, and to provide a classroom structure that facilitates and encourages learning.

Collaboration is implemented according to the needs of each school as well as the resources available to the individual school. In their efforts to work jointly, teachers often work either consultatively or in a coteaching setting.

Consultation

In many schools the demands placed on the special education teacher are so great that it is not feasible to implement a coteaching relationship with the general education teacher. Large schools, schools that serve a significantly large low-incidence population, and any other school settings that serve an exceptionally large number of students with disabilities often require the special education teacher to spend considerable time serving students in a setting that is more restrictive than the general education classroom. In other situations, schools may be so small that special education services are provided on an itinerant basis. This often occurs in rural school districts or in other small school districts. Special education teachers will spend a few days in one school and the remainder of the week in another school. Consequently, this limited time is spent serving the needs of students outside the general education classroom.

When the special education teacher is unable to work directly with students in the general education setting, collaboration with the general education teacher occurs consultatively. The consultation model of service provision typically does not provide the special educator with the opportunity to work directly with students with special needs. Instead, the special educator "consults" with the general educator. Although there may be alternatives, the consultation process usually involves a series of professional tasks. The special educator is likely to observe the student(s) with special needs in the general education classroom in an effort to identify any specific behaviors or skills that may be amenable to classroom intervention. After observing, the special educator meets with the appropriate general education personnel (i.e., classroom teacher, teacher assistant) to discuss specific intervention strategies designed to meet the learning demands of all students, including students with special needs, in the inclusive setting. The general educator then implements the strategies and continues to work with the special educator on an as-needed basis. This process continues as long as necessary to meet the needs of the students who are served consultatively.

Coteaching

Coteaching is undoubtedly the model most often envisioned for an inclusion program. Coteaching occurs when the general and special educators work jointly to meet the needs of all students placed in the inclusion setting. Successful coteachers exhibit certain behaviors, described below, that typically result in effective instruction and classroom management (see, e.g., Friend & Cook, 2003; Keefe, Moore, & Duff, 2004; Murawski & Dieker, 2004).

Most crucially, effective coteachers want to coteach. Teachers who are not interested in coteaching and/or have specific biases against the model or the students involved are likely to be far less successful than other teachers.

Even if teachers want to be in a coteaching situation, it is often necessary for them to receive training in specific strategies that make coteaching work. The general educator, for example, may need additional training on the unique needs of students with disabilities and the specific instructional considerations necessary to meet these needs. The special educator may require training on large group instruction or specific content knowledge that may be the focus of instruction in the general education classroom.

As this instructional knowledge is gained (or regained), coteachers hopefully recognize the positive impact that coteaching can have on the learning of *all* students. Teachers consistently report to us that they are amazed at the impact of the "new" teaching strategies on the students who do not exhibit special learning needs. As teachers learn to appreciate the positive effects of coteaching on the learning of *all* students, they are more inclined to use strategies that would not have been possible in previous situations.

Teachers begin to recognize that there is more than one way of teaching. Different teachers bring different learning styles to classroom instruction. For example, one teacher may be more "lecture" oriented, presenting information verbally while writing using corresponding PowerPoint slides. The coteacher's style may be more conducive to tactile, hands-on activities. An effective lesson may include an introductory lecture on the specific content (i.e., the basis of the material) followed by a project involving the direct implementation of the basics of the material. The lecture is presented by the first teacher described above, and the second teacher leads the project portion of the class. The key is recognizing, not simply that such differences may exist, but that they can and will enhance the learning of all students in the classroom. Classroom instruction would be greatly benefited if all teachers recognized and valued the differences between and among them and their colleagues.

Unfortunately, the ideal classroom does not exist. But without the ideal, it is important for all coteachers to recognize that their input is as important as any other input. Teachers, therefore, must often learn that it is appropriate for them to express their disagreement about a specific lesson or strategy being used. In this situation, it is also important for them to realize that while their disagreement is welcomed and accepted by their colleagues, the point the recommendations presented may not be immediately or directly applied to the lesson. This often creates problems in a coteaching relationship; teachers with less experience may be somewhat hesitant to voice their disagreement. If they do not believe that their input is welcomed or accepted, they may be less likely to provide their perspective in the future. In these circumstances, it is important to reconsider the characteristics of effective collaboration presented earlier in this chapter. The ultimate and, hopefully, obvious goal is for all coteachers to learn to listen, respect, and consider instructional differences as simply instructional differences and not good or bad, right or wrong. They are differences that may work sometimes and may be completely unsuccessful in other circumstances. The comfort level that exists when professionals recognize and accept different ideas is a foundation for successful coteaching.

As teachers develop this comfort level in working with their coteaching colleagues, it is crucial that it extend to potentially frustrating or even embarrassing situations. Aside from the authors of this book, there has never been a teacher who is always "on"! We only wish that this was true. But no human being is always going to be "at the top of his or her game." There are days when doctors make an inaccurate diagnosis or when meteorologists make an inaccurate weather prediction. Such is the case with teachers. Some days just do not go all that well. It is one thing for these days to occur when we are in our own classroom without anyone else watching. However, it is completely different when our coteacher is in the room, observing the "bad day" as it happens! Effective coteachers must be comfortable with saying to their colleagues, "That wasn't a very good lesson." First, the coteacher is probably very aware that the lesson wasn't very effective! Second, it should not matter that this was the case. In a team, one member covers for the other as much as possible and progress continues to be made. Finally, coteachers should always remember that they, too, will have a "bad day" or two throughout the academic year. Once again, teachers report to us that, as they become more comfortable in the coteaching environment and more aware of their coteachers, they use a series of signals to alert their coteachers to the need for change. A specific look may indicate a need to hold a brief meeting to consider the target information. A verbal prompt such as "What do you think, Ms. Jones?" may indicate that "I have forgotten what comes next" and that Ms. Jones needs to jump in and continue with the lesson. When "bad days" occur, the traditional or established roles of each coteacher may change.

Collaborative Roles and Responsibilities of All Those Involved

While the primary participants in an inclusive classroom are the general educator and the special educator, there are other key players in the process. In fact, many teachers believe that the inclusive school's principal plays the most important role in the inclusion process. The principal must give the entire school information regarding the initiation of the inclusion program as well as the guidance and support necessary for the program to be successful. In some cases, the principal is informed by district-level administrators that inclusion will be implemented in his or her school.

Principals themselves are often the professionals who initiate the move toward inclusion. In other circumstances, the principal initiates inclusion based on the input and recommendations from teachers in the school. Regardless, the principal is the person who brings the concept of inclusion forward to the school personnel. Once this has occurred, the principal must continue to support the teachers in their efforts to implement the program. This support may include the provision of appropriate inservice training, planning time before the beginning of the school year as well as during the year itself, the necessary instructional resources, and an ongoing attitude that inclusion is important and can be successfully implemented in the school. In attempting to meet these responsibilities, principals may introduce ideas that might be appropriate in one circumstance and not another. For example, the principal of an inclusive elementary school had some discretionary monies available for a specific academic year. She met with her teachers and suggested two ways to spend these monies. One was to hire another custodian to help with the upkeep of the school. The other was to "buy" a half-time special educator to provide greater support in the classrooms. However, if the half-time special educator was hired, it would be necessary for each class to vacuum their rooms twice a week and to empty their trash each day. By completing these tasks, they would enable the existing custodial staff to continue to meet the needs of the entire school. The teachers at this school overwhelmingly chose to hire the half-time special educator. However, when this alternative was presented to another principal, she believed that it would not work in her school because the custodial staff would not accept the changes and that the likely backlash would be far more consequential than having a half-time special educator.

Parents of all the students in the inclusive setting play an important role as well. They must be viewed as team members who may support the classroom activities in a traditional manner (i.e., overseeing homework completion) or by being open and responsive to questions that their children might have regarding the students in the room or the techniques being used in the classroom. Although the parents will not have the answers to all the questions that might arise, their understanding and support of the inclusive practices will encourage their children and enhance the likelihood of success of the program. In most circumstances, parents of students with and without special needs accept an inclusion program if they are made aware of the program and if the questions they raise are answered fairly and consistently.

The coteachers themselves must establish, understand, and consistently meet the expectations placed upon them in an inclusive setting. The general education teacher is typically the member with specific content knowledge, especially at the middle school or high school levels. This does not suggest that the special educator does not know or understand the content but simply that the general educator receives specific training related to grade-level curriculum. As such, general educators often have the perspective that inclusion is occurring in "their" classrooms and that the special educator is there as support. Coteachers must relinquish the idea of "my student" versus "yours." All students are the responsibility of each professional involved in the classroom. The general education teacher is also the member with the most significant experience teaching in a "large group" setting. This knowledge and experience is crucial in meeting the needs of *all* students; the general educator should serve as the model for day-to-day instruction in the inclusion setting.

The special educator satisfies certain roles in the process as well. Given the nature of training, he or she is often the member with greater knowledge and experience in providing alternative instruction to students. This may include assessment techniques (see Chapter 10 as well as Box 12.1), task analysis, the implementation of learning strategies (see Chapter 8), adaptations to different learning styles, and other techniques designed to present information in ways that may be unique to individual students. As such, the special educator is often responsible for taking the content of a specific lesson and adapting it to meet the needs of the diverse student population present in the inclusive setting.

Box 12.1 Assessment Information: What All Professionals Should Know

Additional personnel may serve specific or general roles in the inclusive classroom. Teacher assistants or paraprofessionals are often responsible for specific instructional elements during the school day. They may provide one-on-one support to students with and without special needs who may not grasp the concept being presented to the large group. They may also participate directly in the classroom instruction by monitoring student work, providing feedback to the students, or presenting specific concerns to the teachers in the classroom. Related services personnel (e.g., occupational therapists, physical therapists, music teachers, art teachers, physical education teachers) may also provide direct support in the inclusion setting or in alternative environments. Nonetheless, the support provided is designed to foster successful inclusion in the general education classroom. For example, an occupational therapist (OT) may provide direct support to a student with fine motor deficits in the inclusive setting or in a pull-out class. Regardless, the focus of the intervention provided by the OT is to enable to student to use the fine motor skills in handwriting in the general education classroom.

Many professionals involved in meeting the needs of students with special needs do not have specific training or background in assessment. Therefore, four broad, general areas of assessment information that may need to be shared with them are provided below. Less information may be required in some circumstances and more in others. The information here is a starting point for the school psychologist, special education teacher, or other professional involved in testing to use in sharing assessment data with school personnel.

1. Specific Tests Used

It may be necessary to list the specific tests that were used to assess the student and to describe what they measure (e.g., cognitive ability, achievement). Sometimes a more detailed description of a test may be necessary; below, an especially detailed description for the *Wechsler Intelligence Scale for Children—Fourth Edition (WISC-IV)* is provided as an example.

The *Wechsler Intelligence Scale for Children—Fourth Edition (WISC-IV)* is an individually administered measure of intellectual ability. Analysis of the individual subtests of the WISC-IV results in the identification of four index scores. The individual scores are further interpreted in a manner that produces a Full Scale Intelligence Quotient. The indexes and individual subtests are described below:

- Index Scores:
  - The *Verbal Comprehension Index (VCI)* is a measure of verbal concept formation, verbal reasoning, and knowledge acquired from one's environment.
  - The *Perceptual Reasoning Index (PRI)* is a measure of perceptual and fluid reasoning, spatial processing, and visual-motor integration.
  - The *Working Memory Index (WMI)* is a measure of one's ability to temporarily retain information in memory, perform some operation or manipulation with it, and produce a result.
  - The *Processing Speed Index (PSI)* measures one's ability to quickly and correctly scan, sequence, or discriminate simple visual information. It also measures short-term visual memory, attention, and visual-motor coordination.

- Individual Subtests:
  - *Similarities*—A series of orally presented pairs of words for which the child explains the similarity of the common objects or

(Continued)

(Continued)

concepts they represent. It measures understanding of relationships, verbal conceptualization (concrete, functional, and/or abstract.)

— *Vocabulary*—A series of orally presented words, which the child orally defines. It measures knowledge of word meaning, fund of information, conceptualization, and language development.

— *Comprehension*—A series of orally presented questions that require the child's solving of everyday problems or understanding of social rules and concepts. It measures the ability to understand social rules and commonsense issues relative to safety and daily living.

— *Digit Span*—A series of orally presented number sequences, which the child repeats verbatim for digits forward and in reverse order for digits backward. It measures short-term auditory memory, attention, concentration, and anxiety.

— *Letter-Number Sequencing*—Measures working memory. The child is presented with a mixed series of numbers and letters and repeats them with the numbers first (in numerical order) and then the letters (in alphabetical order).

— *Block Design*—A set of modeled or printed two-dimensional geometric patterns that the child replicates using two-color cubes. It measures spatial visualization, visual-motor control, and abstract analysis of whole to part and reconstruction.

— *Picture Concepts*—This subtest measures fluid reasoning, perceptual organization, and categorization (requires categorical reasoning without a verbal response). From each of two or three rows of objects, the child selects the objects that go together on the basis of an underlying concept.

— *Matrix Reasoning*—A measure of fluid reasoning is identified through the administration of this subtest. The child is presented with a partially filled grid and selects the item that properly completes the matrix.

— *Coding*—A series of simple shapes (Coding A) or numbers (Coding B), each paired with a simple symbol. The child draws the symbol in its corresponding shape (Coding A) or under its corresponding number (Coding B), according to a key. It measures eye-hand coordination, short-term visual memory, attention, and accuracy.

— *Symbol Search*—A series of paired groups of symbols, each pair consisting of a target group and a search group. The child scans the two groups and indicates whether a target symbol appears in the search group. It measures concentration and attention, speed, accuracy, and anxiety.

2. Definitions of Terminology

The terminology related to assessment, such as the derived standard score that is reported on most individually administered assessment devices, may be unfamiliar to many professionals. It is helpful to use the normal curve to discuss these scores. Also, many teachers may use the terms *percentage* and *percentile* interchangeably. Providing a clear distinction between these may be helpful.

3. Identification Criteria Used to Classify Students

While the various sets of criteria used to classify students tend to be very similar from one school to another, there may be differences. Therefore, it is beneficial to review the specific criteria used by your state/district.

4. Implications of Assessment Results

It may be useful to discuss the implications of assessment results for other professionals. Do the test results indicate a need for additional support? Are there any areas that are particularly glaring in terms of need? What recommendations does the school psychologist (and/or any others involved in the assessment) have about interventions?

Record Keeping for Collaboration

Given the collaboration of so many people in the project of inclusion, it is crucial to establish and maintain an organizational technique that enables coteachers to maintain records of the interventions that are planned, the personnel involved, the role played by the parents, contacts that have been made or that need to be made, and any changes that would be helpful to future intervention. Tables 12.2 through 12.5(B) provide a series of simple yet very effective organizational materials that can help teachers keep up with the daily events that occur in the inclusive classroom. These materials are designed to be practical and easy to implement to facilitate their use on a day-to-day basis. With regard to the forms for records of contacts made within the school, some teachers may prefer to use the format shown in Tables 12.4(A) and 12.4(B) (Option 1). These teachers often maintain notebooks with individual pages allocated for each student. The form shown in Table 12.4(B), for example, gives the follow-up contact regarding Mike Saulson on the same page as the earlier one rather than organizing the record chronologically and listing on the same page all the contacts regarding students that occur at a given time, as in Table 12.5(B). The format used is completely at the discretion of the

Table 12.2 Daily Planning Sheet for the General and Special Educator Team

General Educator:

Special Educator:

Date	What Will Be Taught?	Which Teaching Approach Will Be Used? (e.g., Parallel Teaching?)	What Are the Responsibilities of Each Teacher?	Are Any Specific Materials Needed?	How Will You Evaluate Student Learning?	Will You Give Follow-up Work? To Which Students?
9–15	State history; location of major cities, major businesses in cities.	Parallel teaching	Ms. Jones works with half the class while Ms. Smith works with the other half.	State maps, Internet sites for each city, Chamber of Commerce URL, or printed information.	Fill in spaces on blank map for homework. Have students draw pictures of major businesses and match to cities.	Matt—needs to work on location; highlight a map and the cities located there; using this color cue, ask him to match business to city.

SOURCE: Adapted from Vaughn, Schumm, and Arguelles (1997).

Table 12.3(A) Blank Parent Contact Form

Student's Name	Parents' Names	Date of Contact	How Contact Made? (e.g., Phone, Note, E-mail)	Information Shared With Parents	Feedback Expected From Parents	Feedback Received	Follow-up Steps?

Table 12.3(B) Completed Parent Contact Form

Student's Name	Parents' Names	Date of Contact	How Contact Made? (e.g., Phone, Note, E-mail)	Information Shared With Parents	Feedback Expected From Parents	Feedback Received	Follow-up Steps?
Kathy Doe	M/M John Doe	1/10/06	Note sent with Kathy	Kathy has not turned in her last 4 math homework assignments	Reason(s) for no homework; commitment to completing in the future	M/M Doe will sit each night w/ Kathy to ensure completion of homework; if Kathy says there is no homework, parents will check homework hotline	Ms. Jones will call the Does on or before 1/24/06

Table 12.4(A) Blank Form for Record of Contacts Made Within the School (Option 1)

Student's Name	Date	Who Contacted?	Purpose of Contact	How Was Contact Made?	Response Received?	Feedback Necessary?	Resolution

Table 12.4(B)   Completed Form for Record of Contacts Made Within the School (Option 1)

Student's Name	Date	Who Contacted?	Purpose of Contact	How Was Contact Made?	Response Received?	Feedback Necessary?	Resolution
Mike Saulson	10/12	Ms. Ramirez (Spanish teacher)	Check on Mike's progress; determine if necessary to coteach.	Sent e-mail and left note in her mailbox telling her about the e-mail.	Yes; said Mike is doing much better; now has a 78 average.	Contact again around 11/5 after midterm.	Ms. Ramirez has been using the accommodations that we use in Mike's other classes. Coteaching not necessary at this time.
	10/26	Ms. Ramirez (Spanish teacher)	Check on Mike's progress.	Spoke at faculty meeting.	Yes; said Mike continues to perform adequately.	Contact again around 11/5 after midterm	N/A

Table 12.5(A)   Blank Form for Record of Contacts Made Within the School
(Option 2)

Student's Name	
Date	
Who Contacted?	
Purpose of Contact?	
How Was Contact Made?	
Response Received?	
Feedback Necessary?	
Resolution?	

Table 12.5 (B)   Completed Form for Record of Contacts Made Within the
School (Option 2)

Student's Name	Mike Saulson	
Date	10/12/05	
Who Contacted?	Ms. Ramirez (Spanish teacher)	
Purpose of Contact?	Check on Mike's progress; determine if necessary to coteach.	
How Was Contact Made?	Sent e-mail and left note in her mailbox telling her about the e-mail.	
Response Received?	Yes; said Mike is doing much better; now has a 78 average.	
Feedback Necessary?	Contact again around 11/5 after midterm.	
Resolution?	Ms. Ramirez has been using the accommodations that we use in Mike's other classes. Coteaching not necessary at this time.	

individual teacher. Parent contact forms such as the one shown in Tables 12.3(A) and (B) could also be organized in either format.

WHAT APPROACHES ARE USED TO COMMUNICATE, CONSULT, AND COLLABORATE?

The specific approaches used in an inclusive classroom setting may vary from school to school, room to room, or even day to day. The key to selecting and using an instructional approach is the degree to which the approach will be successful in the specific classroom, with the students placed in the classroom, and with the teachers who are working jointly to meet the needs of these students. The roles of the coteachers are determined by the strengths of each teacher, knowledge of the content being presented, and the teaching styles and individual preferences of the cooperating teachers. Nonetheless, generally several approaches are used in presenting instruction to students in the inclusive classroom (Friend & Cook, 2003; Murawski & Dieker, 2004).

One Teaching, One Assisting

In this format, one teacher is clearly identified as the "lead" teacher. This professional conducts most of the instruction, leads classroom discussions, and responds to most of the students' questions. The second teacher observes and "drifts" throughout the class during instruction. If specific questions arise or any confusion is identified, this teacher is available to respond to the questions or provide individual or small group attention. Many special educators have considered this approach to be the least effective because the special education teacher often assumes the role of a teacher assistant. While assisting is an important role, the training and experience of the special educator are usually beyond those of an assistant. Special education teachers report that they do not feel as if this approach provides them with the professional responsibilities appropriate to the coteaching, inclusion setting. This approach may be used in circumstances in which the special educator is not comfortable in the general classroom setting or is uncomfortable with the content, or when the coteachers are not aware of an alternative.

Station Teaching

This approach typically uses two or more stations at which the students are placed. The coteachers divide the instruction into two segments, with the content presented in two separate sites in the classroom. For example, the special education teacher may present new phonics rules to a small group of students at one station while the general education teacher reviews phonics rules that were previously learned by the class. After a designated period of time, the teachers switch groups and repeat the instruction. Our experience with station teaching suggests that, if possible, it is more effective for the teachers to move than for the students to move. This reduces the transition time and enables students to refocus attention more quickly and consistently. The third station, if appropriate, is available for students to complete independent work. This may include practicing previously learned skills or completing "enrichment" types of activities that extend and expand previous learning.

Parallel Teaching

As the name would suggest, parallel teaching divides the class in half, with each coteacher responsible for instruction to one half of the class. The lesson(s) is jointly planned, and each teacher is essentially teaching the same content. Friend and Cook (2003) suggest that this approach is most successful when groups formed are heterogeneous. This approach is often effective because of the reduced teacher-student ratio. As noted, the lessons typically cover the same material. However, Cook and Friend (1995) offer an alternative that is often appealing to teachers and students. Both teachers present the same background information (e.g., the War in Iraq), but one group receives instruction that focuses on the positive aspects of the United States' involvement in the war while the second group receives instruction focusing on the negative aspects of the United States' involvement. Subsequently, a discussion is designed that provides each group with the opportunity to present its arguments.

Alternative Teaching

This approach usually involves one small group and one larger group of students. Instruction for the first group may focus on reteaching material that was not mastered by students. The second group, presumably made up of students who have learned the previous skills, may begin to preview the material to be covered during the next class period. They may learn new vocabulary, skim a short story, or use specific study techniques to secure an overall understanding of the new chapter that will be introduced in class tomorrow. Students may self-select to participate in the review group if they feel that they have not completely mastered the previous skills.

Team Teaching

Classroom instruction in the team teaching approach is shared by the coteachers. One teacher often lectures while the second teacher demonstrates the concept being presented. Team teaching may also involve a teacher presenting information while the second teacher models effective note-taking skills using the overhead projector.

In addition to the approaches listed above, Murawski and Dieker (2004) present information that specifically considers behaviors in which teachers might be involved during a coteaching situation. For example, if one teacher is passing out papers, Murawski and Dieker suggest that the second teacher review directions or model the first item of the assignment. Another example involves one teacher taking roll while the second teacher is collecting and reviewing the previous night's homework. For more information, see the Resources section below.

WHERE CAN I FIND RESOURCES OR MORE INFORMATION ON COMMUNICATING, CONSULTING, AND COLLABORATING?

Books

Salend, S. J. (2005). *Creating inclusive classrooms: Effective and reflective practices for all students* (5th ed.). Columbus, OH: Pearson.

Journal Articles

Bauwens, J., & Hourcade, J. J. (1997). Cooperative teaching: Pictures of possibilities. *Intervention in School and Clinic, 33,* 81–85, 89.

Keefe, E. B., Moore, V., & Duff, F. (2004). The four "knows" of collaborative teaching. *Teaching Exceptional Children, 36,* 36–42.

Mastropieri, M. A., & Scruggs, T. E. (2001). Promoting inclusion in secondary classrooms. *Learning Disability Quarterly, 24,* 264–274.

Murawski, W. W., & Dieker, L. A. (2004). Tips and strategies for co-teaching at the secondary level. *Teaching Exceptional Children, 36,* 52–58.

Walsh, J. M., & Jones, B. (2004). New models of cooperative teaching. *Teaching Exceptional Children, 36,* 14–20.

Web Sites

Division for Learning Disabilities (DLD) of the Council for Exceptional Children (CEC; www.dldcec.org). One of 17 special interest groups of the CEC, DLD is the largest international professional organization dedicated to improving educational outcomes for individuals with exceptionalities, students with disabilities, and/or the gifted. Since the early 1980s, DLD has worked on behalf of students with learning disabilities and the professionals who serve them.

LD Online (www.ldonline.org). A national educational service of public television station WETA in Washington, D.C. It is the leading information service in the field of learning disabilities, serving more than 200,000 parents, teachers, and other professionals each month.

CHAPTER REFERENCES

Cook, L., & Friend, M. (1995). Co-teaching: Guidelines for creating effective practices. *Focus on Exceptional Children, 28,* 1–16.

Friend, M., & Cook, L. (2000). *Interactions: Collaborative skills for school professionals* (3rd ed.). New York: Longman.

Friend, M., & Cook, L. (2003). *Interactions: Collaborative skills for school professionals* (4th ed.). New York: Longman.

Gable, R. A., Korinek, L., & McLaughlin, V. L. (1997). Collaboration in the schools: Ensuring success. In J. S. Choate (Ed.), *Successful inclusive teaching: Proven ways to detect and correct special needs.* Needham Heights, MA: Allyn & Bacon.

Keefe, E. B., Moore, V., & Duff, F. (2004). The four "knows" of collaborative teaching. *Teaching Exceptional Children, 36,* 36–42.

Murawski, W. W., & Dieker, L. A. (2004). Tips and strategies for co-teaching at the secondary level. *Teaching Exceptional Children, 36,* 52–58.

Vaughn, S., Schumm, J. S., & Arguelles, M. E. (1997). The ABCDEs of co-teaching. *Teaching Exceptional Children, 30(2),* 4–10.

The End Is Just the Beginning!

You are embarking on the most potentially challenging and rewarding part of your career, serving students and including students with disabilities in your classroom. The chapters of this book have given you a peek at the issues you will face. Many more will arise, and your challenges will be as individual as you are. Still, we hope that we have given you some basic information, concepts, and ideas that will help you on your journey. In this chapter, we will present the "big finish," which is really the big beginning.

ENSURING THAT NO CHILD IS LEFT BEHIND

You have probably heard from one or more sources about the No Child Left Behind Act (NCLB), which was proposed by President Bush and made into law by Congress. According to NCLB (2001), "States, school districts, and schools must be accountable for ensuring that all students, including disadvantaged students, meet high academic standards" (p. 5). NCLB holds schools accountable for meeting set standards through annual reading and math assessments in Grades 3 through 8. Depending on whom you talk to, NCLB is the innovation that will guarantee meaningful learning by every child or an impossible goal that will frustrate schools, teachers, parents, and students everywhere. At this point, schools and school systems and states are working to put the law into practice. Of course, they are also trying to ensure that they will meet the qualifications of the law, because not meeting the qualifications leads to dire consequences (loss of jobs, loss of funding, etc.).

The impact of NCLB on special education and individual educational programs (IEPs) is unclear. Some predict that underachievers will make gains as they meet higher expectations. Others warn that the concept of the "individual," so basic to special education programming, will be annihilated in the process of setting the same high expectations for everyone.

Keeping abreast of changes and the impact of NCLB as it pertains to you and your job is a smart thing for you to do. Working with your administrators and doing the work that leads you to become a "highly qualified teacher" is also important. However, these are not the only ways that you can ensure that "no child is left behind." Some guiding principles may help:

1. *You are not alone.* Identify resourceful persons as early as you can. Do not limit yourself to the help you get from obvious mentors; look also for people in your life that can provide wisdom for your job. Likely candidates are your administrators, team leaders, and appointed mentors. There are also "undercover mentors" waiting for you at your school. They may be your teaching assistant, school custodian, cafeteria worker, bus driver, and savvy parents and grandparents. Enlist the support of people with experience in various roles and learn from them.

2. *You need to work as part of a team, and you have something to offer.* You have heard the African proverb "It takes a village to raise a child." Well, it takes a team to teach one, or two, or 33. You cannot do your job by relying totally on yourself. You will need to get help and give help. You do not get out of this responsibility just because you are young and/or inexperienced. No matter how much or how little experience you bring to your job in education, you have something to offer the people on your team. Listen respectfully, speak with confidence (having read this book twice), and work things out with the people who work with you. Make every effort to resolve conflicts between team members, because conflict will likely affect your students.

3. *Consider your related service personnel your support system and safety net.* Your school counselor, school psychologist, diagnostician, social worker, speech clinician, occupational therapist, physical therapist, and other related service personnel are experts in areas critical to your students with special needs. Use their expertise and guidance in any area of your classroom you see fit, from classroom organization to scheduling to lesson planning to assessment to behavior modification.

4. *Reserve a special place in your heart for special teachers.* The special teachers in your school, such as the music teacher, physical education teacher, art teacher, and media coordinator, may be able to inspire your students with

special needs in ways you cannot. They may also see strengths in your students that are not as obvious in the subject area(s) you teach. Good communication and collaboration with these professionals make your job easier.

5. *Be thankful for an administrator who "gets it," and be patient with an administrator who doesn't.* Some administrators have deeply embedded negative attitudes toward including students with special needs in general education classrooms. Some administrators have no problem with certain "types" of special needs (e.g., learning disabilities) but big problems with others (e.g., behavior disorders). As with your colleagues, make every effort to resolve conflict with information and respectful listening. Have someone you trust to keep your confidence to act as a sounding board. Finally, these books will make excellent Christmas presents.

6. *Respect the paperwork.* Exceptional children's paperwork is federal documentation and should be taken seriously. Specific procedures exist for data collection and certain meetings, such as identification and placement, reevaluations, and manifestation determination. Do your part in following procedure correctly, and if you are not sure what to do, ask your exceptional children's contact person at your school.

7. *Make modifications and accommodations a habit.* Students do not learn the same things at the same rate, and nowhere is this more evident than in an inclusive classroom. The more you change your instruction (as needed) so that individuals can be successful, the better you will get at modifications. Special education teachers spend a lot of time learning about modifications that they must quickly put to use. Call upon your special education colleagues to help. Also, as your students figure out that you are willing to make modifications, they may be able to assist you in making modifications for them. The child's first teachers, his or her parents, may also be able to help with modifications. Your openness to ensuring your students' success sends a big message that you are on your students' side.

8. *Ensure your students' safety by sharing information as appropriate.* The adults who have regular contact with a special needs student need to know about health and safety risks for that student. This is not an excuse to gossip, and you should not share more information than is needed. For example, if a student has a seizure in a bus line and has problems communicating, serious injury can result if adults do not know what is happening or do not know how to intervene. Again, your exceptional children's contact person is a good resource for assisting you in schoolwide communication.

9. *You know quite a bit now, but you will keep learning.* Students come and go, parents come and go, and you will learn from all of them. Enjoy yourself and remind yourself that you are making an impact on the future. When in doubt,

10. *Refer to 1.*

Best wishes for your continued success!

Index

Abilities, 196
Academics, 6–7
Accommodations:
  application of, 179-180
  definition of, 178
  equipment/technological assistance, 187–188, 185-187
  presentation, 84
  reasons for classroom use, 178-179
  resources on, 193
  responses, 184-185
  on SAT, 181
  scheduling, 184
  setting, 183
  for students with disabilities, 177-178
  teacher use of, 257
Activities, behavior management, 121, 125–131
Adaptive behavior, 5–6
Adequate yearly progress (AYP), 202
ADHD (Attention Deficit Hyperactivity Disorder), 8
Administrator:
collaboration for inclusion
  classroom, 233-234
  positive attitudes toward
  inclusion, 22–23
  support of lesson plans, 95
  teachers and, 257)
  See also Principal
Advanced organizers, 138-140
Agard, J. A., 21
Agencies, 55-57
Algozzine, B., 114-115
Alternative teaching:
  description of, 66-67, 102
  for inclusive classroom, 251
  reading strategies and, 138
American Psychiatric Association, 8
Anecdotal records, 116-117
Appl, D. J., 106-107
Arguelles, M. E., 104
Articles. See Books/articles
Assessment:
  accommodations, 183-186
  collection of assessment data, 202-208
  comprehensive evaluation, 198
  grading, 209-210
  identification of students with disabilities, 199

important information for teachers, 240-243
  legal considerations, 198, 199-202
  modifications to, 186-187
  No Child Left Behind Act and, 25
  overview of, 196-197
  purposes of, 197
  resources on, 209-210
Attention, orienting strategies for, 155-156
Attention Deficit Hyperactivity Disorder (ADHD), 8
Attentional aids, specific,156-159
Attitudes, 22–23
Autism, 5
AYP (adequate yearly progress), 202

Baker, S., 149–150
Balance, 63
Bean Bag Toss, 160
Beckman, P., 25
Behavior:
  behavioral reasons for special education, 7–8
  classroom rules/procedures, 67–69
  interviews and, 205–206
  observations about, 204–205
Behavior counts, 116, 117–119
Behavior management/motivation:
  aspect of classroom organization, 61
  common activities,125-131
  evaluating success of, 124-125
  reasons for using, 111–112
  resources for, 131–133
  using in classroom, 112–124
Benchmarks, 48–49
Bereiter, C., 149
Billingsley, B. S., 220, 221
Blind, 4
Books/articles:
  accommodations/modifications, 193
  assessment, data collection, grading, 209
  behavior management/motivation, 131–132
  classroom organization, 71–72
  cognitive strategies, 170–173
  communication/consultation/collaboration, 252
  inclusion, 29–30
  Individualized Education Program, 57
  lesson planning, 108
  parent/family assistance, 226

reading strategies, 144–146
special education, 15–16
Boudah, D. J., 143
Boys, 134
Brain injury, 5
Brown, A. L., 149
Bulgren, J. A., 143, 151
Burish, P., 141
Bush, George W., 27, 255

Carlson, E., 41, 42
Cartwright, C. A., 21
Cartwright, G. P., 21
Categories, of special education
students, 2–3
Categorizing, 169–170
CBA (curriculum-based assessment), 207–209
Change, 162–165
Characteristics, assessment of, 196–197
Chard, D. J., 136
Charts:
for observational data analysis, 125
for remedial work with student, 106–107
Chen, L., 41, 42
"Child Find" system, 34
Choral Response,160
Choutka, C. M.:
on instruction modifications, 189
on lesson planning, 101, 102
on modifications, 181
Class body, 60–61
Classroom:
accommodations in, 183–186
behavior management in, 112–124
instruction, IEP connection with, 38–39
modifications to setting, 190
physical layout of, 61–67
reading strategies for, 136–143
See also Inclusion classroom
Classroom organization:
classroom interactions/activities, 67–69
definition of, 59–60
evaluation of, 70
physical layout of classroom, 61–67
reasons for, 60–61
resources on, 71–72
teacher organization, 69
who needs, 69–70
Clustering, 170
Cognition, 5–6
Cognitive strategies:
content enhancement and, 151-153
elaboration strategies, 161-162
evaluation of, 153
imagery strategies, 165-166
mnemonic strategies, 166-169
organizational strategies, 169-170
orienting strategies, 155-156
overview of, 153-154
purpose of, 149-150

reasons for, 150–151
rehearsal strategies, 159–161
resources on, 170–174
specific attentional aids, 156–157
specific problem-solving aids, 158–159
transformational strategies, 162–165
Collaboration:
approaches, 250–252
assessment information, 240–243
collaborative roles, 238–240
consultation and, 235–236
co-teaching, 236–238
in co-teaching model, 67
between home/school, 218–223
for inclusion, 24–25
for inclusive classroom, 230
methods, 232–235
reasons for, 231
record keeping for, 243 - 250
teams for teaching, 256
Communication:
about Individualized Education Program, 43
approaches, 250–252
for collaboration, 230-231, 234
between home/school, 218–220
with parents, 215-216, 224–225
speech, language impairments, 7
Comprehension:
cognitive strategies and, 150
definition of, 135
reading strategies for, 142
Conflict, parent/school personnel, 220–221
Consultation:
approaches, 250–252
for inclusion classroom, 235–236
Contacts forms, 245–250
Content, lesson planning and, 102–103
Content enhancement, 143, 151–153
Content evaluation, 151–152
Continuum of inference, 113, 114
Contracts:
for behavior reinforcement, 126–127
statements for improving social problems, 128
Cook, C. R., 121
Cook, L.:
on classroom arrangements, 66, 67
inclusive classroom approaches, 250, 251
team teaching models, 137–138
Cook, T., 219
Co-teachers:
collaborative roles/responsibilities of, 239-241
grading and, 208,209
inclusive classroom approaches, 250, 252
lesson planning and, 95
Co-teaching:
collaboration and, 236–238
daily lesson plan example for, 104
description of, 67
reading strategies and, 138
Council for Exceptional Children: on Individualized
Education Program, 37

mainstreaming definition, 21
Counts, 116, 117–118
Crews, S. D., 121
Criterion-referenced assessment, 206–207
Criterion-referenced grading, 209
Criterion-referenced tests, 203, 204
Curriculum-based assessment (CBA), 207–208

Daily planning sheet, 244
Darch, C. B., 70
Darling-Hammond, L., 24
Data:
　behavior management and, 112
　in instructional decision-making, 104–107
Data collection, assessment, 202–208
Davern, L., 222
Deafness, 4–5
Decreasing behavior, 128–129
Descriptive articles. See Books/articles
Deshler, D. D., 143, 151
Dieker, L. A.:
　on grading, 208
　inclusive classroom approaches, 250, 252
　on lesson planning, 95
Diliberto, Jennifer, 133–147
Direct instruction programs, 142–143
Disabilities, 2–3
　See also Students with disabilities
Dyson, L. L., 215

Early childhood education, 26
Early Reading First initiative, 134
Education, 1
Education environment. See Settings
Edwards, L. L.:
　on lesson planning, 101,102
　on modifications, 181, 189
18-step lesson plan format:
　rubric, 80–92
　scoring sheet, 93
　of UNC Charlotte, 77, 79
Elaboration strategies, 154, 161–162
Elementary and Secondary Education ACT (ESEA),
　27, 28
Ellis, M., 213, 214
Ellis. E., 143, 168–169
Emmer, E. T., 65–66
Environments:
　accommodations for students
　with disabilities, 183
　of special education, 11–15
Equipment, 185–186
Escobar, M. D., 134

ESEA (Elementary and Secondary Education ACT),
　27, 28
Evaluation:
　assessment tests, 198

of children for disabilities, correct
of classroom organization, 70
of cognitive strategies, 153
of content, 151–152
of reading strategies, 144
Event recordings, 205
Evertson, C. M., 65–66
Exceptional children, 20
Expectations, 188–189

F. A. T. City video (Lavoie), 60
Failure, 111–112
Fair treatment, 60
Falik, L. H., 212
Family, 233
　See also Parents/families, assisting
Fernald, G., 140
Fernald method, 140
First-letter mnemonics, 167–168
Fletcher, J. M., 134
Flexibility, 28
Fluency, 135
Foundation information, 159
Friend, M.:
　on classroom arrangements, 66–67
　inclusive classroom approaches, 250, 251
　team teaching models, 137–138
Fuchs, D., 141, 179
Fuchs, L. S., 141, 179
Funding, 27–28

Gable, R. A., 231, 232
Gearheart, B. R., 21
Gearheart, C. J., 21
General education classroom:
　assessment, legal considerations, 199, 200
　special education in, 11–12
　See also Inclusion classroom
General education curriculum:
　IEP goals/objectives and, 43
　No Child Left Behind Act and, 25–27
General education teacher:
　collaborative roles/responsibilities of, 239–240
　consultation with, 235–236
　co-teaching, 236-238
　IEP development and, 39–41
　inclusive classroom arrangements and, 66–67
　lesson planning and, 95-96
Gerber, P. J., 218
Gersten, R., 149–150
Gifted students, 19–20
Gillingham, A., 140
Gillingham model, 140
Girls, 134
Goals:
　for collaboration, 233
　goal statement in lesson planning, 102-103
　of IEP, 37–39, 45
　in sample IEP, 48
Good, R. H., 136

Gottlieb, J., 21
Graphs, 119–121, 124–125
Great Leaps in Reading (program), 143
Green, M. Y., 44
Gresham, F. M., 121
A Guide to the Individualized Education Program
(U.S. Department of Education), 34–37

Haigh, J.:
    on accommodations, 183
    on assessment modifications, 186
    on modifications, 180,182
Hearing impairment, 4–5
Henker, B., 8
High-inference problems, 115
Horn, J. L., 2

IDEA. *See* Individuals with Disabilities Education Act
IEE (Independent Educational Evaluation), 35
IEP. *See* Individualized Education Program
IFSP (individualized family service plan), 44
Imagery strategies, 154, 165-166
Inclusion:
    classroom organization and, 61
    grading in inclusive setting, 208–209
    history of, 20–22
    IEP and classroom instruction, 38–39
    inclusive classroom arrangements, 66–67
    Individualized Education Program and, 34
    multisensory reading instruction and, 140
    No Child Left Behind Act and, 25–28
    resources on, 28–31
    settings of special education, 11–15
    success factors, 22–25
    types of students, 19–20
Inclusion classroom:
    approaches, 250–252
    collaboration for, 232–235
    collaboration/communication for, 230–231
    collaborative roles in, 238–240
    consultation for, 235–236
    co-teaching, 236–238
    record keeping for collaboration, 243–250
Independent Educational Evaluation (IEE), 35
Individualized Education Program (IEP):
    accommodations included in, 180
    assessment, legal considerations, 198–199
    classroom layout and, 61–62
    classroom rules and, 67–69
    creation of, 34–37
    development of, reduction of paperwork, 41–45
    inclusive classroom instruction and, 38–39
    information in, 37–38
    overview of, 33–34
    participants in
        development of, 39–40
    regulations/guidelines, 45–46
    resources on, 55–58
    sample, 47–55

    strategies for, 41
Individualized family service plan (IFSP), 44
Individuals with Disabilities Education Act (IDEA):
    accommodations/modifications and, 177–178
    assessment, legal considerations, 198, 199–202
    assessment tests, 197, 198
    on IEP assessment, 43
    inclusion and, 20
    See also Public Law 92–140
Individuals with Disabilities Education Act (IDEA)
Amendments of 2004:
    access to general education curriculum and, 25
    Individualized Education Program and, 37
    Individualized Education Program paperwork and,
        41
    learning disabilities definition, 6–7
    special education guidelines, 11
Inference, 196
Instruction:
    accommodations, 183–186
    modifications, 187–192
Instructional delivery, 187
Instructional supports, 152
Interior design, 63–64
Interventions:
    lesson planning and, 105
    observations for planning, 113–121
Interviews:
    assessment data collection with, 205–206
    for intervention planning, 121-124

Jephson, M. B., 221
Jitendra, A. K.:
    on instruction modifications, 191
    on lesson planning, 101,102
    on modifications, 181
Jordan, LuAnn, 133–147

Kame'enui, E. J., 70, 136
Kansas Learning Strategies, 142
Kauffman, J. M., 21
Key word mnemonics, 167
Klein, S., 41, 42
Knowledge, 206
Korinek, L., 231, 232
Kronowitz, E. L., 43
KU-CRL (University of Kansas Center for Research
on Learning), 143
Kukic, M. D., 21

Lake, J. F., 220, 221
Language impairments, 7
Lavoie, Rick, 60
Layout, classroom, 61–67
Learning disabilities, 6–7
Learning gap, 181–182
Learning needs, 3–8
LEAs. *See* Local education agencies
Least restrictive environment:

inclusive setting as, 75-76
mainstreaming, 21
provision of IDEA, 20
for students with disabilities, 199
Leavell, A. G., 189
Legal considerations, assessment,198, 199–202
Lenz, B. K., 143
Lesson content, 96–102
Lesson organization:
  facilitating, 102–107
  factors affecting planning success, 93–94
  inclusive classrooms, organizing lessons in,
    95–102
  Instructional Lesson Plan Rubric, 80–92
  overview of, 75–79
  resources for, 108–109
  Scoring Sheet, 93
LINCS mnemonic, 168–169
Local education agencies (LEAs):
  grants, 27-28
  IEP development and, 37, 46
Locations. See Settings
Low-inference problems, 113, 115
Lyon, G. R., 1134

Mainstreaming, 21
Manset, G., 217
Maroney, S. A., 76
Martin, Casey, 179–180
Mastropieri, M. A., 166
Material. See Lesson content
Materials:
  arrangement of, 65
  modifications, 180–183, 188
  orienting strategies and, 155
Mathematics, 191
McKnight, P. C., 143
McLaughlin, M. J., 179
McLaughlin, V. L., 231, 232
Meetings, 234
Memorization, 158–159
Memory:
  mnemonics strategies, 166–169
  organizational strategies, 169–170
  See also Cognitive strategies
Mental retardation, 5–6
Mercer, A. R.:
  advanced organizer, 140
  on classroom rules/procedures, 67
  on special classroom areas, 66
  on student space, 64–65
Mercer, C. D.:
  advanced organizer, 140
  on classroom rules/procedures, 67
  on special classroom areas, 66
  on student space, 64–65
Metacognition, 149–150
Mind. See Cognitive strategies
Mnemonic strategies, 154, 166–169
Moats, L. C., 134

Modifications:
  application of, 180–183
  to assessment, 186–187
  definition of, 178
  to instruction, 187–192
  reasons for classroom use, 178–179
  resources on, 193
  for students with disabilities, 177–178
  teacher use of, 257
Money, 27–28
Moores, D., 4
Multisensory reading instruction, 140
Murawski, W. W.:
  on grading, 208
  inclusive classroom approaches, 250, 252
  on lesson planning, 95

National Assessment of Educational Progress
(NAEP), 28
National Education Association (NEA), 44
National Information Center for Children and Youth
with Disabilities (NICHCY), 44–45
National Institutes of Child Health and Development
(NICHD), 133-134
National Reading Panel (NRP), 134–135, 137
NCLB. See No Child Left Behind Act
NEA (National Education Association), 44
Needs, 3–8
Negative reinforcement, 125–126
NICHCY (National Information Center for Children
and Youth with Disabilities), 44–45
NICHD (National Institutes of Child Health and
Development), 135–136
No Child Left Behind Act (NCLB):
  assessment, legal considerations, 199, 201, 202
  impact of, 255–256
  inclusion and, 25–27
  reading instruction and, 134
Nolet, V., 179
Normal students, 19–20
Norm-referenced grading systems, 209
Norm-referenced tests:
  educator and, 206
  pros/cons of, 204
  purpose of, 203
North Carolina State Board of Education, 62
NRP (National Reading Panel), 134-135, 137

Objectives:
  of IEP, 38–39, 45
  in sample IEP, 48–49
Observations:
  assessment data collection with, 204–205
  for intervention planning, 113–121
Office of Civil Rights (OCR), 208
OHI (other health impairments), 8, 9
Organizational difficulties, 192
Organizational strategies, 154, 169–171
Organizations:

assessment, data collection, grading, 210
inclusion, 31–32
lesson planning, 108–109
on parent/family assistance, 226–227
special education, 17–18
Orienting strategies, 154, 155–156
Other health impairments (OHI), 8, 9

PA (phonological awareness), 135
Palincsar, A. S., 149
Paperwork:
    for IEP, reduction of, 41–45
    respect for, 257
Parallel teaching:
    description of, 66, 101
    for inclusive classroom, 251
    reading strategies and, 138
Paraphrasing, 162, 163, 164
Parent contact form, 245–246
Parents:
    collaborative roles of, 239
    evaluation of children for
        disabilities and, 34, 35
    IEP development and, 39, 40
    IEP meeting and, 36
    IEP paperwork and, 41
    inclusion success and, 23
    Individualized Education Program and, 37
    information on child's progress, 52–53
    No Child Left Behind Act and, 26–27
    rights of, 201
Parents/families, assisting:
    approaching effectively, 223–226
    considerations about, 211–218
    involvement of, 218–223
    resources for, 226–227
Peer teaching, 140–141
Peltier, G. L., 217
Performance:
    curriculum-based assessment, 207–208
    tests, 206
Permanent records, 117
Phonics, 135, 140
Phonological awareness (PA), 135
Physical disabilities, 63, 64
Physical layout, classroom, 61–67, 190
Physical reasons, for special education needs, 4–5
Planning pyramid, 189
Popp, P. A., 218
Portfolio assessment, 207
Positive attitudes, 22–23
Positive reinforcement, 125–126
Power thinking, 141–142
Presentation, 184
Primary level of intervention, 136
Principal:
    collaborative roles/responsibilities of, 238–239
    No Child Left Behind Act and, 27
    See also Administrator
Prioritizing, 169

Problem-solving aids, specific, 154, 158–159
Procedural facilitators. See Cognitive strategies
Procedural prompts. See Cognitive strategies
Procedures, classroom, 67–69
Professional development, correct
Proportion, 63–64
Public Law 94–142
    inclusion and, 20
    number of special education students and, 9
    special education guidelines, 11
    See also Individuals with Disabilities Education
        Act

Ramsay, E., 121
Reading:
    difficulties, 28
    modifications for difficulties, 191
    No Child Left Behind Act and, 25
Reading, teaching:
    content enhancement, 143
    evaluation of reading strategies, 144
    reading components, 134–135
    reading problems, 133–134
    reading strategies, 136-143
    resources on, 144–147
    students' reading difficulties, sensitivity to,
        135–136
Reading First initiative, 134
Reading First program, 28
Reading strategies:
    advanced organizers, 138–140
    chart of, 139
    direct instruction programs, 142–143
    evaluation of, 144
    multisensory reading
        instructions, 140
    peer teaching, 140–141
    power thinking, 141–142
    University of Kansas Learning Strategies, 142
    use of, 136-138
Reality TV, 223
Records:
    behavior management and, 112
    of behavior observation, 116–118
    for collaboration, 243–250
    on IEP, 43–44
Rehearsal strategies, 154, 159–161
Reinforcement, 125–128
Research articles. See Books/articles
Resources:
    accommodations/modifications, 193
    assessment, data collection, grading, 209–210
    classroom organization, 71–72
    cognitive strategies, 170–174
    communication/consultation/collaboration,
        252–253
    inclusion, 28–32
    Individualized Education Program, 55-57
    lesson planning, 108–109
    reading strategies, 144–147

for schools, 27
special education, 15–18
Respect, 235
Responses:
accommodations, 184–185
assessment modifications, 186–187
instruction modifications, 188
Review:
of IEP, 37
lesson, 104–106
RIDER visual imagery strategy, 142
"Ring strategy," 156
Roeber, E. D., 202
Rosenshine, B., 149, 150
Routines, 152
Rowell, J., 106–107
Rules, classroom, 67, 68–69
Russell, K. P., 221

Safety, student, 257
Salend, S. J., 208, 209
Salvia, J.:
on criterion-referenced assessment, 206
on inference, 196
testing definition, 203
SAT, 181
Scaffolds. *See* Cognitive strategies
Scanlon, D., 149–150
Scardamalia, M., 149
SCENE imagery strategy, 165
Schedule of reinforcement, 127, 128
Scheduling, 184
School environment, 94
See also Settings
Schroll, K., 41, 42
Schulz, J. B., 21
Schumaker, J. B.:
on cognitive strategies, 151
on content enhancements, 143
PENS mnemonic, 167-168
Schumm, J. C., 189
Schumm, J. S., 104
SCOS. *See* Standard course of study
Scruggs, T. E., 166
Searcy, S., 76
Secondary level of intervention, 136
Semmel, M. I., 217
Sensitivity, 135–136
Sensory disabilities, 64
Settings:
accommodations for students with disabilities, 183
modifications to physical setting, 190
of special education, 11–15
Shaping behavior, 129–131
Shaywitz, B. A., 134
Shaywitz, S. E., 134
Sheldon, J. B., 167–168
Siblings, 224
Simmons, D. S., 136
Simplicity, lesson planning, 103–104

Six-point plan:
overview of, 76–77
sample of, 78–79
Skills, 190–192, 196
SLANT mnemonic, 167
Social problems:
behavior management and, 111–112
in inclusive classrooms, 114
reference behaviors for learning disabled students, 115
Special areas, classroom, 65–66
Special education:
definition of, 1
inclusion and, 9–11
legal considerations, 198, 199–202
location of delivery, 11–15
need for, reasons for, 3–8
number of students who receive, 9
recipients of, 2–3
resources, 15–18
steps of process, 34–37
See also Inclusion; Students with disabilities
Special Education Program at University of Northern Iowa, 15, 28
See also Resources
Special education teacher:
collaborative roles/responsibilities of, 238–240
consultation with, 235–236
co-teaching, 236–238
IEP development and, 39
inclusive classroom approaches, 250
inclusive classroom arrangements and, 66–67
lesson planning and, 95–96
Specific attentional aids, 154, 156–157
Specific learning disabilities, students with, 9
Specific problem-solving aids, 156, 160–161 154, 158–159
Speech impairments, 7
Sprick, Randy, 67
Stainback, S., 21
Stainback, W., 21
Standard course of study (SCOS):
lesson plan development of, 75
lesson planning and, 96, 100–101
mathematics example, 97–100
Station teaching:
description of, 66, 101
for inclusive classroom, 250–251
reading strategies and, 137, 143
Stillman, B., 140
Student space, 69
Students:
accommodations/modifications for, 177–178
assessment of, 196–197
classroom organization evaluation and, 70
classroom organization needs, 69–70
classroom organization, reasons for, 60–61
classroom rules/procedures and, 67–69
cognitive strategies, description of, 153–170
cognitive strategies, reasons for, 150–151
collaboration and, 232–235

content enhancement and, 151–153
co-teaching and, 237
IEP focus on, 40–41
IEP participation by, 42–43
inclusion, factors for, 22–25
inclusive classroom approaches and, 250–252
lesson plan success and, 94
lesson planning and,75–76, 101–103
reading difficulties, 133–136
reading strategies for, 136–143
safety of, 257
special education, number receiving, 9–11
special education, reasons for need of, 3–8
special education recipients, 2–3
special education settings, 11–15
special education steps, IEP, 34–37
types of, 19–20 (correct)
without special needs, parents of, 215–217,
    225–226
A Student's Guide to the IEP (National Information
Center for Children and Youth with Disabilities),
44–45
Students with disabilities:
    accommodations for, 179–180, 183–186
    assessment, legal considerations, 198, 199–202
    assessment data collection, 202–208
    assessment of, 196–198, 199
    classroom layout and, 61–67
    inclusion, No Child Left Behind Act and, 25–27
    inclusion history, 20–22
    modifications for, 180–183, 186–192
    problems of parents, 212–215
    use of term, 19–20
Study carrels, 190
Supplies. *See* Materials
Support, 189–190
Swain, J., 219

Tables, 119–120
Teacher Assistance Team (TAT), 35
Teachers:
    accommodations and, 183–186
    assessment data collection, 202–208
    assessment information for, 240–243
    assessment purposes, 197
    classroom layout, 61–67
    classroom organization and, 69
    classroom organization evaluation, 70
    classroom organization for, 60–61
    classroom rules/procedures and, 67–69
    cognitive strategies, description of, 153–170
    cognitive strategies, evaluation of, 153
    cognitive strategies, reasons for, 150–151
    cognitive strategies/content enhancement, 151–154
    collaboration methods, 232–235
    collaboration/communication for inclusive
        classroom, 230–231
    collaborative roles/responsibilities of, 238, 239–
        240

consultation with other teachers, 235–236
co-teachers and lesson planning, 95
co-teaching, 236–238
general vs. special in lesson planning, 95–96
IEP development and, 39–40, 41
IEP development, paperwork reduction, 41–45
in IEP process, 45–46
inclusion, factors for success, 22–25
inclusive classroom approaches, 250–252
lesson plans and, 76, 93–94
modifications and, 186–192
No Child Left Behind Act and, 26, 27
principles for, 256–258
reading, teaching, 133-142
record keeping for collaboration, 243–250
Teaching method, 101–102
Teaching together model:
    description of, 67
    reading strategies and, 138
Team Competition, 160
Team teaching:
    description of, 102
    for inclusive classroom, 252
    reading strategies and, 137–138
Teams. *See* Collaboration
Technological assistance, 185
Terminology, of assessments, 243
Tertiary level of intervention, 136
Testing:
    accommodations, 179–180, 181
    assessment data collection with, 203–204
    definition of, 203
    identification of students with disabilities, 199
    modifications to assessment, 186–187
    No Child Left Behind Act and, 25, 26
    responses accommodations, 84–185
    scheduling accommodations, 184
    setting accommodations, 183
    See also Assessment
Time, 188
Time sampling recording, 205
Tokens, 127
Transformational strategies:
    description/example of, 154
    mnemonic strategies as, 166
    overview of, 162–165
Transition services, 51–52
Traumatic brain injury, 5
Treadway, P. S.:
    on lesson planning, 101, 102
    on modifications, 181, 189
Troha, C., 106–107
Trust:
    for collaboration, 235
    between educators/parents, 217
Turnbull, A. P., 21
Twenty-Second Annual Report to Congress (U.S.
Department of Education, 2000), 9

Unit background, 102–103
University of Kansas, 168–169
University of Kansas Center for Research on Learning (KU-CRL), 143
University of Kansas Learning Strategies, 142
University of North Carolina at Charlotte:
  lesson plan format of, 77–79
  lesson plan rubric, 80–92
  lesson plan scoring sheet, 80–92
U.S. Department of Education:
  IEP development, 39, 45–46
  IEP documentation, 44
  IEP requirements, 37–38
  IEP sample, 47–55
  IEP steps, 34–37
  on inclusion, 21–22
  No Child Left Behind Act and, 25
  number of special education students, 9–11
  special education categories, 2–3
  special education environments, 11–15

Valuation, 221
Variety, 63
Vaughn, S., 104, 189
Vision, 4
Visual imagery strategy, 142
Visually impaired people, 4
Vocabulary:
  definition of, 135
  lesson planning and, 102–103

Walker, H. M., 121
Ward, M. E., 21
Washburn-Moses, L., 180, 182
Web sites:
  on accommodations/modifications, 193
  on assessment, data collection, grading, 210
  on behavior management/motivation, 132
  on classroom organization, 72
  on cognitive strategies, 173–174
  on communication/consultation/collaboration, 252–253
  on inclusion, correct
  on lesson planning, 108
  on mnemonics, 167
  on parent/family assistance, 227
  on reading strategies, 146–147
  on special education, 16–17
Wechsler Intelligence Scale for Children—Fourth Edition (WISC-IV), 241–242
Weishahn, M. W., 21
Welch, M., 78–79
Whalen, C. K., 8
World Association of Persons with Disabilities Newsletter, 17
Worsham, M. E., 65–66
Written language
  difficulties, 192

Youngblood, L. A., 221
Ysseldyke, J. E.:
  on criterion-referenced assessment, 206
  on inference, 196
  testing definition, 203